1,001 FACTS THAT WILL
SCARE THE S#*T
OUT OF YOU

The Ultimate Bathroom Reader

Written by
Cary McNeal

Avon, Massachusetts

Published by
Adams Media, a division of F+W Media, Inc.
57 Littlefield Street, Avon, MA 02322. U.S.A.
www.adamsmedia.com

ISBN 10: 1-60550-624-9
ISBN 13: 978-1-60550-624-1

Printed in the United States of America.

10   9

Library of Congress Cataloging-in-Publication Data
is available from the publisher.

This publication is designed to provide accurate and authoritative information
with regard to the subject matter covered. It is sold with the understanding that
the publisher is not engaged in rendering legal, accounting, or other professional
advice. If legal advice or other expert assistance is required, the services of a com-
petent professional person should be sought.
—From a *Declaration of Principles* jointly adopted by a Committee of the
American Bar Association and a Committee of Publishers and Associations

Many of the designations used by manufacturers and sellers to distinguish their
product are claimed as trademarks. Where those designations appear in this book
and Adams Media was aware of a trademark claim, the designations have been
printed with initial capital letters.

Certain sections of this book deal with activities and devices that would be in viola-
tion of various federal, state, and local laws if actually carried out or constructed.
We do not advocate the breaking of any law. This information is for entertainment
purposes only. We recommend that you contact your local law enforcement officials before undertaking any project based upon any information obtained from
this book. We are not responsible for, nor do we assume any liability for, damages
resulting from the use of any information in this book.

Interior illustrations:
Line art © Clipart.com
Silhouettes © Neubau Welt

This book is available at quantity discounts for bulk purchases.
For information, please call 1-800-289-0963.

Contents

✛✛

Acknowledgments

Writing any book is a massive undertaking, and no author does it alone, even though you certainly feel alone when it's 4:30 on a beautiful sunny spring afternoon and you're stuck inside banging your head against the desk as you try to come up with something funny to say about people being beheaded or bugs that eat human flesh while all your friends and family are outside somewhere having fun without you, usually accompanied by alcohol.

Still, a lot of people made this book happen, and I need to thank them. Especially if I want to get hired again. Those people are:

Holly Schmidt and Allan Penn at Hollan Publishing, for giving me the opportunity to write this book, for believing in me, for coddling me and listening to me whine and bitch about how hard it was and convincing me it would be worth the effort in the end. It was.

Matt Glazer and Paula Munier at Adams Media, for their guidance and patience, and for giving a first-time author a chance.

Kirsten Amman, my researcher, whose task was monumental; yet she did it with vigor and efficiency and glee. For that I could kiss her, but I don't want her boyfriend to beat my ass, so she'll have settle for a heartfelt thank you.

Jenny Bent of The Bent Agency, for her generous and invaluable advice, and Elaine English, my attorney, for reading all the long, wordy documents and knowing exactly which parts were most important.

My friends Don and Danna Calder, for legal assistance, medical supervision, patience, and encouragement, and for entertaining my family while I was holed up writing.

Beverly Linzer Jenkins and Adrianne Gershberg, the funniest chicks I know, for their comic genius and inspiration, and all my friends from List of the Day.

Amy Miller and Tom Jacobsen for their unconditional friendship and for waiting months for me to answer their e-mails and return their phone calls.

Amy Winter, my professional role model and friend, and the entire crew at Wolff Bros Post.

My parents, Perry and Jean McNeal, and the rest of my family for their interest in, and support of, my writing.

My wife Paige and daughter Keaton for loving me no matter what.

Introduction

The world is a frightening place.

But you already knew that; you read it in the paper, hear about it from friends, see it with your own eyes every time you turn on the TV to watch bad singers or dancers subject themselves to abuse from judges with no more talent than the contestants, or see a web video of a teenager shooting a bottle rocket from his ass for amusement, or get plowed from behind in your car by another driver who was texting "LMAO" to his friends instead of noticing that the light had turned red and you had stopped.

If random violence doesn't get you, cancer will. If cancer doesn't, global warming will. If global warming doesn't, bullet ants will. Or botflies. Or lightning. Or tsunamis. Or the Great Pacific Garbage Patch. Or Fijian headhunters. Or just normal everyday activities like drinking water, eating an orange, breathing the air, or having sex with a goat.

Yes, we are in deep doo-doo. You should be scared to death, right?

Wrong.

Okay, sure, this is a book of scary facts, and the more you read, the more afraid you are likely to be. I wouldn't be doing my job if you weren't. But if forewarned is forearmed, then the more you know, the safer you'll feel, even if it's a false sense of security since you can't do a thing about most of what you read here. But who cares, as long as you feel better?

If not—if this information scares the shit out of you—that's okay, too. You're probably reading this on the crapper, anyway, and what better place to be scared shitless? Isn't that the idea, to be shitless? At least you aren't befouling a nice pair of pants. I'm also keeping you regular. You're welcome.

While I'm scaring you, though, I also hope to make you laugh. There's a joke after every fact, for chrissakes. Do you have any idea how hard it is to make jokes about things like a guy getting the wrong testicle removed during surgery? Okay, bad example. But you get the idea: you should laugh when you read this book. If you don't, either you have no sense of humor or I need a new career. I'm too old to start a new career, so the blame falls squarely on you.

Be warned also that you might be offended by this book when I make fun of someone or something you love. Butts of my jokes include doctors, dentists, Latvians, Texans, kids, pets, Deadheads, mothers-in-law, Death Row inmates, Catholics, Pentecostals, Sammy Hagar, Lyle Lovett, the French, Tennessee, fast-food employees, and numerous other people, places and things. I also make ample fun of myself, my wife, my (fictitious) sex life, my home state of Georgia, and other things I hold near and dear. So unbunch your panties and laugh a little. Even you, Sammy Hagar.

Far more offensive than my jokes are the ridiculous things that occur in this world on a daily basis, so read these facts and be afraid, be amused, be annoyed, be aghast, be whatever. You already bought the book and I already got paid, so I don't really care. Sorry, just being honest. (Sort of.)

And remember: front to back, and keep wiping until the TP is clean. Your pal,

Cary McNeal

CHAPTER 1

Are You Gonna Eat That?

The Ugly Truth about Food and Drink

FACT: Bottled drinking water has been marketed as being cleaner and more pure than ordinary tap water, but, in a recent study, a third of bottled water showed significant **chemical or bacterial contamination**, including arsenic, nitrates, carcinogenic compounds, and coliform bacteria. *Probably the bottom third; that kind of stuff tends to sink.*

❯ "Bottled Water: Pure Drink or Pure Hype?" National Resources Defense Council, *www.nrdc.org*.

FACT: Bottled water is rarely tested for purity. An Environmental Working Group study found that ten popular brands were riddled with **chemical pollutants and bacteria**, some as high as tap water. *Hey, you wanted low prices.*

❯ "FDA Should Adopt EPA Tap Water Health Goals for Bottled Water," news release, Environmental Working Group, November 19, 2008, *www.ewg.org*.

❯ "Bottled Water: Pure Drink or Pure Hype?" National Resources Defense Council, *www.nrdc.org*.

FACT: While the results of tap water contamination tests are made public, manufacturers of bottled water **do not divulge** their test results. *Chalk it up to the protection of trade secrets. Every brand of bottled water has its own proprietary blend of pathogens, contaminants, and waste that give the product its uniquely refreshing taste.*

❯ "FDA Should Adopt EPA Tap Water Health Goals for Bottled Water," news release, Environmental Working Group, November 19, 2008, *www .ewg.org*.

FACT: According to government and industry estimates, almost **40 percent** of bottled water is ordinary tap water, often with no additional treatment. *"Additional treatment" = changing out the lawn hose before filling a new batch.*

❯ "FDA Should Adopt EPA Tap Water Health Goals for Bottled Water," news release, Environmental Working Group, November 19, 2008, www.ewg.org.

❯ "Bottled Water: Pure Drink or Pure Hype?" National Resources Defense Council, www.nrdc.org.

FACT: Almost **99 percent** of imported food is never inspected by the FDA or USDA, the two agencies responsible for protecting Americans from tainted products. *They're busy testing bottled water.*

❯ Andrew Bridges, "Imported Food Rarely Inspected," *USA Today*, April 16, 2007, www.usatoday.com.

FACT: One pound of peanut butter can contain up to **150 bug fragments and 5 rodent hairs.** *Up to 150. That means there could only be 120–130. Whew! I was almost disgusted there for a second.*

❯ Stephanie Bailey, "Bug Food: Edible Insects," University of Kentucky College of Agriculture, Entomology Department, www.ca.uky.edu.

❯ "Food Defect Action Levels," U.S. Food and Drug Administration Center for Food Safety and Applied Nutrition, last updated November 2005, www.cfsan.fda.gov.

FACT: One in five office coffee mugs contains **fecal bacteria and *E. coli*,** which can cause diarrhea, food poisoning, and infections. *Not surprising, since most office coffee tastes like shit. Related fact: Three of five office coffee mugs feature sayings that are meant to be funny but aren't, like "Bean me up, Scotty" and "No coffee, no workee."*

❯ Stephanie Muller, "Stay Healthy with Tips from a Germ Freak," *Health Communications Quarterly*, October 19, 2005, www.usjt.com.

❯ "Dr. Germ," Information for News Media, University of Arizona College of Agricultural and Life Sciences, February 17, 2005, www.cals.arizona.edu.

FACT: Vegetarians beware: many low-fat and nonfat yogurts and sweets contain gelatin, which is made from **animal tendons, ligaments, and bones**. *You'd think the crunching would give it away. It must be drowned out by the sound of all those vegetarians patting themselves on the back for being vegetarians.*

> Ayami Chin, "Gross Facts You May Have Never Wanted to Know," Associated Content, May 24, 2007, *www.associatedcontent.com.*

> Ernest R. Vieira and Louis J. Ronsivalli, *Elementary Food Science,* 4th ed. (Springer, 1999), 237.

> Audrey Ensminger, *Foods and Nutrition Encyclopedia,* 2nd ed. (CRC Press, 1994), 1057.

FACT: Fining is a process used by most wineries to **remove particles and impurities** from wine. Typical fining agents include isinglass (a collagen from sturgeon bladders), gelatin, and ox blood. *Whatever impurities are removed by fining, are they worse than fish urine, animal bones and ox blood?*

> Thor Iverson, "Ladybug Marmalade," Stuff Boston, January 12, 2009, *www.stuffboston.com.*

> Emile Peynaud, *Knowing and Making Wine,* trans. Alan Spencer, 2nd ed. (Wiley-IEEE, 1984), 291–294.

FACT: Even when grapes are harvested by hand, some **insects wind up** in the pickers' baskets. Workers simply don't have time to inspect every grape individually as they work. *Consider it fiber. We all need fiber.*

> Thor Iverson, "Ladybug Marmalade," Stuff Boston, January 12, 2009, *www.stuffboston.com.*

> G. L. Creasy, G. I. Creasey, and Leroy L. Creasy, *Grapes* (CABI, 2009), 180.

FACT: Most wines are made from grapes harvested by machines that scythe through everything in their path, including **sticks, insects, rodents, and even larger mammals**, which can make their way into the end product. This is known to wine growers as MOG, or "material other than grapes." *MOG also stands for "Mother of God, I think that was a hoof."*

> Thor Iverson, "Ladybug Marmalade," Stuff Boston, January 12, 2009, *www.stuffboston.com.*

> Ronald S. Jackson, *Wine Science: Principles and Applications,* 3rd ed. (Academic Press, 2008), 335.

> John Smith, "Grapes: MOG," Oakstone Winery, *www.oakstone-winery.com.*

12

FACT: In 2001, the Ontario, Canada wine region was hit by an infestation of ladybugs, which infiltrated many area wineries. When agitated, ladybugs secrete a **strong, foul liquid** containing pyrazine, a flavor similar to rancid peanuts—and one that was perceptible in numerous wines of that vintage. *Rancid Pinot Noir and Bugjolais, for example.*

❯ Thor Iverson, "Ladybug Marmalade," Stuff Boston, January 12, 2009, *www.stuffboston.com.*

❯ "Ladybug, Ladybug, Get Outta My Wine," Canadian Broadcasting Centre News, January 28, 2003, *www.cbc.ca.*

 13

FACT: Molds are tiny organisms with thread-like roots that burrow deep into the foods where they grow. While some molds are safe, like those used to make certain kinds of cheeses—Roquefort, Gorgonzola, Brie—most molds are **unsafe for consumption**, as they can contain *listeria, brucella, salmonella* and *E. coli. Mold is also used to make Frumunda, a briny, piquant cheese from the Nether regions of Crackoslovokia.*

❯ Katherine Zeratsky, "Moldy cheese: Is it unsafe to eat?" Nutrition and Healthy Eating, Expert Answers, Mayo Clinic, *www.mayoclinic.com.*

 14

FACT: **Bacteria multiply** between temperatures of 40° and 140°F, so be careful when reheating food in slow-cookers or chafing dishes. *This is good news for those who like fast-food drive-thrus—the French fries there are usually around 34°F.*

❯ Katherine Zeratsky, "Food Poisoning: How long can you safely keep leftovers?" Nutrition and Healthy Eating, Expert Answers, Mayo Clinic, *www.mayoclinic.com.*

FACT : Parasitic round worms such as *Anisakis simplex*, frequently found in fish, can lead to **anisakiasis in humans**, a condition marked by severe abdominal and gastric pain, nausea, vomiting and abdominal distention, which can last for months. *I think my wife's been cooking with those.*

> R. Wootten and D. C. Cann, "Round Worms in Fish," Food and Agriculture Association of the United Nations, Ministry of Agriculture Fisheries and Food, Torry Research Station, *www.fao.org.*

> Sari Edelstein and others, *Food and Nutrition at Risk in America: Food Insecurity, Biotechnology, Food Safety, and Bioterrorism* (Jones & Bartlett, 2008), 28.

 16

FACT : Long a staple of the American diet and U.S. economy, corn is a **high-carbohydrate, high-glycemic food** that fattens up cattle and does the same to humans who consume it in excess. *If you don't believe me, visit Nebraska.*

> Melissa Diane Smith, "Corn Fed and Fat: The American Problem That is Spreading to Other Countries," News & Notes, Against the Grain Nutrition, July 31, 2008, *www.againstthegrainnutrition.com*

> Audrey Ensminger, *Foods and Nutrition Encyclopedia*, 2nd ed. (CRC Press, 1994).

 17

FACT : Corn is in almost everything we consume. It is the primary food for the chicken, pigs, and cows we eat; the source of corn oils found in many snack foods, margarines, and baked goods; used to make high-fructose corn syrup, the most prevalent, cheapest and, some believe, **most hazardous of all sweeteners**; and the source of numerous food additives. *As a result, corn is found in things that come out of our bodies, too. Like the one you're working on right now.*

> Melissa Diane Smith, "Corn Fed and Fat: The American Problem That is Spreading to Other Countries," News & Notes, Against the Grain Nutrition, July 31, 2008, *www.againstthegrainnutrition.com.*

> Audrey Ensminger, *Foods and Nutrition Encyclopedia*, 2nd ed. (CRC Press, 1994).

FACT: Beef cattle evolved to survive on grass but are regularly fed corn, which has disastrous effects on their digestive systems, requiring a **constant regimen of antibiotics** to keep them healthy. *The antibiotics are clearly working; cows digest things just fine. About every two to three minutes, in fact.*

❯ Michael Pollan, "When a Crop Becomes King," *New York Times*, July 19, 2002, *www .michaelpollan.com.*

❯ Danielle Nierenberg and Lisa Mastny, *Happier Meals: Rethinking the Global Meat Industry* (Worldwatch Institute, 2005), 25.

FACT: Many environmentalists believe salmon farms could have a catastrophic effect on the world's wild salmon populations. Concentrations of solid-waste and nitrogens from farmed pens can **poison marine life**, and many researchers fear that salmon farm escapees could soon overrun and decimate wild stocks. As of 1999, a million salmon had escaped from farms in Puget Sound and British Columbia alone. *Although farmers use dogfish to track the escapees, most ultimately find their way to freedom. Fish that are caught are returned to the farms, where they face intense grilling over an open flame for 8–10 minutes.*

❯ David F. Arnold and William (FRW) Cronan, *The Fishermen's Frontier: People and Salmon in Southeast Alaska* (University of Washington Press, 2008), 187.

FACT: Peanut allergies afflict an estimated 4 million Americans, and can be life-threatening. Almost **half of annual emergency room visits** and two-thirds of deaths due to anaphylaxis are the result of peanut allergies. *On the bright side, if you're a peanut allergy sufferer, you won't have to worry about all those bug fragments and rat hair in peanut butter.*

❯ "Of Mice And Peanuts: A New Mouse Model For Peanut Allergy," Science News, Science Daily, Jan. 14, 2009, *www .sciencedaily.com.*

❯ Kalidas Shetty and others, *Food Biotechnology,* 2nd ed. (CRC Press, 2006), 970.

FACT: Peaches, apples, nectarines, and strawberries are among the **top six "dirtiest" foods**, according to investigations by the Environmental Working Group. More than 90 percent of samples of these fruits tested positive for detectable pesticides, even after being rinsed or peeled. *What, that two-second splash of cold water didn't wash off all the chemicals?*

> "Shopper's Guide to Pesticides," The Environmental Working Group, *www.food news.org.*

FACT: Independent studies show that bell peppers, celery, kale, carrots, lettuce, and potatoes are the vegetables most likely to **expose consumers to pesticides**, despite being rinsed or peeled. *Bell peppers, celery, carrots, lettuce, and potatoes are also the foods most likely to expose family and friends to your lethal flatulence. Who the hell eats kale?*

> "Shopper's Guide to Pesticides," The Environmental Working Group, *www.foodnews.org.*

FACT: Red-colored grocery items like fruit punch and strawberry yogurt are often dyed with carmine, which is made from **ground-up cochineal beetles**. For some, carmine can cause severe allergic reactions and can even lead to anaphylactic shock. *That's too bad, because eating ground-up beetles sounds really great otherwise.*

> Daniel M. Marmion, *Handbook of U.S. Colorants: Foods, Drugs, Cosmetics, and Medical Devices,* 3rd ed. (Wiley-Interscience, 1991), 128.

> J.B. Greig, "Cochineal Extract, Carmine, and Carminic Acid," WHO Food Additive Series 46, Food Standards Agency, London, *www.inchem.org.*

FACT: Citrus Red No.2 is often used to give Florida oranges a brighter, more appealing hue. The same dye has been **banned for use** in food processing because studies have shown that it causes cancer. *Citrus Red No. 2 is also used at spray-on tanning spas to give customers that oh-so-life-like bright orange glow.*

❭ Mike Adams, "Grocery Warning: The Seven Most Dangerous Ingredients in Conventional Foods," (Truth Publishing LLC, 2006), Organic Consumers Association, *www.organic consumers.org.*

❭ Elson Haas and Buck Levin, *Staying Healthy with Nutrition: The Complete Guide to Diet and Nutritional Medicine,* 21st ed. (Celestial Arts, 2006), 447.

FACT: Prior to 2007, Girl Scout cookies were made with **trans fat-filled hydrogenated oil**, though most trans fat has now been removed from the recipes. *Hold on, Sparky. They're still packed with sugar and saturated fat, so it's not a good idea to down an entire box of Tagalong's in one sitting. Even though I have. More than once. Thin Mints, too.*

❭ Mike Adams, "Grocery Warning: The Seven Most Dangerous Ingredients in Conventional Foods," (Truth Publishing LLC, 2006), Organic Consumers Association, *www.organic consumers.org.*

❭ "Thin Mints Recipes," Little Brownie Bakers, *www.little browniebakers.com.*

FACT: A diet high in processed meats like sausage, hot dogs, and luncheon meats **increases the risk of pancreatic cancer**. Chemical reactions that occur during the preparation of these meats yield carcinogens, which could be responsible for the association. *Subway's Jared: "I ate Subway every day for a year and lost 200 pounds. And my pancreas."*

❭ Mike Adams, "Grocery Warning: The Seven Most Dangerous Ingredients in Conventional Foods," (Truth Publishing LLC, 2006), Organic Consumers Association, *www.organic consumers.org.*

❭ "Processed Meat Linked to Pancreatic," Consumer Affairs, April 22, 2005, *www.consumer affairs.com.*

FACT: Mushrooms can kill. The two species most commonly to blame in **mushroom poisonings** are the Death Cap, which contains seven toxins and can be lethal with just one bite, and the Destroying Angel, often confused for an edible white cap mushroom. *Death Cap. Destroying Angel. Who names these things, Dr. Evil?*

❭ Dahlia Rideout, "Ten Dangerous & Deadly Foods," Divine Caroline, *www.divinecaroline .com.*

❭ Ian Robert Hall, *Edible and Poisonous Mushrooms of the World* (Timber Press, 2003).

FACT: Think you're avoiding monosodium glutamate (MSG) by checking product labels? You could be wrong. Food makers now **conceal MSG in packaged foods** by listing it under other names, such as autolyzed or hydrolyzed vegetable protein, torula yeast, soy extracts, yeast extract, and protein isolate. *So the next time you're at a Chinese restaurant, instead of asking for "No MSG, please," say, "No autolyzed or hydrolyzed vegetable protein, torula yeast, soy extracts, yeast extract, and protein isolate, please." And the waiter will still nod and smile as if the MSG wasn't already in the food and he could remove it even if he had any intention of doing so, which he doesn't.*

❯ Mike Adams, "Grocery Warning: The Seven Most Dangerous Ingredients in Conventional Foods," (Truth Publishing LLC, 2006), Organic Consumers Association, *www.organicconsumers.org.*

❯ Myrna Chandler Goldstein and Mark Allan Goldstein, *Controversies in Food and Nutrition* (Greenwood Publishing Group, 2002), 13.

 29

FACT: Blowfish (fugu), a delicacy in Japan and Hong Kong, contains **deadly amounts of tetrodotoxin**, a poison 500 times stronger than cyanide. Several diners die each year from blowfish consumption. *And yet, people continue to eat it. If I'm going to die from eating something, I assure you it won't be fish. Donuts, maybe, or bacon, but not fish.*

❯ Dahlia Rideout, "Ten Dangerous & Deadly Foods," Divine Caroline, *www.divinecaroline.com.*

❯ Jack Jackson, *Complete Diving Manual* (New Holland Publishers, 2005), 177.

❯ Robb Satterwhite, *What's What in Japanese Restaurants: A Guide to Ordering, Eating, and Enjoying,* 2nd ed. (Kodansha International, 1996), 64.

 30

FACT: Because they are filter-feeders, shellfish can accumulate **high levels of toxins** from the algae they consume. Eat enough of them, and you could die. *Lobster and shrimp: two more things I'd rather die from eating than blowfish.*

❯ Dahlia Rideout, "Ten Dangerous & Deadly Foods," Divine Caroline, *www.divinecaroline .com.*

❯ "Various Shellfish-Associated Toxins," Bad Bug Book, U.S. Food and Drug Administration, Center for Food Safety and Applied Nutrition, *www.cfsan .fda.gov.*

31

FACT: Rhubarb leaves contain a high concentration of oxalate, which is **poisonous in large doses**. The stems contain a lower concentration of oxalate, and also act as a good laxative. *Some foods were never meant for human consumption, and rhubarb is at the top of that list. The proof: it either poisons you or makes you crap your pants.*

❯ Dahlia Rideout, "Ten Dangerous & Deadly Foods," Divine Caroline, *www.divinecaroline.com.*

❯ Ian Shaw, *Is it Safe to Eat?: Enjoy Eating and Minimize Food Risks* (Springer, 2005), 127.

32

FACT: Potatoes contain **toxic compounds called glycoalkaloids** that cannot be reduced in cooking. Consumption of high doses of glycoalkaloids can cause diarrhea, vomiting, and, in severe cases, death. *Death by potato. Still better than death by blowfish.*

❯ Dahlia Rideout, "Ten Dangerous & Deadly Foods," Divine Caroline, *www.divinecaroline.com.*

❯ Ian Shaw, *Is it Safe to Eat?: Enjoy Eating and Minimize Food Risks* (Springer, 2005), 127.

33

FACT: Apricot, cherry, and peach pits contain **cyanogenetic glycosides, which release cyanide**. It would take a huge dose to kill you, but there have been reports of children in Turkey suffering from apricot seed poisoning. *In case you needed another reason not to eat a peach pit. Imagine passing that thing.*

❯ Dahlia Rideout, "Ten Dangerous & Deadly Foods," Divine Caroline, *www.divinecaroline.com.*

❯ Y.H. Hui, R. A. Smith, and David G. Spoerke, *Plant Toxicants*, 2nd ed. (Marcel Dekker, 2001), 47.

34

FACT: Chocolate contains the alkaloid theobromine, which in **high doses can be toxic** to humans, and in even small amounts can kill dogs, parrots, horses, and cats. *This means that despite its name, the Kit-Kat candy bar is not a recommended snack for your kittycat. I wonder how many cats have died because of this confusion.*

❯ Dahlia Rideout, "Ten Dangerous & Deadly Foods," Divine Caroline, *www.divinecaroline.com.*

❯ Lewis R. Goldfrank and others, *Goldfrank's Toxicologic Emergencies*, 8th ed. (McGraw-Hill Professional, 2006), 993.

FACT: If not processed properly, tapioca can be toxic; it is made from cassava root, which contains a natural **cyanide-like compound** called linamarin. If the plant is properly dried, soaked, and baked, however, the linamarin is rendered harmless and safe for consumption. *Soaked and Baked—two of my college roommates.*

❯ Dahlia Rideout, "Ten Dangerous & Deadly Foods," Divine Caroline, *www.divinecaroline .com.*

❯ Rudolph Ballentine, *Diet & Nutrition: A Holistic Approach* (Himalayan Institute Press, 1982), 389.

FACT: Bluefin tuna is popular at sushi bars, but it contains **high amounts of mercury**. Mercury poisoning can cause fatigue, memory loss, and numbness in extremities; recent studies also suggest that mercury can increase your risk of cardiovascular disease. *Do not confuse mercury poisoning with Freddie Mercury poisoning, which causes buck teeth, stage theatrics, uncontrollable porn-mustache growth, and a desire to dress like Cap'n Crunch.*

❯ Aaron Casson Trenor, *Sustainable Sushi: A Guide to Saving the Oceans One Bite at a Time* (North Atlantic Books, 2009), 14.

❯ "High Mercury Levels Are Found in Tuna Sushi," *New York Times,* January 23, 2008, *www .nytimes.com.*

FACT: The well-known poison **arsenic is approved by the FDA** as an additive to poultry feed and given to at least 70 percent of chickens raised for consumption in the United States. Arsenic has been linked to cancer, birth defects, diabetes, and death. *Worse, arsenic has almost no taste. They could at least use cyanide, which is every bit as lethal but has the flavor of delicious almonds. And who doesn't love almond chicken?*

❯ "Feeding Arsenic to Poultry: Is this Good Medicine?" Going Green: A Resource Kit for Pollution Prevention in Health Care, Health Care Without Harm,

❯ "Playing Chicken: Avoiding Arsenic in Your Meat," report, Institute for Agriculture and Trade Policy, April 5, 2006, *www.iatp.org.*

FACT: Though banned by all European nations and Canada, the synthetic hormone rBGH (Recombinant Bovine Growth Hormone) is still used by American dairy farmers to boost growth rates and increase body mass of cows, despite being linked to higher risks of **breast cancer and hormonal disorders** in humans who consume milk from those cows. *Got cancer?*

❯ Samuel S. Epstein, *Cancer-Gate: How to Win the Losing Cancer War* (Baywood Publishing Company, 2005), 223.

FACT: Overconsumption of purine-rich foods like lobster, foie gras, and liver can lead to gout, a type of arthritis. **Attacks can last for weeks**, and can damage joints, tendons, and other tissues. *Gout has been called the "rich man's disease" because of its association with fine foods like lobster and foie gras. But, gout can also be caused by excessive alcohol use; this type is known as "poor man's gout." Those of us in the middle class are in the clear.*

> "Gout—Topic Overview," WebMd, *www.webmd.com.*

> "Gout," The Free Dictionary Medical-Dictionary, *http://medical-dictionary.thefree dictionary.com.*

> "Gout," The-Family-Doctor. com, *www.the-family-doctor .com.*

FACT: Commercial livestock and poultry farmers routinely feed antibiotics to animals that are not sick to help them grow larger, or as a pre-emptive measure to make up for stressful, crowded, and unsanitary living conditions. But antibiotic overuse builds resistance to the drugs, and can lead to consumer goods contaminated with **drug-resistant, disease-causing bacteria**. *What about the stressful, crowded, and unsanitary office conditions facing the average American worker? Companies need to start giving drugs to their employees, but not antibiotics. I mean good stuff—Xanax, Valium, Percocet, Thorazine. It would certainly make the day go by quicker.*

> "Antibiotic Overuse in Food Animals," Institute for Agriculture and Trade Policy, *www.iatp.org.*

FACT: *Campylobacter* is a bacteria that can cause **fever, diarrhea, and abdominal cramps**. Most raw poultry meat carries *campylobacter*, making consumption of undercooked chicken the main source for this infection. *Campylobacter* does not commonly cause death. *But consuming it will make you beg for death.*

> "Campylobacter General Information," Centers for Disease Control and Prevention, Department of Health and Human Services, *www.cdc.gov.*

FACT: *E. coli* O157:H7 is a bacterial pathogen found in cow feces. Consuming water or food contaminated with even **a tiny amount of bovine waste** can lead to bloody diarrhea, abdominal cramps, temporary anemia, and kidney failure. *Bloody diarrhea: because neither bloody stool nor diarrhea is enough fun on its own.*

> "Foodborne Illness," Content Source: National Center for Immunization and Respiratory Diseases: Division of Bacterial Diseases, Centers for Disease Control and Prevention, Department of Health and Human Services, October 25, 2005, *www.cdc.gov.*

FACT: A century ago, the most common foodborne diseases were typhoid fever, tuberculosis, and cholera. Today, we have **a new list of food infections** to worry about, including recent discoveries like *cyclospora*, a diarrhea-causing parasite found in Guatemalan raspberries. *"Guatemalan raspberries" is also the nickname of this explosive type of diarrhea. "Start the game without me. I got the Guatemalan raspberries."*

> "Foodborne Illness," Content Source: National Center for Immunization and Respiratory Diseases: Division of Bacterial Diseases, Centers for Disease Control and Prevention, Department of Health and Human Services, October 25, 2005, *www.cdc.gov.*

FACT: In 2008, a Nebraska policeman was awarded $40,000 after he sued a Taco Bell/KFC restaurant that served his family **food containing an employee's urine and spit**. His son was hospitalized with gastroenteritis and dehydration following the meal. The employee who contaminated the food was fined $100 but kept his job. *If you want to hide spit or piss in food, Taco Bell and KFC are the places to do it.*

> "Family wins $40,000 over urine-tainted food," MSNBC.com, July 14, 2008, *www.msnbc.msn.com.*

FACT: The term "natural" (or "all-natural") has **no nutritional meaning** and is not defined or regulated by the FDA, so packaged goods and restaurants can use the term at will. For example, fast-food chain Arby's claims to serve "100 percent all-natural chicken," but uses artificial flavoring. *Consumer food products, now made with 100 percent all-natural bullshit!*

❯ "Sixteen Secrets The Restaurant Industry Doesn't Want You To Know," MSNBC.com, December 13, 2007, *www.msnbc.msn.com.*

❯ "'All natural' claim on food labels is often deceptive," NaturalNews.com, March 21, 2005, *www.natural news.com.*

❯ Lorraine Heller, "'Natural' will remain undefined, says FDA," FoodNavigator-USA.com, January 4, 2008, *www.foodnavigator-usa.com.*

FACT: One serving of Aussie Cheese Fries at Outback Steakhouse contains 2,900 calories—an entire day's **recommended calorie intake** for the average person. *No worries, mate, they'll go right through ya. Cheese fries are only rented, not bought.*

❯ "Sixteen Secrets The Restaurant Industry Doesn't Want You To Know," MSNBC.com, December 13, 2007, *www.msnbc.msn.com.*

FACT: Many of the "low-fat" menu items at Applebee's restaurants contain over 500 calories; the "low-fat chicken quesadillas," for example, weigh in at a whopping **742 calories and 90 grams of carbohydrates** per serving. *Applebee's slogan: "Welcome to the neighborhood." Of people who think they are dieting but aren't.*

❯ "Sixteen Secrets The Restaurant Industry Doesn't Want You To Know," MSNBC.com, December 13, 2007, *www.msnbc.msn.com.*

FACT: A medium fruit-and-yogurt smoothie at Dunkin' Donuts contains **four times as much sugar** as a chocolate-frosted cake doughnut. *Good, I'd rather have the doughnut anyway.*

❯ "Sixteen Secrets The Restaurant Industry Doesn't Want You To Know," MSNBC.com, December 13, 2007, *www.msnbc.msn.com.*

FACT: The Omelette Feast at International House Of Pancakes contains **1,335 calories and 35 grams of saturated fat:** that's one and a half times your recommended daily fat requirement and three times the suggested daily cholesterol intake. *Hint: Avoid menu items that include the words feast, monster, explosion, blowout, or eat-a-palooza.*

❯ "Sixteen Secrets The Restaurant Industry Doesn't Want You To Know," MSNBC. com, December 13, 2007, *www.msnbc.msn.com.*

 50

FACT: Despite its extensive menu, chain restaurant T.G.I. Friday's only makes nutritional data available for "low-fat" dishes (under 500 calories and 10 grams of fat each). There are **only three such selections** on the entire menu. *On the bright side, your server today is wearing 87 pieces of "flair."*

❯ "Sixteen Secrets The Restaurant Industry Doesn't Want You To Know," MSNBC.com, December 13, 2007, *www .msnbc.msn.com.*

CHAPTER 2

Every Little Thing We Do Is Tragic

Human (Mis) Behaviors

FACT: More American teenagers are killed in **car accidents** than by any other cause, accounting for more than one in three fatalities. Risk of accident is highest in the first year that a teen drives, and increases with the number of teenage passengers in a car with an unsupervised teen driver. *Risk of accident is also high in the last year that a person drives, and increases with the number of imaginary passengers in the car.*

❯ "Teen Drivers: Fact Sheet," Motor Vehicle Safety, Centers for Disease Control and Prevention, January 26, 2009, *www .cdc.gov.*

FACT: Roughly 100 people die every year by **choking on ball-point pens**. *Even more tragic: it's usually the only pen they have on them, so they can forget writing a quick farewell note to their loved ones as they are choking.*

❯ Mitchell Symons, *This Book: . . . of More Perfectly Useless Information* (HarperCollins, 2005).

FACT: Some scientists view love in terms of addiction, and they might be right. One study discovered that monogamous pairing is based in the **same region of the brain as drug addiction**. Losing your love can be like experiencing withdrawal. *And for some, getting divorced can feel like taking ecstasy.*

❯ Susana Martinez-Conde and Stephen L. Macknik, "Optical Illusions and the Illusion of Love," *Scientific American*, February 12, 2009, *www.sciam.com.*

FACT: Studies that examined what victims of a heart attack were doing and feeling in the hours preceding the event found **acute emotional stress** to be a common trigger. In one study, more than half of subjects reported being very upset or under great stress in the 24 hours before their attack. *But probably not as upset as they were during and after the attack.*

❯ Michael Feld and Johann Caspar Rüegg, "Head Attack," *Scientific American*, June 2005, *www.sciam.com.*

FACT: Eating and drinking while driving is a serious problem. Most incidents occur while **drivers are on their way to work**. If they spill something on their work clothes, they're more likely to try to remove the stain, become distracted, and cause an accident. *Hence these ridiculous wrinkle- and stain-resistant clothes that retailers are selling now. Sorry, guys, if I want a shirt that wears like a cardboard box, I'll just Scotchgard it myself.*

> "The 10 Most Dangerous Foods to Eat While Driving," Insurance.com, March 2, 2007, www.insurance.com.

FACT: A 2000 survey on driving habits ranks tuning the radio as the most common distraction, with over **60 percent of drivers** admitting that they do it. Other distractions noted include eating while driving (57 percent do it), and turning around to talk with passengers (56 percent). Surprisingly, only a third of drivers listed talking on a cell phone as a distraction. *Because the other two-thirds of cell users aren't distracted at all. They give the phone call their full attention while barreling their car through anything in the way: stop signs, yield signs, road construction crews, aging pedestrians, dogs, children, the blind, traffic cops, bicyclists, unicyclists, juggling unicyclists, mimes, midget parades, clown funerals, etc.*

> "The 10 Most Dangerous Foods to Eat While Driving," Insurance.com, March 2, 2007, www.insurance.com.

FACT: From 2005 to 2006, black Americans had **higher depression rates** (8.0 percent) than whites (4.8 percent). For both whites and blacks living below the poverty line, rates of depression were higher than those with higher incomes. *Now we know why Navin Johnson was so bummed out in* The Jerk. *He was black and poor.*

> "Morbidity and Mortality Weekly Report: Quick Stats," Centers for Disease Control and Prevention, October 3, 2008, www.cdc.gov.

FACT : Studies show that 87 percent of people fear getting trapped in **dull conversations** at dinner parties. *If someone is boring you to tears, interrupt and ask if he would mind calling you on your cell phone. Tell him you want to check reception. When he does, and your phone rings, answer it and say, "Hello?" Then cover the mouthpiece and say to him, "I need to take this, sorry," then begin an imaginary conversation and continue it until he gets annoyed and walks away.*

> Richard Wiseman, *Quirkology: How We Discover the Big Truths in Small Things* (Basic Books, 2008).

FACT: President Ronald Reagan allowed

astrologers to influence

some of his decisions, including the timing of international summits, presidential announcements, and the schedule of Air Force One. *I'll take astrologers over Karl Rove.*

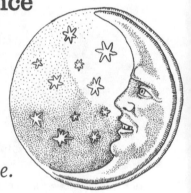

> Richard Wiseman, *Quirkology: How We Discover the Big Truths in Small Things* (Basic Books, 2008).

FACT : The TV viewing habits of millions of Americans fit **the criteria for substance abuse**, with numerous similar dependency symptoms, such as the inability to control viewing, using TV as a sedative, feeling lack of control while watching, angry feelings for watching too much television, and being upset when unable to watch. *"I can quit anytime I—oh, look, Family Guy's on!"*

> "Television & Health: Television Statistics," Compiled by TV-Free America, *www.csun .edu.*

61

FACT: More fast-food employees were murdered on the job in 1998 than police officers. An average of four to five fast-food workers are **killed every month**, usually during robberies, as fast food is largely a cash business and most restaurants have large amounts on site at any given time. *Not surprising. I want to murder an employee almost every time I eat fast food. Not for the money, though . . . just on principle.*

❯ Eric Schlosser, *Fast Food Nation: The Dark Side of the All-American Meal* (Houghton Mifflin Harcourt, 2001).

62

FACT: Women with cosmetic breast implants are three times more likely than other women **to take their own lives**, and are also three times as likely to die from alcohol and drug use. Why? Researchers suspect that many of these women had pre-existing body image and self-esteem issues before getting the implants. *Nah, the researchers—obviously female—are just jealous of women with fabulous racks.*

❯ Maggie Fox, "Breast Implants Linked with Suicide in Study," Reuters, Aug 8, 2007, *www .reuters.com*.

63

FACT: English teen Natalie Cooper is unable to eat **anything but Tic-Tacs**, and throws up anything else she tries to ingest. Cooper must be fed a special formula through a tube to her stomach in order to survive. *She'd have great breath if it weren't for all the puking.*

❯ "The teenage girl who can only eat Tic Tacs," *The Daily Mail*, February 9, 2008, *www .dailymail.co.uk*.

64

FACT: In 2008, drunken Jersey City, New Jersey councilman Steven Lipski was arrested in Washington, DC for **urinating from a night club balcony** onto concertgoers watching a Grateful Dead cover band. *They're Deadheads—they should be used to smelling like pee. I hope Lipski hit the band while he was at it. The only thing worse than The Dead is a Dead cover band.*

❯ Rich Schapiro, "Jersey City Councilman Steven Lipski is No. 1 threat at Washington club," *NY Daily News*, November 9, 2008, www.nydailynews.com.

65

FACT: In an October 2008 presidential debate, "Joe the Plumber" was mentioned twenty-six times, while more serious campaign issues like the troubled U.S. economy and Iraq were only mentioned **sixteen times and six times**, respectively. *If only those other issues would disappear as quickly as Joe did.*

> Posted by Brian Montopoli, "Joe The Plumber's Chat With Couric," CBS News, October 16, 2008, *www.cbsnews.com.*

 66

FACT: Six-year-old Bennett Christiansen made headlines in 2008 when he was **approved for his first credit card**. Bank of America gave Christiansen a $600 credit limit even after he gave his actual birth date and listed his income truthfully as "$0" on the card application. *"What's in your jammies?"*

> Leah Hope, "Six-Year-Old Approved for Credit Card," ABC Local, Chicago, June 18, 2008, *http://abclocal.go.com.*

 67

FACT: When Shanta Dargbeh's ex-boyfriend took someone else to the prom in 2008, the New Jersey teen **set fire to his home**, burning it to the ground. *Nice going, Carrie. Note to self: never cross a Jersey girl.*

> Associated Press, "Trenton Police Say Spurned Girl Set House on Fire," NJ.com, May 24, 2008, *www.nj.com.*

 68

FACT: In 2008, a fifty-year-old woman from Saudi Arabia demanded a divorce in 2008 after her husband **lifted her veil** to view her face while she was asleep. She had concealed her face from him for thirty years. *Because she looks like Jamie Farr.*

> "Divorce for Looking at Wife's Face," *The Daily Telegraph,* May 21, 2008, *www.news.com.au.*

FACT: In January 2008, domestic violence expert Dean Tong was **arrested for assaulting his wife**. This was Tong's third arrest, and his second involving domestic violence. *How do you think he became an expert?*

> Susan Wilson, "Update: Abuse Expert Arrested on Abuse Charge Releases Statement," Tampa Bay's 10 News, *www.wtsp.com*.

> Melanie Brooks, "Author Under Arrest Talks Exclusively with 10 News," 10Connects.com, *www.wtsp.com*.

 70

FACT: A retired teacher in California admits that he taught high school for seventeen years **without knowing how to read or write**. *Neither could his students, so it all worked out.*

> Charisse Yu, "Retired Teacher Reveals He Was Illiterate Until Age 48," 10 News San Diego, February 14, 2008, *www.10news.com*.

71

FACT: A man nearly died at an airport security checkpoint in Nuremberg in 2007 **after drinking a full liter of vodka** rather than surrendering it before taking his flight. The man became severely impaired and had to be taken to a hospital and treated for alcohol poisoning. *Unfortunately, he was one of the pilots, so the flight was delayed until someone else could be called in to take his place.*

> Associated Press, "Man Chugs Down Liter of Vodka in Airport Line," *USA Today*, December 12, 2007, *www.usatoday.com*.

FACT: In 2004, a Syracuse, New York woman required emergency surgery and hospitalization after the **bit of a dentist's drill flew off and lodged near her eye**. At the time of the accident, her dentist was dancing to the song "Car Wash" on the radio. The patient later sued the dentist for more than half a million dollars. *The story has a happy ending. The patient is fine and the dentist got his wish: he's working at the car wash.*

❯ Associated Press, "Disco-Dancing Dentist Sued for Drilling Disaster," MSNBC.com, November 2, 2007, www.msnbc.msn.com.

FACT: A California dentist, Dr. Mark Anderson, was accused in 2007 of **fondling the breasts** of twenty-seven patients. Although he claimed that these "chest massages" were an effective treatment for TMJ, Anderson was later convicted of eleven counts of felony sexual battery. *Now he's working at the car wash with the other ex–dentist, presumably as a wax applicator. Wax on, wax off.*

❯ Associated Press, "Dentist Accused of Fondling Female Patients Argues Massages Appropriate," ABC Local News, http://abclocal.go.com.

❯ Hudson Sangree, "Woodland Dentist Mark Anderson Found Guilty in Fondling Case," *Sacramento Bee*, www.sacbee.com.

FACT: A New York man faced arrest in Times Square in 2004 **for doing nothing**. A police officer charged Matthew Jones with "disorderly conduct" because "numerous pedestrians in the area had to walk around him." Jones maintains he was simply "standing around" talking to friends. *If standing around doing nothing is a crime, I know a lot of people who should be in jail.*

❯ Nicholas Confessore, "A Times Square Pedestrian Is Giving No Ground," *New York Times*, October 18, 2007, www.nytimes.com.

75

FACT: A woman in Pennsylvania was cited for disorderly conduct in 2008 for **swearing at an over-flowing toilet**. The off-duty police officer who lived next door took offense at the language. *If he thought the language was offensive, he should've seen what was clogging the toilet.*

❯ Associated Press, "Scranton Woman Who Swore at Toilet Settles Lawsuit," Pennlive .com, October 22, 2008, *www .pennlive.com.*

 76

FACT: 40 percent of women admit that they **have thrown footwear** at a man. *Women love shoes, so if she's willing to hurl one at you, you know she's pissed.*

❯ Bernice Kanner, *Are You Normal about Sex, Love, and Relationships?* (Macmillan, 2004).

 77

FACT: A Nevada couple were charged in 2007 with child neglect after their kids became malnour-ished **while the couple played online video games** for days at a time. Their eleven-month-old's hair was so matted her head had to be shaved, and her twenty-two-month-old brother had difficulty walking due to lack of muscle development. *Video games may or may not be addictive, but being an asshole certainly is.*

❯ Associated Press, "Parents Neglect Starved Babies to Feed Video Game Addiction," Fox News, July 14, 2007, *www .foxnews.com.*

FACT: In 2005, a fifty-seven-year-old woman **gave birth to her own granddaughter**, a baby conceived with an egg donated by her twenty-seven-year-old daughter. *Let me guess: Arkansas?*

> Lucy Lawrence, "Woman of 57 Who Gave Birth to Her Own Granddaughter," *Sunday Mirror,* August 14, 2005.

 79

FACT: In 2007 a British climber reached the summit of Mt. Everest, but ran out of air during his descent. **As many as forty climbers passed the dying man**, unwilling to risk using up their own oxygen to help him. *They'll need it in Hell.*

> Associated Press, "As Others Pass, Climber Dies Alone on Mount Everest," ESPN, May 27, 2006, *http://sports.espn.go.com.*

 80

FACT: In 2006, Claude Allen, a former domestic policy adviser for President George Bush, was charged for **stealing $5,000 worth of items** from several Washington DC-area stores. *It sounds worse than it was. All he stole was a coat rack from Pottery Barn and a set of bookends from Restoration Hardware.*

> John Files and Robert Pear, "Former White House Aide Is Arrested on Theft Charges," *New York Times,* March 11, 2006, *www.nytimes.com.*

FACT: A former U.S. soldier who was wounded in Iraq was **billed for his bloody body armor** that was discarded as a biohazard. The man, who left the Army because of his injury, had to borrow $700 from friends to make the payment before the Army would discharge him. *Oh, and thanks for serving!*

❯ Allison Barker for the Associated Press, "Wounded Soldier Made To Pay For Armor Pulled Off His Bleeding Body," *The Huffington Post,* February 8, 2006, *www.huffingtonpost.com.*

FACT: Multimillionaire David Pizer has arranged to **freeze his body in liquid nitrogen** when he dies in hopes of being brought back to life someday. Pizer has also left his entire fortune to himself. *I hope he's not counting on his heirs to unfreeze him.*

❯ James Langton, "Rich Freeze Their Assets for Chance to Live Again," *Telegraph UK,* January 30, 2006, *www.telegraph.co.uk.*

FACT: A French woman who survived the first face transplant in history in 2006 **took up smoking again** once she regained feeling in her mouth and lips. *She spent months in the hospital and had umpteen surgeries after having half of her face chewed off by her dog while she was passed out after attempting suicide with a handful of sleeping pills. Let the woman have a damn cigarette.*

❯ Ariane Bernard and Craig S. Smith, "French Face-Transplant Patient Tells of Her Ordeal," *New York Times,* February 7, 2006, *www.nytimes.com.*

FACT: In 2006, a forty-one-year-old British woman married what she called "the love of my life": **a male dolphin named Cindy**. The woman had met Cindy fifteen years before and said it was "love at first sight." *I'm not sure what's more disconcerting, the marriage or the fact that someone would name a male dolphin "Cindy."*

❯ Associated Press, "With This Herring I Thee Wed," MSNBC.com, Jan. 3, 2006, *www.msnbc.msn.com.*

FACT: To fight loneliness, one Navy wife in Georgia **purchased a mannequin dressed like a sailor** in 2005 to stand in for her husband, who was serving at sea. The woman takes the mannequin to dinner, movies, and shopping. *Okay, if your wife can replace you with a mannequin and be happy, you must be one boring motherfucker.*

> "Navy Wife Finds a New Man-Nequin," MSNBC.com, December 14, 2005, *www.msnbc.msn.com.*

FACT: A prominent cause of divorce among older Japanese couples is **"retired husband syndrome."** Doctors first described the syndrome when wives began showing irritability, ulcers, rashes, and other stress symptoms when made to manage their recently retired husbands who have nothing to do but bark orders at them all day long. *By the time you read this, "retired husband syndrome" will have been renamed "dead retired husband syndrome."*

> "Retired Husband Syndrome," ABC News, January 11, 2006, *http://abcnews.go.com.*

FACT: A gunshot wound in his leg didn't keep a Tampa, Florida pizza delivery man from finishing his rounds in 2005. Dedication to his work compelled Thomas Stefanelli to deliver four more pizzas before calling for help after **being shot in a robbery attempt.** *Tom came in second in the Employee Of The Year contest, edged out by a co-worker who refused bathroom access to a guy who wasn't a paying customer.*

> Associated Press, "Bullet Won't Stop This Pizza Delivery Man," MSNBC.com, June 8, 2005, *www.msnbc.msn.com.*

FACT: Purdue University researchers say most drivers have no problem exceeding the speed limit by **up to 20 mph** and see no risk in doing so. *You know who will be glad to hear this? Sammy Hagar.*

❯ Keith Barry, "Study Shows Drivers Feel Free to Ignore Speed Limits." Wired.com, November 14, 2008, *www .wired.com.*

FACT: Trichotillomania is a behavioral disorder that makes people **rip their own hair out**, pulling it from the scalp, eyebrows, eyelashes, and more, with bald patches as result. The condition affects as many as 9 million Americans; 90 percent of adult sufferers are women. *All of them mothers, I bet.*

❯ "What Is Compulsive Hair Pulling?," Trichotillomania Learning Center, *www.trich.org.*

FACT: Chronic skin picking (CSP) is a serious but largely misunderstood human behavioral problem. **CSP sufferers obsessively pick, scratch, and rub their skin,** often in an attempt to remove small irregularities or perceived imperfections. This behavior can result in skin discoloration, scarring, or even severe tissue damage. *Chronic nit-picking (CNP) is a serious but largely tolerated human behavioral problem. CNP sufferers obsessively pick, nag, harangue, and correct others, particularly spouses, children, and coworkers, often in an attempt to remove small irregularities or perceived imperfections.*

❯ "What Is Chronic Skin Picking?," Trichotillomania Learning Center, *www.trich.org.*

91

FACT: People who have borderline personality disorder (BPD) suffer from mood instability, troubled personal relationships, and an inability to control their emotions and impulses. BPD affects up to **10 percent of all patients under psychiatric care.** *And about 80 percent of psychiatrists giving that care.*

❯ Andreas Meyer-Lindenberg, "The Roots of Problem Personalities," *Scientific American*, April 2009, *www.sciam.com.*

❯ "Borderline Personality Disorder," National Institute Of Mental Health, *www.nimh.nih.gov.*

 92

FACT: Foreign Accent Syndrome (FAS) is an extremely rare brain disorder that causes sufferers to **speak involuntarily in a foreign accent.** The illness is the result of trauma affecting the area of the brain that controls speech. *I think my hillbilly cousin has this. Every once in a while he'll say something that sounds vaguely like English.*

❯ Andrea Canning, "Foreign Accent Syndrome Gives Sufferers an International Sound," ABC News, November 13, 2008, *http://abcnews.go.com.*

 93

FACT: The rare neurological disorder Alien Hand Syndrome (AHS) **causes the sufferer's hands to move independently**, without his control over the action. People with AHS have been known to punch or choke themselves and tear at their clothing without meaning to do so, and may even need to use the healthy hand to curb the alien hand. The condition typically arises after trauma to the brain, brain surgery, or stroke. *"Let's all give it up for E.T.!" (audience applauds). That's what I thought Alien Hand Syndrome was.*

❯ "Definition of Alien hand syndrome," Medicine.net, December 15, 2000, *www.medterms.com.*

❯ Charles W. Bryant, "How Alien Hand Syndrome Works," HowStuffWorks.com, *www.health.howstuffworks.com.*

❯ "Alien Hand Syndrome: Nerve Impulses Can Cause Movement Even When Person Is Unaware," Science Daily, July 17, 2007, *www.sciencedaily.com.*

FACT: The Bible is the **most shoplifted book**. *At least the right people are getting it.*

> Jerry MacGregor and Marie Prys, *1001 Surprising Things You Should Know about the Bible* (Fall River Press, 2006).

 95

FACT: People with Cotard's syndrome can suffer from a variety of delusions, which range from **a belief that they are missing body parts or vital organs** to thinking that they are dead, have lost their soul, or do not even exist. The illness is found mostly in individuals with schizophrenia or bipolar disorder. *You have to exist to be able to think you don't exist, DUH! Schizos are stupid.*

> J. Pearn and C. Gardner–Thorpe, "Jules Cotard (1840–1889): His life and the unique syndrome which bears his name," *Neurology*, May 14, 2002, 1400–1403, *www.ncbi .nlm.nih.gov.*

 96

FACT: People who experience Capgras' delusion are convinced that others, usually those closest to them, **have been replaced by identical impostors**. The condition affects both sexes, but occurs more frequently in women. *Particularly when their husbands make dinner or take the kids to the park without being asked.*

> H. D. Ellis and others, "Reduced autonomic responses to faces in Capgras delusion," *Proceedings, Biological Sciences,* July 22, 1997, 1085–1092, *www .pubmedcentral.nih.gov.*

> "Capgras Syndrome," Disorder Info Sheet, Psychnet.com, *www .psychnet-uk.com.*

 97

FACT: Piblokto, or Arctic hysteria, is a mental disorder that affects people living in the Arctic Circle, typically Inuit women. It is marked by **frenzied, disturbed behavior** such as uncontrolled screaming, running wildly, or removing one's clothing in frigid weather; memory loss; seizures; and other symptoms reminiscent of epilepsy. *They also drink a shitload of tequila, which doesn't help.*

> Emilio F. Moran and Rhonda Gillett-Netting, *Human Adaptability: An Introduction to Ecological Anthropology,* 2nd ed. (Westview Press, 2000).

> "Arctic Hysteria," Sarah Efron, Journalist, July/August 2003, *www.sarahefron.com.*

98

FACT : Exploding Head Syndrome is a rare phenomenon in which a person approaching deep sleep **experiences a loud bang in his head** that sounds like a bomb exploding or similarly loud noise. Though the event seems to originate from inside the head, it is an illusion and does no physical damage to its victim. *Exploding Head Syndrome sounds a lot like a hangover.*

❯ "Exploding Head Syndrome," American Sleep Association, September, 2007, *www.sleep association.org.*

 99

FACT : Body Integrity Identity Disorder, also known as Amputee Identity Disorder, is a psychological condition that **causes sufferers to seek amputations for cosmetic reasons**: they want their bodies to match the idealized image they have of themselves as amputees. *Doctors are stumped as to the cause of the disorder. They continue the necessary legwork to arm themselves with the facts before they will go out on a limb and theorize about causation, as they are determined not to come up short and have their efforts cut off at the knees.*

❯ "Body Integrity Identity Disorder," Body Integrity Identity Disorder, *www.biid.org.*

 100

FACT : In April 2009, a Louisiana man was arrested for stabbing his sixty-three-year-old brother **after the two argued over a can of pork and beans**. The victim was treated for multiple stab wounds to his arm and shoulder. The two men had been drinking when the fight began. *Alcohol and beans—always a recipe for trouble.*

❯ "Man Allegedly Stabs Brother Over Pork and Beans," Yahoo News, April 16, 2009, *www.news.yahoo.com.*

CHAPTER 3

Totally Gross Anatomy

*The Human
Body Exposed*

101

FACT: If you sneeze hard enough, you can fracture a rib. But try to suppress a sneeze and you might **rupture a blood vessel in your head or neck** and drop dead. *If you try to suppress a fart and a sneeze at the same time, you could blow your head off like a champagne cork.*

> Cameron Tuttle, *The Paranoid's Pocket Guide* (Chronicle Books, 1997).

102

FACT: While pubic lice primarily infect pubic hair, they can also **be found in thigh, chest, and facial hair**, including eyelashes. *How pubic lice might end up on one's face I will leave to you to deduce.*

> James G.H. Dinulos, MD, "Lice," Merck Manuals Online Medical Library, September 2008, *www.merck.com.*

103

> Matthew Fox, *The A.W.E. Project: Reinventing Education, Reinventing the Human* (Wood Lake Publishing, 2006).

FACT: The human stomach must produce a new lining every day to protect itself from **its own acid**. *Which somehow reminds me of Groucho Marx's quote, "I don't care to belong to any club that would have me as a member."*

34   the human body exposed

FACT: The acid in your stomach is so powerful that it can **dissolve a razor blade** in less than a week. *You should still be careful when eating them, though.*

> Matthew Fox, *The A.W.E. Project: Reinventing Education, Reinventing the Human* (Wood Lake Publishing, 2006).

FACT: If a boy is born without testosterone, **his genitalia will mimic that of a female**: the scrotum forms labia majora—the outer lips of a vagina—and the penis becomes a sort of clitoris. *That's the guy you don't want to tell to go fuck himself, because he might try.*

> Ruth K. Westheimer, *Sex for Dummies*, 3rd ed. (For Dummies, 2006).

FACT: The skin is the largest organ in the human body, **covering about twenty square feet** in an adult male. It also constantly regenerates; a person sheds around forty pounds of skin in his lifetime. *Some people can shed it all at once by just shaking their dandruff-ridden heads.*

> Robert Dolezal, *Reader's Digest Book of Facts* (Readers Digest, 1987).

> Mitchell Symons, *That Book: . . . of Perfectly Useless Information* (HarperCollins, 2004).

FACT: We grow in our sleep, and wake up every morning **about eight millimeters taller** than the night before. However, we return to our former height as gravity compresses our cartilage discs back into place throughout the next day. *It's like "morning wood" for the entire body.*

> Robert Dolezal, *Reader's Digest Book of Facts* (Readers Digest, 1987).

FACT: The pressure exerted by a pumping human heart can **squirt blood thirty feet**. *Research is limited, though, so if you ever lose a limb unexpectedly, grab a tape measure and see how far your blood squirts before you pass out and die. Don't forget to write it down, too.*

> Mitchell Symons, *That Book: . . . of Perfectly Useless Information* (HarperCollins, 2004).

FACT: You can find 20 million microscopic animals **living on a square inch** of human skin. *Skin sounds like Tokyo.*

> Mitchell Symons, *That Book: . . . of Perfectly Useless Information* (HarperCollins, 2004).

FACT: The average human body radiates enough heat in thirty minutes to **boil two pints of water**. *But only if you're not looking. A watched body won't boil.*

> Robert Dolezal, *Reader's Digest Book of Facts* (Readers Digest, 1987).

FACT: The postage stamp-sized foreskin from a circumcised baby takes just twenty-one days to grow enough skin to **cover three basketball courts**. Such laboratory-grown skin is used to treat burn patients. *This is why you should never call a burn victim "dickhead." You could be right.*

> Robert Dolezal, *Reader's Digest Book of Facts* (Readers Digest, 1987).

112

FACT: Though female ovaries generate almost half a million eggs, **only about
400 of them** will ever get the chance to be
fertilized. *It's like being called for jury duty, except
the eggs probably don't sit there whispering to themselves, "Please don't pick me, please don't pick me."*

> Robert Dolezal, *Reader's
Digest Book of Facts* (Readers
Digest, 1987).

113

FACT: Human saliva helps keep the
mouth's pH balance slightly alkaline.
If it didn't, the mouth would create an
**acidic environment that would rot away
your teeth**. *If the acid is that strong, you won't
need teeth.*

> Kathleen McGowan, "The
Biology of . . . Saliva," Discover,
October 2005, *www.discover
magazine.com*.

114

FACT: There are **over 700 species of bacteria** that thrive in the thirty-three square
inches of the average mouth, making it
the most unsanitary part of your entire
body. *Surely the rectum runs a close second.*

> "Grossology Gross Facts,"
Denver Museum of Natural Science, *www.dmns.org*.

115

FACT: The types of bacteria in the
human mouth **vary among the world's
population**. North Americans, South
Americans, and Swedes harbor different
bacteria. *I think I need to swap spit with a Swedish woman so we can compare bacteria.*

> Kathleen McGowan, "The
Biology of . . . Saliva," Discover,
October 2005, *www.discover
magazine.com*.

F A C T : When full, the bladder expands to roughly **the same size as a softball**. *But it feels like a basketball. Made of lead.*

> Truman Hedding, "Nineteen Things You Didn't Know About The Human Body," *www.truman hedding.com.*

F A C T : By the time you're an adult, you're likely to have **about 5 million hairs** growing out of your skin—the same number as a gorilla. *Or Robin Williams.*

> "Human Hair," Discovery Channel, *http://.yucky.discovery .com.*

F A C T : Male testicles create **10 million new sperm cells** every day, enough to repopulate the planet in just six months. *Some men try, too.*

> Robert Dolezal, *Reader's Digest Book of Facts* (Readers Digest, 1987).

F A C T : Being "scared to death" can happen. The body's protective mechanism, the fight-or-flight response, pumps adrenaline into the blood, causing the nervous system to increase blood flow to muscles, dilate the pupils and, in some cases, evacuate the bowels. But **adrenaline is toxic in large amounts** and can cause death if it floods the heart unchecked. *So being "scared shitless" isn't just hyperbole, either.*

> Coco Ballantyne, "Can a person be scared to death?" *Scientific American*, January 30, 2009, *www.sciam.com.*

120

FACT: Strong positive or negative emotions—ecstasy, grief, excitement—**can lead to sudden cardiac death** via ventricular fibrillation (irregular heartbeat), as in the case of people who have died during sexual intercourse or when frightened. *Or when frightened during sexual intercourse, which happens more often than you might think. At least it does to me.*

❯ Coco Ballantyne, "Can a person be scared to death?" *Scientific American*, January 30, 2009, *www.sciam.com*.

121

FACT: A study in Germany found an **increase in sudden cardiac death** on days that the German soccer team was playing in the World Cup championship. *If they ever win one, that number will go up, as thousands more Germans will die of shock.*

❯ Coco Ballantyne, "Can a person be scared to death?" *Scientific American*, January 30, 2009, *www.sciam.com*.

122

FACT: Some people are born with **extra nipples (polythelia) or even extra breasts (polymastia)**. Extra or "accessory" breasts are most commonly found in the armpits, but can develop anywhere along mammary ridges, which extend from the armpits to the upper thighs. *And, by the way, we still don't know why men have a mammary ridge, just that they do. "I have nipples, Focker. Are you gonna milk me?"*—Meet the Parents.

❯ Leonard V. Crowley, *An Introduction to Human Disease: Pathology and Pathophysiology Correlations*, 7th ed.(Jones & Bartlett, 2006).

❯ Susan Van Houten, "Accessory nipples (polythelia) and breast tissue (polymastia)," University Health Systems Of Eastern Carolina, March 21, 2003, *www.uhseast.com*.

FACT: Breast cancer isn't just a women's disease. **Men can get it, too**, though they do so much less frequently, about one man for every 100 women. Also, unlike women, men typically only get the disease after age fifty. *Sounds to me like a good excuse to go into the mobile mammography bus and scope out some bare boobs.*

❯ Gerard M. Doherty and Lawrence W. Way, *Current Surgical Diagnosis & Treatment*, 12th ed. (McGraw-Hill, 2005).

FACT: More than **90 percent of women have asymmetrical breasts**. While most asymmetry is slight and inconspicuous, women with significantly mismatched breasts can suffer mental and emotional anguish. *Especially if you call them "Feldmans" or ask if one breast is adopted.*

❯ Dimitrije E. Panfilov, *Cosmetic Surgery Today*, trans. Grahame Larkin (Thieme, 2005).

FACT: Humans shed about **1.5 million skin flakes every hour**. Bath sponges and washcloths can be filled with these flakes and their accompanying *staphylococcus aureus*, a common skin bacteria that can cause infection if it ends up in the wrong part of the body. *In other words, don't wash your crack with someone else's loofa unless you want to spend the next six months scratching it.*

❯ Philip M. Tierno, *The Secret Life of Germs: What They Are, Why We Need Them, and How We Can Protect Ourselves against Them* (Simon & Schuster, 2004).

FACT: Only 10 percent of the cells in our bodies are actually human. The rest are the **90 trillion bacteria that live on or in us**, covering our bodies from head to toe. *Only 5 percent of the cells in Christopher Walken's body are actually human. The rest are from an alien world.*

❯ Rose George, *The Big Necessity: The Unmentionable World of Human Waste and Why It Matters* (St. Martin's Press, 2008).

❯ Garry Hamilton, "Insider Trading," New Scientist, June 26, 1999, *www.newscientist.com*.

FACT: Less sleep disturbs normal metabolism, which **contributes to obesity, diabetes, and cardio-vascular disease**. People who averaged just five hours of sleep a night also showed a higher level of ghrelin, a hormone the stomach releases to signal hunger. *People who average just five hours of sleep a night also show a higher level of ghrouch, a hormone that makes you want to kick someone's ass when they say, "You look tired."*

❯ Rick Nauert, PhD, "Childhood Obesity from Lack of Sleep?" PsychCentral, October 24, 2006, http://psychcentral.com.

FACT: All humans exist for **half an hour** as a single cell at conception. *Some of us stay that way.*

❯ Truman Hedding, "Nineteen Things You Didn't Know About The Human Body," www.truman hedding.com.

FACT: *The British Medical Journal* has estimated that smoking one cigarette **takes eleven minutes off the life** of an average person. *Too bad those eleven minutes don't disappear right as you're smoking, say, during* The English Patient.

❯ Mary Shaw, Richard Mitchell, and Danny Dorling, "Time for a smoke? One cigarette reduces your life by 11 minutes," *British Medical Journal*, January 1, 2000, www.pubmedcentral.nih.gov.

FACT: The 250,000 pores that exist on the soles of the feet secrete almost ¼ **cup of sweat** every day. *Oh, is that all? No wonder they smell so good.*

❯ "Grossology Gross Facts," Denver Museum of Natural Science, www.dmns.org.

FACT: Continuous farting for **six years and nine months** would create energy equal to that of an atomic bomb. *I need to hook my child up with the Defense Department.*

❯ Mitchell Symons, *That Book: . . . of Perfectly Useless Information* (HarperCollins, 2004).

FACT: Your body produces enough saliva during your lifetime to fill **two swimming pools**. *Luckily, most swimming pools are already filled with saliva, so yours isn't needed.*

❯ Mary M. Bauer, *The Truth About You: Things You Don't Know You Know* (VanderWyk & Burnham, 2006).

FACT: An "Extreme Gulp" drink sold at 7-11 convenience stores **has twice as much liquid** as the average human stomach can hold. *Which is why no one holds it. And why I sit on the end of the row at the movies.*

> James Bevan, *Handbook of Anatomy and Physiology* (New York: Simon & Schuster, 1978) 45.

> Peter Strupp and Alan Dingman, *Fat, Dumb, and Ugly: The Decline of the Average American* (Simon & Schuster, 2004).

FACT: The human liver performs no fewer than **500 different functions**. If a portion of it were removed, the liver would continue to work and would rapidly grow back to its normal size. *Well, depending on the size of the portion. Don't go lopping off huge chunks of your liver to give away, okay?*

> Mary M. Bauer, *The Truth About You: Things You Don't Know You Know* (VanderWyk & Burnham, 2006).

FACT: The average human swallows about a **quart of snot** every day. *What's really cool is when you can hear people sucking it out of their sinuses and swallowing. I love that sound, especially in restaurants.*

> "Grossology Gross Facts," Denver Museum of Natural Science, *www.dmns.org*.

FACT: Seventy percent of people admit to picking their nose; 30 percent of those confess to **eating what they picked**. *100 percent of people admit to puking when they read that.*

> "Grossology Gross Facts," Denver Museum of Natural Science, *www.dmns.org*.

137

FACT: People who live in big cities make **more ear wax**. *Ah, okay. No wonder big city folks never stop when I try to ask them for directions. They can't hear me. Whew! I was starting to think maybe they were just assholes.*

> "Grossology Gross Facts," Denver Museum of Natural Science, *www.dmns.org.*

138

FACT: Believe it or not, **fresh urine is cleaner** than saliva or your facial skin. Healthy urine is sterile and contains little or no bacteria when it leaves your body. *Being cleaner than spit isn't really a bragging point.*

> "Grossology Gross Facts," Denver Museum of Natural Science, *www.dmns.org.*
> "Bacteria in Urine, No Symptoms," University Of Michigan Health System, *www.med.umich.edu.*

139

FACT: Research suggests that marital discord makes wounds heal more slowly. A recent study showed that couples with consistently hostile behaviors healed at a **40 percent slower rate** than low-hostility couples. *Which means you're gonna have that shoe mark on your forehead for a while, bud.*

> J.K. Kiecolt-Glase, "Hostile Marital Interactions, Proinflammatory Cytokine Production, and Wound Healing," *Archives of General Psychiatry*, December 2005, http://.archpsyc.ama-assn.org.

140

FACT: Goose bumps are caused by piloerection, a fight-or-flight reflex that once **made us seem bigger to predators** and kept us warm by making our hair stand straight up. We lost the fur in evolution, but not the reflex. *And I'm okay with that. If I get cold, I'd rather put on a sweater than be a sweater.*

> Mitchell Symons, *That Book: . . . of Perfectly Useless Information* (HarperCollins, 2004).
> "What causes goose bumps?" Advice, Mens Health, *www.menshealth.com.*

FACT : The average human loses **85,000 brain cells** each day, but only regenerates 50 new ones. *Which is a lot like my 401(k)— except for the regenerating part.*

❯ "Statistically Speaking: Brains Made To Order," *Popular Science*, September 2005.

FACT : Babies are **born without kneecaps**—sort of. They have cartilage in their kneecaps which does not ossify into bone until 3–5 years of age. *This explains why infants are notorious gamblers. They don't have to worry about having their kneecaps broken if they don't pay their bookies.*

❯ Noel Botham, *The Ultimate Book of Useless Information: A Few Thousand More Things You Might Need to Know (But Probably Don't)* (Perigee, 2007).

❯ Tom Scheve, "Do Babies Have Kneecaps?" HowStuffWorks.com, *www.health.howstuffworks.com*.

FACT : Your nose can remember **50,000 different scents**. *So, unlike a dog, once you sniff someone's crotch, you'll remember the smell and won't have to sniff them again later. That's a good thing, because sticking your nose in someone's crotch is a good way to get thrown out of a bar, trust me.*

❯ "Sixteen Unusual Facts About The Human Body," HowStuff Works.com, *www.health .howstuffworks.com*.

FACT: About 1 in 2,000 babies is **born with teeth**. If the teeth are membranous, they will be reabsorbed into the body. If fixed firmly, don't remove them, or no other teeth will reappear in their place until the permanent teeth start to come in at age six or seven. *It's easy to spot a baby with teeth. He's the one drinking from a bottle instead of breastfeeding.*

> Adele Pillitteri. *Maternal & Child Health Nursing: Care of the Childbearing & Childrearing Family,* 5th ed. (Lippincott Williams & Wilkins, 2006).

FACT: The occurrence of Type 2 Diabetes in children, once unheard of, has risen **45 percent** in this country in the last ten years, largely due to soaring obesity rates among our kids. *Too bad they don't let kids play dodgeball in school anymore. They'd have a lot more targets than when I was a kid.*

> Katherine Robertson, "Is Your Child a Health Statistic? 4 Scary Facts, 8 Real Solutions," Gaiam Life, *www.life.gaiam.com.*

> "Diabetes Rates Are Increasing Among Youth," NIH News, National Institutes Of Health, November 13, 2007, *www.nih.gov.*

FACT: Diagnoses of Attention Deficit/Hyperactivity Disorder (AD/HD) have risen by **9 million new cases** in the last ten years, and the condition now affects 4–12 percent of American children. *Researchers also discovered tha—hey, look, a seagull!*

> Katherine Robertson, "Is Your Child a Health Statistic? 4 Scary Facts, 8 Real Solutions," Gaiam Life, *www.life.gaiam.com.*

> Victoria Clayton, "Who's to blame for the rise in AD/HD?" MSNBC.com, September 8, 2004, *www.msnbc.msn.com.*

FACT : Copremesis, or fecal vomiting, is not a myth: **a bowel obstruction can cause feces to be drawn into the stomach** from the intestine by spasmodic contractions of the gastric muscles, which the stomach then attempts to expel through vomiting. *That explains some people's breath.*

> "Fecal Vomiting," Dorland's Medical Dictionary, *www.merck source.com.*

> "Fecal Vomiting," Medical Dictionary, *www.medical-dictionary.com.*

> "Fecal Vomiting," Poop Report, *www.poopreport.com.*

FACT : Smegma is a white, foul-smelling, cheese-like secretion sometimes found under the foreskin in males and around the clitoris in females. Smegma is **produced by body oils and the bacteria that feed on them**. Some studies have suggested a link between smegma and penile and cervical cancer. *You had me at "cheese-like."*

> "What is smegma?" Net DoctorUK, *www.netdoctor.co.uk.*

> "Teen Talk: Smegma," Planned Parenthood, *www.teenwire.com.*

> "What are the risk factors for penile cancer?" Cancer.org, *www.cancer.org.*

FACT : A person can live without eating for weeks, but will only survive **eleven days without sleep**. *People around those who haven't slept, however, will only survive a day or two.*

> "Sixteen Unusual Facts About The Human Body," How Stuff Works, *www.health.how stuffworks.com.*

FACT : The human brain stops growing **at the age of eighteen**. *Probably because most eighteen-year-olds know everything by then. If you don't believe me, ask them.*

> Facts Library, FactLib.com, *www.factlib.com.*

CHAPTER 4

Was It Bad for You, Too?

Everything You Never Wanted to Know about Sex and Love

FACT: Up to 20 percent of Americans have genital herpes, **which has no cure** and is easily transmitted through sexual contact. *Genital herpes: the gift that keeps on giving.*

> "Genital Herpes—CDC Fact Sheet," Centers for Disease Control and Prevention, Division of STD Prevention, National Center for HIV/AIDS, Viral Hepatitis, STD, and TB Prevention, January 4, 2008, *www.cdc.gov.*

FACT: Of people who use dating personal ads, **35 percent** are married. *Hey, we all forget things sometimes.*

> Bernice Kanner, *Are You Normal about Sex, Love, and Relationships?* (Macmillan, 2004).

FACT: Two out of three middle class nineteen-year-old males confess to having gotten a date drunk **to coerce her into having sex**. Two out of five have used verbal intimidation, and almost one in five have used force or threats. Nearly 60 percent of female college students say that they have had intercourse against their will. *The rest of us just worked the pity angle. Tears are surprisingly effective at getting a girl in bed.*

> Bernice Kanner, *Are You Normal about Sex, Love, and Relationships?* (Macmillan, 2004).

FACT: Only **15 percent of sexually active adults** have been tested for HIV, says the National Center for Health Statistics. *The other 85 percent are certain they don't have it. No, really, there's no way they could possibly have it, so why bother with that annoying condom?*

> Bernice Kanner, *Are You Normal about Sex, Love, and Relationships?* (Macmillan, 2004).

FACT: 12 percent of men surveyed say they would not tell a partner **if they were HIV-positive**. *At least not until after they've had sex. That would just kill the mood.*

> Bernice Kanner, *Are You Normal about Sex, Love, and Relationships?* (Macmillan, 2004).

FACT: Eight percent of people admit to **having sex with a cousin**, and six percent confess to doing it with a sibling or half-sibling. *Hard to say what's more troubling: the fact that they do it or that they admit it.*

> Bernice Kanner, *Are You Normal about Sex, Love, and Relationships?* (Macmillan, 2004).

FACT: Two out of three men say they would have **sex for cash**, and 16 percent of them would do it for $150 or less. *The third guy is lying.*

> Bernice Kanner, *Are You Normal about Sex, Love, and Relationships?* (Macmillan, 2004).

FACT: In an international survey, 14 percent of people admit to **having slept with a friend's lover** behind his (or her) back. *The trick is to be very quiet and pray he doesn't roll over.*

> Bernice Kanner, *Are You Normal about Sex, Love, and Relationships?* (Macmillan, 2004).

FACT: Erectile dysfunction (ED) affects approximately **18 million** American men. *If my name were Ed, I'd be pissed that they call this ED. Especially if I had it.*

> "Natural Viagra? 'Horny Goat Weed' Shows Promise In Lab Studies," Medical News Today, September 25, 2008, *www.medicalnewstoday.com.*

FACT: Although the penis is not a bone, **it can still be fractured**. A fracture can occur when the erect penis endures blunt trauma during sexual intercourse or other physical activity. A cracking sound can be heard, followed by pain and swelling that causes the shape of the penis to become distorted. Surgery is often required to repair the damage. *Every man reading this just clenched his legs together.*

> Klemen Jagodič and others, "A Case of Penile Fracture with Complete Urethral Disruption during Sexual Intercourse: A Case Report," *Journal of Medical Case Reports*, May 2, 2007, *www.medicalnewstoday.com.*

FACT: One study reports that autoerotic asphyxia, or cutting off oxygen to the brain to achieve greater sexual satisfaction, **claims the lives of 500–1,000 men** in this country each year. *Would someone please tell these guys that "choking the chicken" is just an expression?*

❯ Simon LeVay, PhD, "The Science of Sex: Breathless," October 31, 2000, *www.nerve .com.*

FACT: Some women are **allergic to their male partner's semen**, a condition known as human seminal plasma hypersensitivity. Sufferers complain of symptoms such as wheezing, itching, hives, swelling, chest tightness, vomiting, and diarrhea. Severe reactions can cause loss of consciousness and even death from anaphylactic shock. *God, don't tell my wife about this condition. She's just looking for an excuse.*

❯ Charles Downey, "Could You Be Allergic to Sex?," Swedish Medical Center, May 13, 2008, *www.swedish.org*

FACT: We've all heard the jokes, but **sexual headaches are a real illness** that affects about one in 100 people, either as a dull ache in the neck and head that builds with sexual excitement, or as a sudden and/or severe headache during orgasm. *Don't tell my wife about this one, either.*

❯ Mayo Clinic Staff, "Sex Headaches," Mayo Foundation for Medical Education and Research, Feb. 21, 2008, *www .mayoclinic.com.*

FACT: Yeast infections aren't just a problem for women; **men can get them, too**, as a result of prolonged antibiotic use, diabetes, an impaired immune system, or, in rare cases, from unprotected sex with a partner who has a yeast infection. *But men already scratch their junk all the time, so no big deal.*

❯ Michael A. Sommers, *Yeast Infections, Trichomoniasis, and Toxic Shock Syndrome* (Rosen Publishing Group, 2007).

❯ "Male Yeast Infections," Mayo Clinic, *www.mayoclinic .com.*

FACT: Overweight men are more likely to have **poor semen quality**. *But fat guy sperm are jovial and mischievous, and always good for a laugh.*

> Associated Press, "Another Reason to Watch Your Waist: Bad Sperm," MSNBC.com, July 9, 2008, *www.msnbc.msn.com.*

FACT: The FDA estimates that **4 to 5 million men** suffer from low testosterone, but that only 5 percent of them seek treatment. Testosterone production declines naturally with age, and at least one study suggests that the condition can shorten a man's life span. *Yeah, well, what's the point of living without a sex drive?*

> Bernice Kanner, *Are You Normal about Sex, Love, and Relationships?* (Macmillan, 2004).

FACT: Andropause, **a male form of menopause**, can affect men over forty. The condition, which can affect mood, memory, and overall health, is marked by a decline in testosterone production, as well as fatigue, depression, and sexual problems. *Some call these conditions "being over forty."*

> Bernice Kanner, *Are You Normal about Sex, Love, and Relationships?* (Macmillan, 2004).

> "Low Testosterone Could Kill You," ABC News, June 6, 2007, *http://abcnews.go.com.*

> Eric R. Braverman, *Younger You: Unlock the Hidden Power of Your Brain to Look and Feel 15 Years Younger* (McGraw-Hill Professional, 2006).

> "Male Menopause," Cleveland Clinic, *www.my.clevelandclinic.org.*

FACT: Some men can experience retrograde ejaculation, or "dry orgasms," when **semen travels backwards into the bladder** instead of being expelled. The illness can be congenital, or caused by medications, diabetes, or damage to nerves and muscles that control the opening of the bladder. It isn't harmful, but it can cause male infertility. *You'd think that any orgasm would be good. You'd be wrong.*

❯ "Richard D. McAnulty and M. Michele Burnette, *Sex and Sexuality: Sexual Function and Dysfunction* (Greenwood Publishing Group, 2006).

❯ "Retrograde Ejaculation," Mayo Clinic, *www.mayoclinic.com*.

FACT: Sexual dysfunction, which includes erectile dysfunction, premature ejaculation, dyspareunia (vaginal pain during intercourse), low sexual desire, and other conditions, occurs in **31 percent of men and 43 percent of women**. *Men, if you experience vaginal pain during intercourse, talk to your gynecologist. Or a shrink.*

❯ Glen O. Gabbard, Judith S. Beck and Jeremy Holmes, *Oxford Textbook of Psychotherapy* (Oxford University Press, 2007).

FACT: Premature ejaculation is the **most commonly reported sexual dysfunction in men**, affecting one in five. Some researchers attribute the problem to unhealthy masturbation habits and sexual insecurities. *Don't confuse premature ejaculation with premature evacuation—being so nervous about sex that you crap yourself.*

❯ Glen O. Gabbard, Judith S. Beck and Jeremy Holmes, *Oxford Textbook of Psychotherapy* (Oxford University Press, 2007).

FACT: A recent study comparing the effectiveness of oral contraceptives as they relate to body mass index (BMI) shows that obese or overweight women are up to **70 percent more likely to experience contraception failure** and resulting pregnancy than women of average weight. *Fortunately, obese people start with the most effective contraceptive of all: obesity.*

❯ Larissa R. Brunner Huber and Jessica L. Toth, "Obesity and Oral Contraceptive Failure: Findings from the 2002 National Survey of Family Growth," *American Journal of Epidemiology*, June 29, 2007, *http://contraception.about.com*.

FACT: Keeping a condom in your wallet is a bad idea. The constant friction and temperature changes **can create microscopic tears** in the condom that allow sperm to get through. *No one who carries a condom in his wallet should be procreating anyway, at least not until he finishes high school.*

> David Zieve, Greg Juhn, and David R. Eltz, "Condoms," Medline Plus, U.S. National Library of Medicine, February 19, 2008, *www.nlm.nih.gov.*

FACT: The sudden appearance of a sexually transmitted disease (STD) in a monogamous couple does not necessarily indicate infidelity by either partner. Some infections **can lie dormant for years** after initial exposure. *That's what I told my wife right before she hit me. I guess she wasn't convinced.*

> Lois White and Gena Duncan, *Medical-Surgical Nursing: An Integrated Approach,* 2nd ed. (Cengage Learning, 2002).

FACT: Persistent Sexual Arousal Syndrome (PSAS) is a medical condition where a woman experiences "spontaneous, intrusive and unwanted" **feelings of arousal in the genital area without sexual desire.** PSAS can continue for days or months, is not abated by sexual activity, and causes distraction and psychological distress in sufferers. *Congratulations, ladies. Now you know what it's like to be a man.*

> Sandra Leiblum, "About PSAS," Persistent Sexual Arousal Syndrome, *www.psas .dreamhosters.com.*
>
> "Medical Mystery: Persistent Sexual Arousal Syndrome." ABC News, February 21, 2008, *http:// abcnews.go.com.*

FACT: Human males, like rats, moths, and butterflies, give off a scent that has a physiological and psychological effect on the opposite sex. Researchers discovered that androstadienone, a chemical found in male sweat, **raises levels of the hormone cortisol in women,** resulting in enhanced mood and sexual arousal. *My wife does get pretty excited when she sees a moth.*

> "Male sweat boosts women's hormone levels,"Physorg.com, February 7, 2007, *www.physorg .com.*

FACT: According to one researcher, women have a higher likelihood than men to settle for a **mediocre sex life and unmet emotional needs**. Most keep their dissatisfaction a secret from their partners, often due to a fear of emotional hurt or abandonment. *Mediocre sex is better than no sex at all, isn't it? That's what I tell my wife.*

❯ Jeanna Bryner, "Women Settle for Mediocre Sex, Scientist Finds," LiveScience, AOL Health, February 14, 2007, *www.reference.aol.com.*

 177

FACT: A study reveals that a cluster of genes linked to reproduction could predict **the likelihood that a woman will cheat on her mate**. In a survey of romantically involved couples, women whose major histocompatibility complex (MHC) genes were similar to those of their mates reported decreased attraction to those partners. *See, West Virginia, nature doesn't want you to be turned on by your relatives.*

❯ Jeanna Bryner, "Genetic Test Could Reveal A Cheating Heart," LiveScience, AOL Health, February 13, 2007, *www.reference .aol.com.*

 178

FACT: Use of an oral contraceptive might affect a woman's ability to sniff out a partner. In a study where women were asked to sniff men's sweaty shirts, those on the pill typically chose odors that were **genetically similar to their own** as being the most attractive. Human beings are inclined to go for genetically dissimilar mates. *Obviously, this doesn't apply to those people who admitted having sex with their cousins.*

❯ Jeanna Bryner, "Genetic Test Could Reveal A Cheating Heart," LiveScience, AOL Health, February 13, 2007, *wwwreference .aol.com.*

❯ "The Facts of Life: Attraction," *The Independent*, September 13, 2008, *www.independent.co.uk.*

179

FACT: Several traditional herbs are being studied for their aphrodisiac properties, including yohimbe, tribulus, and maca. Combinations of these are sold as "natural Viagra," but be wary: **their effectiveness is unproven**, and some, like yohimbe, a type of tree bark, can be lethal if consumed in large quantities. *Tree bark? Dude—spring for the Viagra.*

❯ "Top 10 Aphrodisiacs," LiveScience, AOL Health, *www.reference.aol.com.*

180

FACT: The **average size of an erect penis is five inches**, while the average flaccid penis is three and a half inches. Drugs and devices advertised to increase penis size are dismissed as scams. *But you can't blame a guy with a three-inch dong for trying.*

❯ Rob Baedeker, "Sex: Fact And Fiction," WebMD, *www.men.webmd.com.*

181

FACT: While a penis pump can be an effective treatment for erectile dysfunction, a pump will not permanently increase the size of your organ. In fact, a penis pump can **cause numbness and permanent damage** if improperly used. *If I were a penis pump manufacturer, I'd try to use the hit song, "Pump Up The Jam," in my commercials, except I'd change it to "Pump Up The Ham." I think that would be memorable and sell a lot of pumps.*

❯ "Penis Pumps for Erectile Dysfunction: Improve Your Sexual Function," Mayo Clinic, *www.mayoclinic.com.*

182

FACT: Homosexuality **stayed on the list of mental illnesses** of the American Psychiatric Association until 1973. *As did witchcraft, hysteria, alcoholism, left-handedness, drapetomania, and demonic possession. Turns out the list had not been updated since '57. 1857.*

❯ Robert E. Hales and others, *The American Psychiatric Publishing Textbook of Psychiatry,* 5th ed. (American Psychiatric Publishing, 2008).

FACT: During World War I, the French recorded more than **1 million cases of syphilis and gonorrhea**, and the British suffered a loss of 23,000 men on average for seven-week hospital stays due to STDs. *Well, the French are known as lovers. I'm not sure what got into the British.*

> Allan M. Brandt, *No Magic Bullet: A Social History of Venereal Disease in the United States Since 1880* (Oxford University Press, 1987).

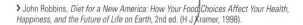

FACT: The average U.S. male's sperm count has declined **30 percent** in the last three decades. *I blame global warming. Or scrotal warming. I'm sure they are related. I should ask Al Gore.*

> John Robbins, *Diet for a New America: How Your Food Choices Affect Your Health, Happiness, and the Future of Life on Earth*, 2nd ed. (H J Kramer, 1998).

FACT: The sale of sex toys and vibrators is **banned in Alabama and Mississippi**. *Good call. We don't really want to encourage sexual activity in those states, as it could lead to procreation.*

> Associated Press, "Appeals Court Overturns Texas Ban on Sex Toys," MSNBC.com, February 13, 2008, *www.msnbc.msn.com*.

186

FACT: Though treatable today through medical advancements, **impotence has been considered grounds for divorce** in many different cultures for centuries. *Can you really call a bunch of dudes sitting around playing music and singing about how much they love their Viagra a medical advancement? Or the guy who can't stop smiling because he always has a boner?*

❯ Angus McLaren, *Impotence: A Cultural History* (University of Chicago Press, 2007).

187

FACT: "Beer goggles" aren't just a myth: **People do appear more attractive** after a few drinks, according to researchers at the University of Bristol in England. *Students who had consumed alcohol rated pictures of people their own age as being more attractive than did participants who had no alcohol. Booze: helping ugly people get laid since the dawn of time.*

❯ "The Facts of Life: Attraction," *The Independent*, September 13, 2008, *www.independent.co.uk.*

188

FACT: Wearing too much makeup can mask the scent that **attracts men to women during ovulation**. An experiment found that a woman's armpit scent was at its most attractive to men between the end of her cycle and ovulation, but that this smell is easily obscured by cosmetics. *Trying to describe when an armpit scent is at its most attractive is like trying to say when vomit is at its tastiest.*

❯ "The Facts of Life: Attraction," *The Independent*, September 13, 2008, *www.independent.co.uk.*

FACT: Not all people are attracted to other humans. There are believed to be around forty *objectum sexuals* in the world who feel attraction, arousal, love, and even commitment for **an object instead of another person**. Swede Eija-Riitta Berliner-Mauer, for example, has been "married" to the Berlin Wall since 1979. *Nobody has the heart to tell her they tore it down.*

> "The Facts of Life: Attraction," *The Independent*, September 13, 2008, www.independent.co.uk.

FACT: According to a study in Wales, sexual activity seems to have a preventative affect on male health. In several southern Welsh villages, **risk for mortality was 50 percent lower** for men with higher frequency of orgasm. *I'm telling my wife about this.*

> "Sex and Death: Are They Related? Findings from the Caerphilly Cohort Study," *BMJ*, December 20, 1997, www.bmj.com.

FACT: In his landmark sex studies, researcher Alfred Kinsey found that **26 percent of women had engaged in extramarital sex** by their forties, and that as many as one in six women aged twenty-six to fifty were engaged in extramarital sex at any given time. *Many of them with Kinsey himself.*

> "Data from Alfred Kinsey's Studies," The Kinsey Institute for Research in Sex, Gender, and Reproduction, Inc., www.kinsey institute.org.

FACT: Kinsey also estimated that **half of all married males** engaged in extramarital sex during their marriages. *Kinsey didn't say which half had extramarital sex, but I'm guessing it was from the waist down.*

> "Data from Alfred Kinsey's Studies," The Kinsey Institute for Research in Sex, Gender, and Reproduction, Inc., www.kinseyinstitute.org.

FACT: Traumatic Masturbatory Syndrome (TMS) is the habit of masturbating in **a face-down position against a bed or floor**, which puts excessive pressure on the penis, and can interfere with sexual relations. The most common problems TMS sufferers have are inorgasmia—inability to reach orgasm during intercourse—or delayed orgasm. Many TMS sufferers also experience erectile dysfunction. *TMI.*

> "Facts about Traumatic Masturbatory Syndrome," Healthy Strokes, *www.healthystrokes .com.*

FACT: Many popular antidepressants, particularly selective serotonin reuptake inhibitor medications like Zoloft, Prozac, and Paxil, **can lower libido** and prevent orgasm. *But then, depression isn't exactly an aphrodisiac.*

> "Can Antidepressants Affect Orgasm?" Ask Dr. Laura Berman, Everyday Health, *www.every dayhealth.com*

FACT: More than half of the women surveyed by Shere Hite in 1994 **admitted faking orgasm**, while fewer than half reported being brought to orgasm by a male partner through intercourse. *I have no problems with a fake orgasm as long she sells it.*

> "Eleven Key Things About Orgasms," *The Observer*, February 11, 2001, *www.observer .guardian.co.uk.*

FACT: Masturbation was considered a sin in the late 1800s and early 1900s. Before the 1960s, **excessive masturbation was thought to be a mental condition**, a fixation on immature or undesirable behavior that led to adult sexual dysfunction. *It's probably still a sin, but nobody cares anymore.*

> "Masturbation: Techniques and Tips For Men And Women," Sexual Health Resource, *www .sexual-health-resource.org.*

197

FACT: The most common sexually transmitted infection is genital human papillomavirus, also known as HPV. About **20 million Americans** are presently infected with HPV, with 6.2 million more becoming infected every year. At least half of sexually active men and women will acquire the infection in their lifetime. *I was getting worried until I read "sexually active." I'm safe.*

> "Sexually Transmitted Diseases: HPV," Centers For Disease Control And Prevention, *www.cdc.gov*.

 198

FACT: On any given day, about **400 million people across the globe** will have sexual intercourse, which means that about 4,000 people are probably having sex right now. *Sadly, I am not one of them. Don't laugh—neither are you.*

> "Ten Strange Sex Facts," Seduction Labs, *www.seductionlabs.org*.

 199

FACT: The sexually transmitted disease chlamydia is caused by the bacterium *Chlamydia trachomatis*. Symptoms of chlamydia are usually mild, but serious cases can lead to irrevocable damage to the reproductive organs, chronic pelvic pain, and infertility, **without a woman ever recognizing the problem**. *That's two more votes for masturbation.*

> "Sexually Transmitted Diseases: HPV," Centers For Disease Control And Prevention, *www.cdc.gov*.

 200

FACT: As much as **6 percent** of the world's population—more than 400 million people—suffer from addiction to sex. *Probably the same 400 million who got it on today.*

> "Sex Addiction," SexHelp.com, *www.sexhelp.com*.

CHAPTER 5

Will You Survive the 9-to-5?

More Reasons to Hate Your Job, Your Boss, and Your Idiot Coworkers

FACT: Office desks have **400 times more bacteria** than toilet seats. *So, be safe and eat your lunch on a toilet instead of at your desk.*

> "Average Desk Harbors 400 Times More Bacteria Than Average Toilet Seat," Medical-NewsService.com, March 31, 2002, *www.medicalnewsservice .com.*

FACT: Telephones carry **the most germs in an office**, followed by desks, microwave door handles, water fountain handles and computer keyboards. *You know what, just move your entire office to the bathroom.*

> "Average Desk Harbors 400 Times More Bacteria Than Average Toilet Seat," Medical-NewsService.com, March 31, 2002, *www.medicalnewsservice .com.*

FACT: The place where you rest your hands on your desk is home to **10 million bacteria** at any given time. *Well, not anymore. Seven million of them just moved to your hand.*

> "Average Desk Harbors 400 Times More Bacteria Than Average Toilet Seat," Medical-NewsService.com, March 31, 2002, *www.medicalnewsservice .com.*

FACT: In a 2008 report, the AFL-CIO claimed that regulatory activity at the Occupational Safety and Health Administration (OSHA) **ground to a halt during the Bush Administration**, with dozens of OSHA and Mine Safety and Health Administration (MSHA) standards pulled from the regulatory agenda.

> "'Death on the Job' Report, 2008: The Toll of Neglect," American Federation of Labor—Congress of Industrial Organizations, *www.aflcio.org.*

205

FACT: The 2008 AFL-CIO report also claimed that new workplace hazards such as **pandemic flu and bioterrorist threats** aren't adequately addressed by government labor policies. *What? The Bush Administration put the interests of big business ahead of the needs of the American worker? No way!*

❯ "'Death on the Job' Report, 2008: The Toll of Neglect," American Federation of Labor—Congress of Industrial Organizations, *www.aflcio.org.*

 206

FACT: At its current understaffed levels, it would take the Occupational Safety and Health Administration (OSHA) **133 years to inspect each of the workplaces** in its jurisdiction just once. *That's 133 years per staff member, so 266 years total.*

❯ "'Death on the Job' Report, 2008: The Toll of Neglect," American Federation of Labor—Congress of Industrial Organizations, *www.aflcio.org.*

 207

FACT: In 2006, **over 11,000 workers** were made ill or injured on the job every day. *Working every day makes me ill, too.*

❯ "'Death on the Job' Report, 2008: The Toll of Neglect," American Federation of Labor—Congress of Industrial Organizations, *www.aflcio.org.*

FACT: An estimated **50,000 to 60,000 workers** die every year from occupation-related diseases. *Is not giving a shit considered an occupation-related disease? Because that affects a lot more than 60,000, I bet.*

❯ "'Death on the Job' Report, 2008: The Toll of Neglect," American Federation of Labor—Congress of Industrial Organizations, www.aflcio.org.

FACT: Work-related stress can be **as damaging to health** as cigarette smoking. *But if you handle that stress with a smoke break, they cancel each other out.*

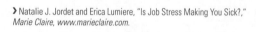

❯ Natalie J. Jordet and Erica Lumiere, "Is Job Stress Making You Sick?," *Marie Claire*, www.marieclaire.com.

FACT: Workplace stress is a near epidemic in the United States, thanks largely to a struggling economy and corporate downsizing. A recent survey recorded **half of respondents feeling too much pressure** at work. *You want pressure? Try writing 1,001 jokes.*

❯ Natalie J. Jordet and Erica Lumiere, "Is Job Stress Making You Sick?," *Marie Claire*, www.marieclaire.com.

211

FACT: The chronic stress of a high-pressure job has been shown to **double the risk of a heart attack**. Chronic stress may also result in alcoholism, hypertension, and severe depression, and can make your joints ache, your hair fall out, and even stop your period. *So that bald drunk lady at work who's always crying and giving away her tampons? Give her a break; she's under a lot of stress.*

> Natalie J. Jordet and Erica Lumiere, "Is Job Stress Making You Sick?," *Marie Claire, www .marieclaire.com.*

 212

FACT: About **1.7 million workplace violence incidents** occur in the U.S. every year. 18,700 of them are committed by the victim's intimate partner. *Don't forget: Friday is Bring Your Batterer To Work Day!*

> "Domestic Violence in the Workplace Statistics," American Institute on Domestic Violence, *www.aidv-usa.com.*

 213

FACT: An estimated **1 million workers** are assaulted on the job every year in the United States. *I know at least nine people I'd like to add to that total.*

> Barbara Kate Repa, *Your Rights in the Workplace*, 8th ed. (Nolo, 2007).

 214

FACT: The U.S. Postal Service reported 500 cases of employees being violent toward supervisors in **a recent span of just eighteen months**, and an additional 200 cases of supervisors being violent toward employees in that same period. *Where do you think the term "going postal" came from?*

> Barbara Kate Repa, *Your Rights in the Workplace*, 8th ed. (Nolo, 2007).

215

FACT: In August 1986, U.S. Postal Service worker Patrick Henry Sherrill—or "Crazy Pat," as he was called—**shot and killed 14 coworkers** in the Edmond, Oklahoma post office where he was employed, including a supervisor who had criticized his work. *Hmm, I wonder why they called him "Crazy Pat."*

❯ Jacob V. Lamar Jr., "'Crazy Pat's' Revenge," *Time*, June 24, 2001, *www.time.com*.

❯ Charles Montaldo, "It's Official: 'Going Postal' Is Epidemic," About.com, *www.about.com*.

216

FACT: In 1976, the typical CEO earned **thirty-six times** the salary of his average worker. Today, the average CEO makes 369 times what an average worker makes. *Both of them are unemployed now, and 369 times zero is zero.*

❯ Steven Greenhouse, *The Big Squeeze: Tough Times for the American Worker* (Random House, 2008).

 217

FACT: There were over **600 workplace homicides** in this country in 2007. *I wonder how many of those were CEOs.*

❯ Steven Greenhouse, *The Big Squeeze: Tough Times for the American Worker* (Random House, 2008).

❯ "TED: The Editor's Desk: Workplace Homicides in 2007," Bureau of Labor Statistics, August 26, 2008, *www.bls.gov*.

 218

FACT: One study suggests that **Californians are more likely to be murdered at work** than in a motor vehicle accident while commuting to work. *Some Californians probably wouldn't mind being murdered during their commute.*

❯ Barbara Kate Repa, *Your Rights in the Workplace*, 8th ed. (Nolo, 2007).

219

FACT: Fatalities at construction sites are most frequently caused by falls, accounting for one–third of construction-related deaths each year. The Bureau of Labor Statistics reports no fewer than **442 construction workers were killed by accidental falls** on the job in 2007. *As opposed to intentional falls. "I'm bored. I'm gonna do some falls. Be back in ten."*

❯ "Preventing Fatal Falls in Construction," Occupational Safety & Health Administrations, U.S. Department of Labor, September 25, 2008, *www.osha.gov.*

 220

FACT: Almost 6,000 Americans— **about seventeen per day—** suffered fatal injuries on the job in 2006. *Some people will do anything to get out of work.*

❯ Tyche Hendricks, "Workplace Deaths Rise in California, Nation," *San Francisco Chronicle,* April 29, 2008, *www.sfgate.com.*

 221

FACT: Falling from the roof is a specific concern at construction sites. Roof falls were the **most prevalent type of deadly falls in 2007**, and resulted in 686 fatalities from 2003 to 2007. *Because of this, the Department of Labor recommends that construction workers avoid falling accidentally, especially from roofs.*

❯ "Preventing Fatal Falls in Construction," Occupational Safety & Health Administrations, U.S. Department of Labor, September 25, 2008, *www.osha.gov.*

222

FACT: A 2006 government study named agriculture, forestry, fishing and hunting as **the most dangerous occupations in the United States**, with an average of 30 deaths each per 100,000 workers. *After a coworker went on a murderous rampage, Melvin quit his office job and became a farmer—then ran himself over with a combine and died a week later.*

❯ Tyche Hendricks, "Workplace Deaths Rise in California, Nation," *San Francisco Chronicle*, April 29, 2008, *www.sfgate .com*.

 223

FACT: In 2007, a laundry employee at Cintas Corp. in Oklahoma was killed when **he fell into an industrial dryer** while attempting to free a wad of clothes that had jammed a conveyor belt. *On a happier note, he did manage to free the clothes, saving the company about $35.*

❯ Tyche Hendricks, "Workplace Deaths Rise in California, Nation," *San Francisco Chronicle*, April 29, 2008, *www.sfgate .com*.

 224

FACT: In its 2008 Death on the Job Report, the AFL-CIO ranked commercial fishing as the occupation with **the highest fatality rate**, with almost 150 deaths on the job per 100,000 workers. *The fatality rate for the fish is even higher.*

❯ "'Death on the Job' Report, 2008: The Toll of Neglect," American Federation of Labor—Congress of Industrial Organizations, *www.aflcio.org*.

FACT: In a 2004 survey, 17 percent of men said they had been **sexually harassed on the job**, but 60 percent of them did nothing about it. *Those 60 percent are the ones who liked it.*

> "Interoffice Romance Survey," Lawyers.com, August 12, 2004, *www.research.lawyers.com.*

> "Sexual Harassment In The Workplace," Sexual Harassment Support, *www.sexualharass mentsupport.org.*

FACT: On January 2, 2006, a coal mine exploded in Sago, West Virginia, **trapping thirteen miners for nearly two days**. All but one of the miners died. A series of subsequent mine disasters in 2006 claimed forty-seven more lives. *Mine disasters, not mime disasters. Sorry. Disappointing, I know.*

> "'Death on the Job' Report, 2008: The Toll of Neglect," American Federation of Labor—Congress of Industrial Organizations website, *www .aflcio.org.*

FACT: Workplace injuries come at a high cost to employers. According to a 2007 Workplace Safety Index from Liberty Mutual Insurance, the most disabling injuries **cost U.S. employers over $48.3 billion** in workers' compensation claims. *But don't worry, I'm sure they won't pass on those costs to customers.*

> "'Death on the Job' Report, 2008: The Toll of Neglect," American Federation of Labor—Congress of Industrial Organizations, *www.aflcio.org.*

FACT: In Japan, suicide resulting from overwork, or karojisatsu, is **an officially recognized and compensated occupational hazard**. By some estimates, 5 percent of all suicides in Japan are "company related." *"Where's Hiro? He's supposed to lead this meeting." "He killed himself, sir." "Ah, dedication. I like it. Give him a raise."*

> "Crying shame," *Hazards Magazine*, January-March 2008, *www.hazards.org.*

FACT: From 2001 to 2002, Japan saw a record 690 claims of karoshi—death by overwork. Of these, 143 were confirmed cases: **96 from stroke and 47 from sudden heart attack**. The numbers were even higher in 2003, with 819 claims, 160 of which were compensated. *That means 659 claims—80 percent—were rejected. The Americanization of Japan is complete.*

❯ Rory O'Neill, "Drop Dead," *Hazards Magazine*, July–September 2003, *www.hazards.org*.

FACT: Claims of karoshi jumped after Japan modified a rule to include the effects of cumulative fatigue. A worker who dies after **routinely working eighty or more overtime hours a month** is now eligible to be considered a case of karoshi. *If I had to work eighty or more overtime hours a month, I would welcome death.*

❯ Rory O'Neill, "Drop Dead," *Hazards Magazine*, July–September 2003, *www.hazards.org*.

FACT: China also has a word for **death by overwork**: guolaosi. *Named after that hard-working American actor, Bela Guolaosi.*

❯ Rory O'Neill, "Drop Dead," *Hazards Magazine*, July–September 2003, *www.hazards.org*.

FACT: A study published in 2002 concludes that workers who perform meaningless work with minimal chance for input were **at higher risk of dying young**. *In other words, everyone but CEOs and a few VPs.*

❯ Rory O'Neill, "Drop Dead," *Hazards Magazine*, July–September 2003, *www.hazards.org*.

233

FACT: A report by the *American Journal of Epidemiology* states that long-term strain on the job is **more harmful for the heart** than aging thirty years or gaining forty pounds. *And not nearly as fun. I'll take the forty pounds instead. Pass the biscuits.*

❯ Paul A. Landsbergis and others, "Life-Course Exposure to Job Strain and Ambulatory Blood Pressure in Men," *American Journal of Epidemiology*, June 2003, *www.aje.oxford journals.org.*

❯ Rory O'Neill, "Drop Dead," *Hazards Magazine*, July–September 2003, *www.hazards.org.*

234

FACT: Workplace homicide can happen anywhere. In 2007, **the frequency of on-the-job murders** involving police officers and supervisors of retail sales workers both increased significantly. *I worked in retail once, but it was the customers, not the supervisors, that I wanted to kill. Wait—no, I wanted to kill them both.*

❯ "TED: The Editor's Desk: Workplace homicides in 2007," Bureau of Labor Statistics, August 26, 2008. *www.bls.gov.*

235

FACT: A 2003 UK study shows that working for an unfair or unreasonable boss can result in **dangerously high blood pressure**. *It can also result in a dangerously high likelihood that someone will bring a gun to work and cap his ass.*

❯ Rory O'Neill, "Drop Dead," *Hazards Magazine*, July–September 2003, *www.hazards.org.*

236

FACT: In 2003, 1,400 government employees in India **committed suicide or died from starvation**. They had not been paid in more than a decade. The state officials responsible were charged with theft, reportedly using employee funds for lavish foreign trips. *So impatient. They couldn't wait one more day for their paychecks?*

> Agence France-Presse, "World Briefing | Asia: India: Inquiry Into Deaths Of Government Workers," *New York Times*, November 14, 2003, *www .nytimes.com.*

 237

FACT: In a 2004 poll, 12 percent of respondents confessed to **having sex in the workplace**, while another 10 percent said they fantasized about it. *Jack and Elaine often worked late, leveraging each other's assets and pumping up the bottom line.*

> "Poll: American Sex Survey: A Peek Beneath The Sheets," ABC News, October 21, 2004, *http:// abcnews.go.com.*

 238

FACT: Researchers concluded in a 2008 study that bullying at work, such as persistent criticism of work, belittling comments, and withholding resources, is **more harmful to employees than sexual harassment**. *Belittling comments, persistent criticism and withholding "resources"? Sounds more like marriage than the workplace.*

> M. Sandy Hershcovis and Julian Barling, "Bullying More Harmful Than Sexual Harassment On The Job, Say Researchers," ScienceDaily, March 9, 2008, *www.science daily.com.*

 239

FACT: Layoffs and a sluggish economy are contributing to frequent outbreaks of "desk rage" in America, with employees arguing and breaking down under pressure. Ten percent of Americans work in **places where physical violence occurs because of stress**, and 42 percent say that verbal abuse and yelling occurs in the workplace. *The economy is slowing? I hadn't noticed.*

> "'Desk Rage' on the Rise," HR Business and Legal Reports, December 14, 2001, *www .hr.blr.com.*

FACT: Workplace bullying affects **25 to 30 percent of employees** at some time during their careers. *Instead of lunch money, they take your parking spot.*

> Jeanna Bryner, "Strange News, Study: Office Bullies Create Workplace 'Warzone'," LiveScience, October 31, 2006, *www.livescience.com.*

 241

FACT: In March 2009, a Louisiana high-school teacher was arrested for obscenity after three students and another teacher witnessed him **masturbating in a classroom**. *I guess he hadn't heard: spanking in schools was outlawed years ago.*

> "Higgins Teacher Arrested For Obscenity," WWLTV.com, March 20, 2009, *www.wwltv.com.*

 242

FACT: A *New York Times* study of rampage killings found that although most perpetrators of workplace massacres made specific threats or exhibited clear warning signs, **these warnings were ignored or dismissed**. *Office Droid 1: "Someone left a decapitated animal head on my desk." Office Droid 2: "Really? Somebody wrote 'DIE' in blood on my office door." Office Droid 1: "Hmm, weird. Hey, wanna go get a smoothie?" Office Droid 2: "Sure!"*

> Katherine M. Ramsland, *Inside The Minds Of Mass Murderers: Why They Kill* (Greenwood Publishing Group, 2005).

FACT: In 2008, a factory worker in Henderson, Kentucky killed his supervisor and six employees at the plant where he worked after getting into an argument about **not using his cell phone on the assembly line and not wearing safety goggles.** *The worker shot himself after the rampage, but put on his goggles first, because sparks and gunpowder from a gun can injure your eyes.*

❯ Eric Boehlert, "Rampage Nation: The Press No Longer Cares About Epic Gun Violence," Workplace Violence News, March 24, 2009, *www.work placeviolencenews.com.*

❯ "Six Dead after Workers Argue," AJC.com, June 26, 2008, *www.ajc.com.*

FACT: Occupational fraud schemes are most commonly committed by the accounting department or upper management. **Executive frauds are particularly costly**, resulting in a median loss of $850,000. *I know lots of executive frauds. I've worked for several of them.*

❯ "2008 Report to the Nation on Occupational Fraud and Abuse," Association of Certified Fraud Examiners, *www.acfe.com.*

FACT: Hourly wages for 80 percent of U.S. workers have risen **by just 1 percent** after inflation since 1979. *Hey, we got a raise!*

❯ Steven Greenhouse, *The Big Squeeze: Tough Times for the American Worker* (Random House, 2008).

FACT: One out of three companies that go bankrupt each year do so as **a result of employee theft**. Almost 80 percent of workers admit that they have, or would consider, stealing from their employers. *If a few filched Post-It Notes and paper clips can drive a company out of business, they probably weren't going to last long, anyway.*

❭ Nicole Jacoby, "Battling Workplace Theft," CNN Money, August 19, 1999, *www.money.cnn.com*.

FACT: Employees who steal rarely do so because of need. In one poll, almost half of respondents said **they stole from their employer out of greed**. Another 43 percent did so out of vindictiveness or "to get even." *Get even for what? You got a 1 percent raise!*

❭ Nicole Jacoby, "Battling Workplace Theft," CNN Money, August 19, 1999, *www.money.cnn.com*.

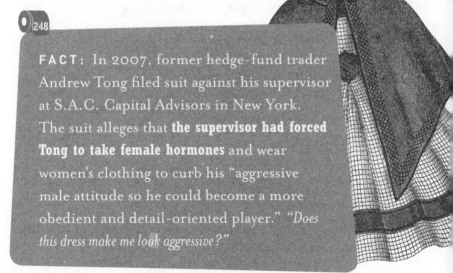

FACT: In 2007, former hedge-fund trader Andrew Tong filed suit against his supervisor at S.A.C. Capital Advisors in New York. The suit alleges that **the supervisor had forced Tong to take female hormones** and wear women's clothing to curb his "aggressive male attitude so he could become a more obedient and detail-oriented player." *"Does this dress make me look aggressive?"*

❭ "The Top 20 Sexual-Harassment Cases of All Time," HR World, *www.hrworld.com*.

249

FACT: A UK woman claims that **she was fired from her job in 2007 for chronic flatulence**. The unnamed woman, who suffers from irritable bowel syndrome, says she was frequently harassed and taunted about her problem by coworkers before being terminated. *That really stinks. What a bunch of asses. There's a happy ending, though: she found work at the gas company.*

❯ Lucy Thornton, "Woman Fired Over Farting Claims," Mirror. co.uk, May 12, 2007, *www .mirror.co.uk*

250

FACT: In 2005, two former gorilla caretakers requested over $1 million worth of damages in a wrongful termination and sexual discrimination suit against The Gorilla Foundation in Woodside, California. The suit claimed that the two women were pressured to comply with famed gorilla Koko's alleged **sign-language request that they display their breasts**. When they refused, the suit says, the two were fired. *The fourteen-year-old sign-language interpreter was not named in the suit and kept his job.*

❯ "The Top 20 Sexual-Harassment Cases of All Time," HR World, *www.hrworld.com.*

❯ "Suit Says Gorilla Foundation Employees Urged To Undress For Koko," FindLaw.com, March 11, 2005, *www.findlaw.com.*

CHAPTER 6

We Be Illin'

The Sickening Truth about Your Health

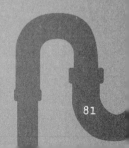

FACT : *Demodex* mites, or follicle mites, live in human skin. By some estimates, **you have a colony of 1,000 to 2,000 living in your skin right now**. When you touch someone or share fabrics with them, you're trading follicle mites. *Unless you touch someone's heart, in which case you don't give them follicle mites, but a warm fuzzy feeling inside. It's a figure of speech, you see.*

> Yezid Gutiérrez, *Diagnostic Pathology of Parasitic Infections with Clinical Correlations*, 2nd ed. (Oxford University Press, 2000).

FACT : Two of the most damaging human parasites are the malaria-causing *Plasmodium* and the flatworm *Schistosoma*, which causes schistosomiasis, **an illness that damages internal organs** and can negatively impact cognitive development and growth in children. *Damn plasmodium. I knew I should've gone with the LCD instead. I bet those don't give you malaria.*

> "Parasite," Microsoft Encarta Online Encyclopedia 2008, *www.encarta.msn.com*.
> "The Carter Center Schistosomiasis Control Program," The Carter Center, *www.carter center.org*.

FACT : Humans develop schistosomiasis after contact with water containing snails infected by human waste. **Snail larvae infiltrate the body and grow into adult worms** up to half an inch long. They live in the bloodstream and can cause inflammation, organ enlargement, intestinal bleeding, bladder cancer, and death. *I'll take death. Thanks.*

> Coco Ballantyne, "Worms 'N Us: A Look at 8 Parasitic Worms That Live in Humans," *Scientific American*, February 5, 2009, *www.sciam.com*.

FACT: Approximately half the world's population is infected with **large roundworms, hookworms, or whipworms**. A Columbia University parasitologist calls them the "unholy trinity." *I prefer to think of them as the intestinal worm version of the Marx brothers: Groucho (roundworm), Harpo (hookworm), and Chico (whipworm). The tapeworm, a less common intestinal parasite, is Zeppo, who didn't always appear with the other three.*

❯ Coco Ballantyne, "Worms 'N Us: A Look at 8 Parasitic Worms That Live in Humans," *Scientific American*, February 5, 2009, *www.sciam.com*.

FACT: Hookworms attack the lungs, where their larvae cause coughing and shortness of breath, and the small intestine, where **they suck blood from the intestinal walls** and cause abdominal pain and anemia. *Nothing that a pack or two of unfiltered Kools can't fix.*

❯ Coco Ballantyne, "Worms 'N Us: A Look at 8 Parasitic Worms That Live in Humans," *Scientific American*, February 5, 2009, *www.sciam.com*.

FACT: Approximately **740 million people worldwide** are plagued with hookworm, according to the World Health Organization. *They're the pale ones coughing up larva and bent double with stomach pain.*

❯ Coco Ballantyne, "Worms 'N Us: A Look at 8 Parasitic Worms That Live in Humans," *Scientific American*, February 5, 2009, *www.sciam.com*.

FACT: Ascariasis is the most common worm-related infection found in humans. Symptoms such as fever, shortness of breath, and wheezing result from roundworm larvae infesting the lungs. The larvae then migrate to the intestines, where **they grow to resemble foot-long earthworms**. *Once again, I will take death over a foot-long earthworm in my ass, thanks.*

❯ Coco Ballantyne, "Worms 'N Us: A Look at 8 Parasitic Worms That Live in Humans," *Scientific American*, February 5, 2009, *www.sciam.com*.

FACT: Ascariasis affects as many as **1.5 billion people worldwide**, causing 60,000 deaths per year. *The ones who don't die always have bait at the ready if they want to fish.*

> Coco Ballantyne, "Worms 'N Us: A Look at 8 Parasitic Worms That Live in Humans," *Scientific American*, February 5, 2009, *www.sciam.com.*

259

FACT: About 800 million people worldwide are infected with whipworm, which can cause diarrhea, weight loss, and anemia. In severe instances rectal prolapse can occur, **in which the walls of the rectum protrude from the anus**. *You might know rectal prolapse by its colorful street name: ass tulip.*

> Coco Ballantyne, "Worms 'N Us: A Look at 8 Parasitic Worms That Live in Humans," *Scientific American*, February 5, 2009, *www.sciam.com.*

260

FACT: Unlike most parasitic worms that inhabit the intestines, lymphatic filariae live in the body's lymph system, where they can cause swelling of the legs, arms, breasts, and, in men especially, the genitalia. More than **120 million people worldwide** are infected, a third of them disfigured by the condition. *No man I know would object to enlarged genitalia.*

> Coco Ballantyne, "Worms 'N Us: A Look at 8 Parasitic Worms That Live in Humans," *Scientific American*, February 5, 2009, *www.sciam.com.*

261

FACT: Every time your heart beats, **it pumps a quarter of your blood to the head**. Brain cells then process 20 percent of the oxygen and food your blood contains. Conditions that disrupt circulation, such as heart disease, diabetes, and stroke appear to increase the chances of developing dementia and Alzheimer's disease. *It's like getting free sprinkles on your sundae. Except it's a shit sundae, and the sprinkles are maggots.*

❯ "Risk Factors," Alzheimer's Association, www.alz.org.

 262

FACT: Humans with failing kidneys can't survive long without an organ transplant or dialysis, a process by which **a machine filters waste from the blood**. Nitrogen in the form of urea builds up quickly in the blood and becomes toxic. *Dialysis sounds fun. Another one for the bucket list.*

❯ Constanza Villalba, "Ten Lessons Medicine Can Learn from Bears," *Scientific American*, January 6, 2009, www.sciam .com.

 263

FACT: According to a researcher at the Michigan Sinus Center, you can stay healthy and combat allergy symptoms by **rinsing the nose with salt water**. *I've heard that a colonic is also good for you, but I won't be doing that, either.*

❯ "Twenty-five Things You Probably Didn't Know About Your Body and Health," MSN Health, www.health.msn.com.

 264

FACT: Sickle cell disease is one of the most common genetic illnesses in America. Researchers estimate that it plagues more than 70,000, and that **over 2 million carry the gene** that could pass this affliction on to their children. *And I used to bitch about getting my dad's ugly feet.*

❯ "What You Don't Know About Sickle Cell Disease," Centers for Disease Control and Prevention, www.cdc.gov.

265

FACT: Jaundice is a common condition that occurs in about **60 percent of newborn babies**, but one that can indicate kernicterus, a devastating brain ailment. *Ever hear the Old West legend of Jaundiced Jake? Probably not—he was yella.*

> "Most Parents Unaware of Possible Brain Damage from Untreated Jaundice," Centers for Disease Control and Prevention, *www.cdc.gov*.

266

FACT: Traumatic brain injury (TBI) is a serious health problem for people aged seventy-five and older, as they have the highest rates of TBIs and **tend to recover more slowly or die from their injuries**. TBI symptoms are subtle, and may not even appear until days or even weeks after the injury occurs. *The rate of TBI in America is still TBD. Consider it TBA until further notice.*

> "Help Seniors Live Better, Longer: Prevent Brain Injury," Centers for Disease Control and Prevention, *www.cdc.gov*.

267

FACT: Blowing your nose when you have a cold might feel good, but it can actually worsen your condition. **Blowing generates enormous pressure and propels mucus into the sinuses**, spreading viruses or bacteria and potentially causing further infection. *What's the alternative? Just letting the snot run down your face?*

> Anahad O'Connor, "The Claim: Never Blow Your Nose When You Have a Cold," *New York Times*, February 9, 2009, *www.nytimes.com*.

268

FACT: **Bacteria can grow and divide every twenty minutes**, turning one bacterial cell into 16 million in just eight hours. *Bacteria sound a lot like trivia facts.*

> Michael Stringer and C. Dennis, *Chilled Foods: A Comprehensive Guide*, 2nd ed. (Woodhead Publishing, 2000).

269

FACT: Belly button lint is made up of **clothing fibers, dead skin, and more**. You should keep your navel clean and dry to prevent infection from *candida*, a type of fungus. *That's why I call it navel jam. Lint doesn't fully capture the variety and complexity of the recipe.*

❯ Perry Garfinkel, *The Male Body: An Owner's Manual: The Ultimate Head-to-Toe Guide to Staying Healthy and Fit for Life* (Rodale, 1996).

 270

FACT: Erectile dysfunction (ED) is a man's inability to keep an erection long enough to perform sexual intercourse. As many as 80 percent of men seventy-five and older have erectile dysfunction, **but the problem can occur at any age**. Causes include lung, liver, heart, or kidney disease; endocrine system disorders such as diabetes; side effects of antidepressants and other medications; substance or alcohol abuse; and anxiety and depression. *They should call premature ejaculation "projectile dysfunction (PD)," just for the sake of consistency.*

❯ "Erectile Dysfunction," Mayo Clinic, *www.mayoclinic.com.*

 271

FACT: High heels are blamed by orthopedists for chronic back problems and postural difficulties. Wearing high-heel shoes regularly causes the tendon in the leg to shrink, making it painful to wear flat shoes. Some even blame **high heels for problems with the internal organs in the abdomen**, since the distortion of posture pushes the pelvic region out of normal alignment. *But they're so comfortable.*

❯ Robin Tolmach Lakoff and Raquel L. Scherr, *Face Value, the Politics of Beauty: The Politics of Beauty* (Routledge, 1984).

FACT: Never share mascara, as this is the most common way that **people pass on eye infections like conjunctivitis** (pinkeye), which is highly contagious. *I hope* The Cure's *Robert Smith is reading this.*

❭ Stephen W. Moore, H. Winter Griffith, and Kenneth Yoder, *Complete Guide To Symptoms, Illness & Surgery* (Perigee, 2006).

FACT: Up to **8 percent of American adults** suffer from toenail fungus. *Up to 100 percent of American adults suffer from the urge to hork when they see the commercial where the little cartoon fungus creature lifts up a toenail and climbs under it.*

❭ "Impact 07—Dermatology," Bay Bio, 2007, *www.baybio.org.*

FACT: A sneeze expels germ-filled droplets **up to thirty feet**. The water content of the droplets evaporates quickly, but thousands of virus cells remain suspended in the air and can infect others. *This is why I like to sneeze in people's hair. No germs are suspended in the air, plus it's fun to watch the reactions, especially from strangers.*

❭ Jana Balaram, *Preventive and Social Medicine* (B. Jain Publishers, 2002).

FACT: If you wear a ring, the number of germs living beneath it could be as high as **the entire population of Europe**. *The smell is probably just as bad, too.*

❯ "Kitchen Habits Causing Food Poisoning Peril," FoodLink Press notice, Food and Drink Federation, June 12, 2006, *www.fdf .org.uk.*

FACT: The Centers for Disease Control ranked the United States 29th in the world **in infant mortality for 2004.** The United States fell from 12th in 1960 to 23rd in 1990, and is currently tied with Poland and Slovakia for infant mortality. *Yes, but we kick their asses in soccer, so it evens out.*

❯ Kim Krisberg, "U.S. Lagging Behind Many Other Nations on Infant Mortality Rates: Healthy Behavior, Healthier Babies," *The Nation's Health*, American Public Health Association, February 2009, *www.apha.org.*

FACT: **The infant mortality rate in America** in 2005 was 13.68 deaths per 1,000 live births among blacks, 8.06 among American Indians and Alaska natives, 8.3 among Puerto Ricans, and 5.76 among whites. *I bet being .68 dead hurts. I think I'd rather just be fully dead.*

❯ Kim Krisberg, "U.S. Lagging Behind Many Other Nations on Infant Mortality Rates: Healthy Behavior, Healthier Babies," *The Nation's Health*, American Public Health Association, February 2009, *www.apha.org.*

FACT: The March of Dimes released the inaugural Premature Birth Report Card in November 2008, **giving the United States a D**. The study states that the leading cause of death in an infant's first month is preterm birth (prior to thirty-seven weeks). *So when people say they are proud to be an American, what they really mean is that they're just glad to be alive at all.*

❯ Kim Krisberg, "U.S. Lagging Behind Many Other Nations on Infant Mortality Rates: Healthy Behavior, Healthier Babies," *The Nation's Health*, American Public Health Association, February 2009, *www.apha.org.*

279

FACT: Tennessee's state health department reports that the 2006 **infant mortality there surpassed the national rate by over 31 percent**, with the black infant death rate over twice as high as the white infant death rate. *See? Even babies don't want to live there.*

❯ Kim Krisberg, "U.S. Lagging Behind Many Other Nations on Infant Mortality Rates: Healthy Behavior, Healthier Babies," *The Nation's Health*, American Public Health Association, February 2009, *www.apha.org*.

280

FACT: Ten percent of U.S. adults eighteen and older—or about 24 million people—experienced **serious psychological distress in 2008**, for which less than half received mental health services. *That's where liquor comes in.*

❯ "Question of the Month: What Percentage of U.S. Adults Experienced Serious Psychological Distress in the Past Year?" *The Nation's Health*, American Public Health Association, February 2009, *www.apha.org*.

281

FACT: Mental health concerns are one of

Americans' top reasons for seeking medical treatment.

Depression and other mental problems prompted 156 million of us to visit doctors, clinics, and hospitals in 2005. *And twice that many to visit liquor stores.*

❯ "Question of the Month: What Percentage of U.S. Adults Experienced Serious Psychological Distress in the Past Year?" *The Nation's Health*, American Public Health Association, February 2009, *www.apha.org*.

282

FACT: Poisoning was **the second most common cause of deadly injury** in the United States in 2004, following vehicular crashes. *What if you are poisoned and then crash your car and die? I bet those are hard to categorize.*

> "QuickStats: Death Rates from Poisoning, by State—United States, 2004," *Morbidity and Mortality Weekly Report,* September 14, 2007, Centers for Disease Control and Prevention, *http://wonder.cdc.gov.*

 283

FACT: **Nearly 70 percent** of poisoning deaths in 2004 were ruled accidental. Another 19 percent were suicides, while the rest were categorized as homicides or undetermined. *What some call accidental is really just Darwinism at work—cleaning out the gene pool and what not.*

> "Question of the Month: "What is the second leading cause of death by injury in the United States?" *The Nation's Health,* May 2008, *www.apha .org.*

 284

FACT: A December 2008 report by Trust for America's Health warns that **budget cuts could stymie our nation's preparedness for emergencies.** The report was issued within days of an independent commission on weapons of mass destruction's warning about the likelihood of a nuclear or biological attack on America within the next five years. *Here's the good news: I just saved some money on my car insurance.*

> Teddi Dineley Johnson, "Budget Cuts Threaten Nation's Public Health Preparedness: Report Calls Biological Attack Likely," *The Nation's Health,* February 2009, *www.apha.org.*

 285

FACT: Tuberculosis (TB) is among **the most widespread and frequently fatal infectious diseases** in the world. TB is caused by *Mycobacterium tuberculosis,* which infects an estimated one-third of the world's population. *TB also stands for Tampa Bay and their NFL team, the Buccaneers, whose players are among the most fatal to your fantasy football team.*

> "Plan to Combat Extensively Drug Resistant Tuberculosis," *Morbidity and Mortality Weekly Report,* Centers for Disease Control and Prevention, February 13, 2009, *www.cdc.gov.*

286

FACT: From 1985–1992, **the United States experienced an unprecedented TB resurgence**, accompanied by a substantial number of patients who did not respond to traditional treatment and died. Doctors soon determined that these individuals had multi-drug-resistant TB, a new strain of the disease. *TB or not TB? That was the question.*

> "Plan to Combat Extensively Drug Resistant Tuberculosis," *Morbidity and Mortality Weekly Report*, Centers for Disease Control and Prevention, February 13, 2009, www.cdc.gov.

287

FACT: From 2005 to 2006, age-adjusted death rates for diabetes declined over 5 percent for whites and blacks. But **rates for black males have generally increased**, now surpassing rates for black females. *I always pronounced it "dia-bee-tees," but then I heard that old guy on the TV commercial call it "dia-beetus," and now I just don't know what to believe anymore.*

> M.P. Heron and others, "Deaths: Preliminary Data for 2006," *National Vital Statistics Report*, Centers for Disease Control and Prevention, June 11, 2008, www.cdc.gov.

288

FACT: A study published in March 2009 reported overweight eighteen-year-old men were as likely **to die by sixty as occasional smokers**; obese young men, much like heavy smokers, doubled the risk of dying early. *So you have a choice, young fatties: donuts or cigarettes. It's a tough one, I know. Good luck.*

> Roni Caryn Rabin, "Obese Teens as Likely as Smokers to Die Early, Study Finds," *New York Times*, March 3, 2009. www.nytimes.com.

289

FACT: In 2005—the most recent year numbers were available—over 186,000 women and 1,700 men were reported with breast cancer; roughly **20 percent of them** died from the disease. *Just one more reason not to grow man breasts (or "moobs"), fellas.*

> "U.S. Obesity Trends 1985–2007," Centers for Disease Control and Prevention, Division of Nutrition, Physical Activity and Obesity, National Center for Chronic Disease Prevention and Health Promotion, July 24, 2008, www.cdc.gov.

FACT: A 2007 report showed just one U.S. state with an obesity rate under 20 percent: Colorado. Thirty U.S. states had **an obesity rate equal to or greater than 25 percent**, and three states—Alabama, Mississippi, and Tennessee—were at or above 30 percent. *They will change their name from the Bible Belt to the Loosened Belt.*

> "U.S. Obesity Trends 1985–2007," Centers for Disease Control and Prevention, Division of Nutrition, Physical Activity and Obesity, National Center for Chronic Disease Prevention and Health Promotion, July 24, 2008, *www.cdc.gov.*

291

FACT: In humans with celiac disease, the body's immune system damages the lining of the small intestine when it processes gluten, **hindering the body's ability to absorb nutrients from food** and causes numerous digestive problems. Untreated celiac disease can be life-threatening. *Other names for celiac disease are celiac sprue and gluten intolerance, but I like to call it "pootin' gluten."*

> "What I Need to Know about Celiac Disease," National Digestive Diseases Information Clearinghouse, National Institute of Diabetes and Digestive and Kidney Diseases, National Institutes of Health, *www.digestive.niddk.nih.gov.*

> "Celiac Disease Facts," University of Maryland Center for Celiac Research, *www.umm.edu.*

292

FACT: Up to **70 million Americans** are affected by digestive diseases such as pancreatitis, cirrhosis, gastritis, reflux, viral hepatitis, and more. *And you don't want to sit near any of them, trust me.*

> "Digestive Disease Statistics," National Digestive Diseases Information Clearinghouse, National Institute of Diabetes and Digestive and Kidney Diseases, National Institutes of Health, *www.digestive.niddk.nih.gov.*

FACT: Eating disorders such as **anorexia and bulimia** can cause low blood pressure, diabetes, heart and kidney problems, brain damage and death. *Other than that, they're harmless.*

> "Eating Disorders," Medline Plus, National Institutes of Health, Department of Health & Human Services, February 27, 2009, *www.nlm.nih.gov.*

FACT: About **5 million Americans** suffer from heart failure; 300,000 of them die each year. *I assume they're including the dead ones in the "suffer from" number.*

> "Heart Failure," Medline Plus, National Institutes of Health, Department of Health & Human Services, *www.nlm.nih.gov.*

FACT: Conditions that affect less than 200,000 people nationwide are **characterized as orphan diseases**. These include Lou Gehrig's disease, cystic fibrosis, Tourette's syndrome, and lesser-known conditions such as Job syndrome, Hamburger disease, and gigantism. Collectively orphan disease plagues up to 25 million in the U.S. *Huh, I always thought orphan diseases were things like lice and rickets.*

> Carol Rados, "Orphan Products: Hope for People With Rare Diseases," *FDA Consumer Magazine*, November-December 2003, *www.fda.gov.*

FACT : The medical condition known as heart failure does not mean that your heart has arrested or is about to quit working, but that the **organ isn't pumping enough blood** through the body. *Either way, it sucks.*

❯ "Heart Failure," Medline Plus, National Institutes of Health, Department of Health & Human Services, *www.nlm.nih.gov.*

FACT : Humans can grow horns. Called cutaneous horns, they grow when the skin surface thickens, typically in response to disease. *I'm pretty sure my old boss had some but not because she was diseased—because she was the Devil.*

❯ Diane Mapes, "These Aren't Devil's Horns, They're Real," The Body Odd, MSNBC.com, *www.bodyodd.msnbc.msn.com.*

FACT : A ninety-two-year-old Chinese woman recently gave birth to **a sixty-year-old baby**. *No baby wants to come out of the womb, but some are a little more stubborn than others. Oh, and by the way—ouch.*

❯ Diane Mapes, "The Curious Case Of The Stone Baby," The Body Odd, MSNBC.com, *www.bodyodd.msnbc.msn.com.*

299

FACT: A sixty-year-old British woman **cannot recognize voices**, even those of family members. She can't comprehend who is talking to her unless she can see the speaking person's face. Even if her child calls on the telephone, it is as if she is hearing that voice for the first time. The only exception is Sean Connery's voice. *But only when he says, "Suck it, Trebek."*

❯ Brian Alexander, "Unable To Recognize Voices, Unless It's Sean Connery," The Body Odd, MSNBC.com, *www.bodyodd .msnbc.msn.com.*

300

FACT: Researchers in Germany have discovered that, if exposed to an unpleasant smell, **sleepers will have bad dreams**. When exposed to pleasant smells of roses, the opposite occurred and their dreams were subsequently positive. *That is, if you consider dreaming that you're a gardener positive.*

❯ Mark Leyner and Billy Goldberg, "Bad Smells Can Give You Nightmares," The Body Odd, MSNBC.com, *www.bodyodd.msnbc.msn.com.*

CHAPTER 7

And in My Spare Time, I Enjoy Dying

Bad News about the Things You Do for Fun—or Used To

301

FACT: Boating accidents claim **an average of 700 lives** each year. *The majority of them on water.*

> "Water-Related Injuries: Fact Sheet," Home & Recreational Safety, Centers for Disease Control and Prevention, *www.cdc.gov.*

302

FACT: Finger holes in bowling balls have been found to contain **"substantial" amounts of fecal contamination**. *Pooping into those little holes isn't easy, either, believe me. But when you gotta go, you gotta go.*

> Philip M. Tierno, *The Secret Life of Germs: What They Are, Why We Need Them, and How We Can Protect Ourselves Against Them* (Simon & Schuster, 2004), 108.

303

FACT: The CDC estimates that **3.8 million sports and recreation-related concussions** happen in the United States each year. *They can only estimate because no one at the CDC has ever set foot on a sports field.*

> "Learn to Prevent & Recognize Concussions," National Center for Injury Prevention and Control, National Center for Health Marketing, Division of eHealth Marketing, *www.cdc.gov.*

304

FACT: Between two and three jockeys are killed each year—the same number of players who have died in professional baseball's entire history—making **horse racing one of the most dangerous sports**. *Some years it's 2.5, if a jockey is really small.*

> Noel Botham, *The Best Book of Useless Information Ever: A Few Thousand Other Things You Probably Don't Need to Know (but Might as Well Find Out)* (Perigee, 2007).

> "Baseball-Related Deaths Uncommon," *Tulsa World*, July 24, 2007, *www.tulsaworld.com.*

FACT: The game "hot cockles" was very popular around Christmas in medieval times. It entailed **taking turns striking a blindfolded player**, who had to guess the name of the person who was doing the hitting. *I usually dread my mother-in-law's Christmas visit, but that just changed. "Who wants to play a fun game?"*

❯ Noel Botham, *The Best Book of Useless Information Ever: A Few Thousand Other Things You Probably Don't Need to Know (but Might as Well Find Out)* (Perigee, 2007).

FACT: A NASCAR fan once sent **over half a million e-mails** to FOX network for airing a baseball game instead of a scheduled race. *FOX cared.*

❯ Noel Botham, *The Best Book of Useless Information Ever: A Few Thousand Other Things You Probably Don't Need to Know (but Might as Well Find Out)* (Perigee, 2007).

FACT: Roughly 20 percent of all traumatic brain injuries to children and adolescents in the United States are caused in some way **by sports and recreational activities**. Most occur during bicycling, skateboarding, or skating. *However, the number of injuries involving unicycles has increased 100 percent in the last decade, from one to two. But both were nerds, so who cares?*

❯ "Sports Injury Statistics," Children's Hospital Boston, *www.childrenshospital.org.*

FACT: About 3 million youth aged fourteen and under are hurt annually during sports or recreational activities; more than 25 percent of those are treated in hospital emergency rooms. Most injuries occur as a result of falling down, being struck by an object, collisions, and overexertion during unorganized or informal sports activities. *The sooner a kid becomes acquainted with pain, the better.*

> "Sports Injury Statistics," Children's Hospital Boston, *www.childrenshospital.org.*

FACT: Sixty percent of sports-related injuries **occur during practice**. *We call that a learning curve, and for things like rock-climbing, hang-gliding, and pole vaulting, it's a drag.*

> "Sports Injury Statistics," Children's Hospital Boston, *www.childrenshospital.org.*

FACT: The severity of sports-related injury **increases with age**. *The severity of a lot of things increases with age.*

> "Sports Injury Statistics," Children's Hospital Boston, *www.childrenshospital.org.*

FACT: Before puberty, girls and boys suffer the same risk of sports injuries, but during puberty, **boys suffer more injuries**, and more severe injuries, than girls. *Probably because during puberty, boys are trying harder than ever to impress those girls.*

> "Sports Injury Statistics," Children's Hospital Boston, *www.childrenshospital.org.*

312

FACT: Baseball has **the highest fatality rate** among sports for children ages five to fourteen, with three to four deaths each year. *From what, boredom?*

❯ "Sports Injury Statistics," Children's Hospital Boston, *www.childrenshospital.org.*

313

FACT: Many rugby song lyrics and the particular plays within the game (presumably jokingly) **glorify raping other men's girlfriends and mothers.** *I've known a few rugby players. They weren't joking.*

❯ Sara L. Crawley, Lara J. Foley, and Constance L. Shehan, *Gendering Bodies* (Rowman & Littlefield, 2007), 187.

314

FACT: NFL players in prestigious and popular roles as scorers—running backs, quarterbacks, wide receivers—appear to be **overrepresented in domestic violence and sexual assaults** committed against women. *Overrepresented legally, that is, like O.J. in his first trial, when he had about seventeen lawyers.*

❯ Sara L. Crawley, Lara J. Foley, and Constance L. Shehan, *Gendering Bodies* (Rowman & Littlefield, 2007), 187.

315

FACT: A Washington, D.C.-based study on the correlation between admissions to emergency rooms and outcomes for Washington Redskins' football games showed that admissions of female victims of stabbings, gunshots, assaults, and other **violence actually increases when the team wins**. *Which, luckily, doesn't happen very often.*

❯ Sara L. Crawley, Lara J. Foley, and Constance L. Shehan, *Gendering Bodies* (Rowman & Littlefield, 2007), 187.

 316

FACT: Boxers and participants in violent team sports **often suffer very high incidence of permanent injuries**, disabilities, alcoholism, drug abuse, obesity, and heart problems. *Really? Because Muhammad Ali seems just fine to me.*

❯ Sara L. Crawley, Lara J. Foley, and Constance L. Shehan, *Gendering Bodies* (Rowman & Littlefield, 2007), 187.

 317

FACT: In Ancient Greece, **boxing was a more brutal sport** than it is today. Fighters wore leather straps to protect their fists, and the contest did not end until one of the fighters was unconscious or, in some cases, dead. *Yes, that sounds totally different from modern boxing. Wait. No, it doesn't.*

❯ "The Most Brutal," Ancient Sports, *www.Ancientsports.net.*

❯ Waldo E. Sweet and Erich Segal, *Sport and Recreation in Ancient Greece: A Sourcebook with Translations* (Oxford University Press, 1987).

FACT: In boxing, a "knockout" is synony-
mous with cerebral concussion, which can lead to
short- or even long-term amnesia and confusion.
Another concern is that **the neurological damage is
cumulative** and makes the boxer increasingly vulner-
able to future injury and permanent neurological
trauma. *Amnesia might not be a bad thing, in this case. Who
wants to remember getting his ass kicked?*

❯ Julian E. Bailes and Arthur L. Day, *Neurological Sports Medicine: A Guide for Physicians and Athletic Trainers* (Thieme, 2001).

FACT: Another popular violent sport in ancient
Greece was pankration, **a hybrid of wrestling and
boxing with no protective gear and no rules**, save a
ban on gouging of eyes and biting. *We still have this.
It's called the Ultimate Fighting Championship. But I think they
allow biting and eye–gouging now. And wedgies.*

❯ "The Most Brutal," Ancient Sports, *www.ancientsports.net*.

❯ Waldo E. Sweet, Erich Segal, *Sport and Recreation in Ancient Greece: A Sourcebook with Translations* (Oxford University Press, 1987).

FACT: Ancient Egyptian sports and games were brutal.
In Fishermen's Jousting, teams of fishermen would
knock their opponents out of their boats. Since many
fishermen were unable to swim,
drownings often resulted. *Because the best sport
for guys who can't swim is one where they try to
knock each other off paper boats into the water.*

❯ "The Most Brutal," Ancient Sports, *www.ancientsports.net*.

❯ Steve Craig, *Sports and Games of the Ancients* (Greenwood Publishing Group, 2002), 6.

321

F A C T : Chariot racing in ancient Rome was brutal. Drivers wrapped the reins of the chariot around their arms and could not let go if they crashed, **allowing them to be dragged behind their horses** unless they could free themselves. Many charioteers carried small knives for this purpose. *Then they realized a better solution: find a new hobby. One that doesn't involve chariots.*

❯ "The Most Brutal," Ancient Sports, *www.ancientsports.net.*

❯ Eckart Köhne, Cornelia Ewigleben, and Ralph Jackson, *Gladiators and Caesars: The Power of Spectacle in Ancient Rome* (University of California Press, 2000).

322

F A C T : Spanish-style bullfights are **a gruesome tradition**. Picadors (lance-yielding men on blind-folded horses) and banderilleros (men on foot who wield sticks with harpoon points) stab a bull in the back and neck. When the bull is weakened, the matador forces a few charges from the bull for show, then kills it with a sword and cuts off the ears or tail as trophies. *Well that sounds like fun. I have to take the kids.*

❯ "What is wrong with bullfight-ing?" League Against Cruel Sports, *www.league.org.uk.*

 323

F A C T : Six people died in bullfights in 2004. *What a shame. That there weren't more.*

❯ "What is wrong with bullfighting?" League Against Cruel Sports, *www.league.org.uk.*

 324

F A C T : Since 1924, **thirteen people have been killed in Pamplona**, Spain's annual "Running of the Bulls" at the San Fermin festival. Injuries have persisted in recent years despite the government's attempts to make the event safer by coating the streets with a special anti-slip paint. *One year, instead of anti-slip paint, they covered the street with butter and banana peels just for fun. The number of injuries increased a bit.*

❯ Damien Simonis, Susan For-syth, and John Noble, *Spain*, 6th ed. (Lonely Planet, 2007).

325

FACT: If you ascend too quickly while scuba diving, you risk lung over-expansion, a condition that occurs when air is inhaled underwater and not exhaled while rising to the surface. The air in the lungs expands as the diver ascends, and can result in **potentially lethal air bubbles in the blood**. *That doesn't sound painful.*

❯ "Decompression Symptoms: The Bends," eMedicineHealth, *www.emedicinehealth.com.*

326

FACT: Scuba divers who ascend too quickly also risk decompression sickness, or "the bends," which occurs when nitrogen that builds in tissues during the dive is forced back into the blood stream too quickly, **resulting in nitrogen bubbles in the blood**. The condition is extremely painful and potentially fatal. *Like any of this will matter the next time you're diving and a fifteen-foot shark starts circling. You'll ascend so fast you'll look like Shamu coming out of the water.*

❯ "Decompression Symptoms: The Bends," eMedicineHealth, *www.emedicinehealth.com.*
❯ Bruce Iliff, "The Bends In Scuba Diving," suite101.com, *www.suite101.com.*

327

FACT: Research by the National Spinal Cord Injury Statistical Center shows that **18 percent of spinal cord injuries are sports-related**, with close to 8,000 injuries each year. This is likely a gross underestimate, however, as an additional 20 patients per million die before reaching the hospital. *People without medical coverage will do anything to avoid a high hospital bill.*

❯ Randolph W. Evans, *Neurology and Trauma*, 2nd ed. (Oxford University Press, 2006).

328

FACT: One study showed that over half of **sports-related catastrophic spinal cord injuries resulted from diving accidents**, most of them during unsupervised or unsponsored activities in which alcohol was a factor. *"Hey y'all, watch this!"*

❯ Randolph W. Evans, *Neurology and Trauma* 2nd ed. (Oxford University Press, 2006).

 329

FACT: From 1982 to 1997, cheerleading accounted for 57 percent of the **catastrophic injuries and fatalities** among young female athletes. *When did cheerleaders become "athletes"?*

❯ Jean O'Reilly and Susan K. Cahn, *Women and Sports in the United States: A Documentary Reader* (UPNE, 2007).

 330

FACT: Stingers are injuries to the nerves in the neck and shoulder that cause **painful electric sensations to radiate through one of the arms**. If not properly diagnosed and treated, stingers, which are usually sports-related, can lead to persistent pain and permanent nerve damage. *They might want to rethink that name. Talk about an understatement.*

❯ "The Stinger," North American Spine Society Public Education Series, North American Spine Society, 2006, www.spine.org.

 331

FACT: From 1973 to 1975, there were **eighty-one known fatalities from hang-gliding**, usually involving massive head, neck, and chest trauma that included shattered skulls and ruptured aortas, heart lacerations, and pulmonary collapse. The majority of injured hang-gliders arrived at the hospital deceased. Of thirty-seven fatal injuries, 20 percent involved alcohol. *Alcohol and hang-gliding—great idea!*

❯ Julian E. Bailes and Arthur L. Day, *Neurological Sports Medicine: A Guide for Physicians and Athletic Trainers* (Thieme, 2001).

FACT: Rowing is a taxing sport with a **significant incidence of injury among participants**, ranging from spondylolysis, a stress fracture to one of the vertebrae, to disc disease, chronic pain from a damaged disc. Both conditions can lead to other injuries and degeneration in the spine. *Row, row, row your boat, Paddles in a line, Push 'em up, pull 'em back, Snap your goddamn spine.*

> Julian E. Bailes and Arthur L. Day, *Neurological Sports Medicine: A Guide for Physicians and Athletic Trainers* (Thieme, 2001).

> "Spondylolysis and Spondylolisthesis," American Academy of Orthopaedic Surgeons, www.orthoinfo.aaos.org.

> "Degenerative Disc Disease," Cedars-Sinai Medical Center, www.csmc.edu.

FACT: Sports shooters, especially those who use indoor small-bore rifle ranges, **risk lead absorption and intoxication**, known to cause symptomatic neuropathy, which can be damaging to the brain, nerves, and more. *Neuropathy is a nervous disorder—not really something you want in a guy walking around with a loaded gun.*

> Julian E. Bailes and Arthur L. Day, *Neurological Sports Medicine: A Guide for Physicians and Athletic Trainers* (Thieme, 2001).

FACT: Skiing carries a high risk of injury to the nervous system that can result in quadriplegia and death.

Recreational skiers can easily reach speeds of up to 40 mph

when traveling downhill, which can lead to injuries similar to those seen in car accidents. *If you don't believe it, ask Sonny Bono. Oh, wait, never mind. He's dead.*

> Julian E. Bailes and Arthur L. Day, *Neurological Sports Medicine: A Guide for Physicians and Athletic Trainers* (Thieme, 2001).

FACT : The use of trampolines carries a great risk for catastrophic injury. In one study, **thirty-two out of fifty instances** of spinal cord injury in gymnastics involved trampolines. *Still, they're a lot safer now than when I was a kid. We didn't have safety nets or spring covers, and the trampolines were made of asbestos, covered in lead paint, and often surrounded by a ring of fire or piranha-filled water or land mines. I saw a lot of good kids go down.*

❯ Julian E. Bailes and Arthur L. Day, *Neurological Sports Medicine: A Guide for Physicians and Athletic Trainers* (Thieme, 2001).

FACT : Golf may be considered a benign sport, but it carries risk of injury and death, most often from lightning, power lines, heart attack, and heat stroke. **Other deaths have occurred from freak injuries.** In one instance, an angry golfer killed his caddie by swinging a club at him after missing a shot, and another player broke his club on a tree, only to have it rebound and impale him. *No one who has played golf considers it a benign sport.*

❯ Julian E. Bailes and Arthur L. Day, *Neurological Sports Medicine: A Guide for Physicians and Athletic Trainers* (Thieme, 2001).

FACT : In the United States, at least seven fatalities and numerous severe injuries have been reported among **bungee jumpers using a hot air balloon as a platform**. In two instances, no one noticed that the balloon lost altitude, making the jump cord too long, and the jumpers hit the ground. *Oops. I hope they got a refund.*

❯ Julian E. Bailes and Arthur L. Day, *Neurological Sports Medicine: A Guide for Physicians and Athletic Trainers* (Thieme, 2001).

FACT: Bow-hunter's stroke is caused by **the narrowing or obstruction of main arteries** supplying blood to the brain stem or cerebellum. This can be caused by forcibly turning your head to one side, commonly on a head rotation of 90 degrees or more to the left, as an archer does when aiming. *The most common cause of death during archery remains the same as always: letting someone try to shoot an apple off the top of your head.*

> Julian E. Bailes and Arthur L. Day, *Neurological Sports Medicine: A Guide for Physicians and Athletic Trainers* (Thieme, 2001).

FACT: No one would consider lawn darts dangerous—unless he knew that the sport has been associated with skull-penetrating injuries, **half of which cause permanent neurological impairment**. In fact, the head is the most common body part to sustain injury, usually in children. *Of course it is. Head shots are worth fifty points, plus an extra ten if you hit them in the face.*

> Randolph W. Evans, *Neurology and Trauma*, 2nd ed. (Oxford University Press, 2006).

FACT: Injuries in equestrian sports are almost **twenty times more common** than injuries in motorcycling. *Except when you're thrown from a horse, you don't bounce off the windshield of a car or skid 200 yards down the asphalt on your face.*

> Randolph W. Evans, *Neurology and Trauma*, 2nd ed. (Oxford University Press, 2006).

FACT: Noodling is **a dangerous type of bare-hand fishing** used to catch large—and powerful—catfish in underwater holes. Noodlers have been drowned, suffered broken bones, and been severely bitten by turtles, beavers, snakes, and muskrats. Noodling is illegal in thirty-seven states. *Even more dangerous is canoodling. Catfish aren't affectionate, and unwanted advances will earn you a bite or a barb.*

> "How Noodling Works," HowStuffWorks.com, *www.howstuffworks.com.*

FACT: Children spend **greater time watching TV** than all other activities, except sleep. *Do you know what babysitters charge these days?*

> Huston and Wright, "Television and Socialization of Young Children," in *Tuning In to Young Viewers*, ed. T. MacBeth (Thousand Oaks, CA: Sage, 1996), 37–60.

FACT: In 2007, **forty-five people were struck and killed by lightning** in the United States, a quarter of them in or near water. *Better to be struck and killed than struck and not killed, don't you agree? If you live through that, you're probably going to be really skittish for a while. Your hair will never be right again either, I bet.*

> "Lightning Safety," National Weather Service, *www.lightningsafety.noaa.gov*.

FACT: Each year about fifty to seventy confirmed shark attacks and **five to fifteen shark-attack fatalities** occur around the world. *Numbers are on the rise. I'm wondering what makes for an unconfirmed shark attack. If a person has a huge chunk of meat ripped out of his ass, does anyone really suspect a sea bass?*

> Brian Handwerk, "Shark Facts: Attack Stats, Record Swims, More," National Geographic News, June 13, 2005, *www.news.nationalgeographic.com*.

345

FACT: Collisions with motor vehicles cause over **90 percent of deaths** from bicycle-related injuries. *And it's not the people in the motor vehicles who die, in case you were wondering.*

> "Bicycle Injury: A Nationwide Problem," Alaska Department of Transportation, August 2003, *www.dot.alaska.gov.*

346

FACT: Over 400,000 children go to the emergency room for **bicycle-related injuries each year**; children account for 70 percent of all bike injuries treated. *Clowns, monkeys, Shriners, and village idiots account for the rest.*

> "Bicycle Injury: A Nationwide Problem," Alaska Department of Transportation, August 2003, *www.dot.alaska.gov.*

347

FACT: There were **850 hunting accidents** in this country in 2002, more than 10 percent of them fatal. *Beer + redneck + loaded weapon ≠ "accident."*

> "IHEA Hunting Statistics," Hunting for Tomorrow, December 10, 2005, *www.huntingfortomorrow.com.*

348

FACT: In 2008, a seventeen-year-old boy was killed at Six Flags Over Georgia amusement park after **being decapitated by a roller coaster**. The teen and a friend had climbed over two well-marked six-foot security fences as a short-cut into the park when the victim was struck. *Six Flags' "No cutting in line" policy is a bit more strict than most amusement parks.*

> "Boy Decapitated by Roller Coaster at Six Flags Over Georgia," *Atlanta Journal-Constitution,* June 29, 2008, *www.ajc.com.*

349

FACT: At the Middle Tennessee District Fair in Lawrenceburg, a sixty-year-old woman was severely injured when she **fell thirty feet from the top of a ferris wheel** and landed on the spokes close to the center wheel axle. Witnesses told investigators that the woman was standing up and waving right before she fell from the gondola. *I bet she saw a guy selling cotton candy and was trying to get his attention.*

❯ "Woman, 60, in Critical Condition after Fall from Ferris Wheel," RideAccidents.com, September 28, 2007, *www.rideaccidents.com.*

350

FACT: A thirty-two-year-old woman fell from a roller coaster at Holiday World & Splashin' Safari theme park in Santa Claus, Indiana in 2003 and was killed. The equipment **malfunctioned at the highest point of the roller coaster**, when riders feel the most "air time," or zero-gravity feeling as a roller coaster train crests a hill. The victim fell from the last seat of the train car and plunged sixty to eighty feet to her death. *You'd think nothing bad could happen in a town called Santa Claus. You'd be wrong.*

❯ "Woman, 32, Killed in Fall from Roller Coaster at Holiday World," RideAccidents.com, May 31, 2003, *www.rideaccidents.com.*

CHAPTER 8

Let Me Hear Your Potty Talk

The Straight Poop on Going to the Bathroom

FACT: The germs on your fingers **double after using the toilet**, but almost 50 percent of men and 25 percent of women do not wash their hands after going to the bathroom. *That's why they call bowls of loose candy in restaurants and offices "fecal mints."*

❯ Katy Holland and Sarah Jarvis, *Children's Health for Dummies* (For Dummies, 2006).

FACT: Simply washing your hands with soap and water after going to the bathroom **reduces the spread of diarrheal diseases by almost half.** *The simple act of diarrhea is enough to convince me to wash my hands with soap.*

❯ "Poo Facts," Poo Productions Advocacy Group, *www.poo productions.org.*

FACT: Flushing the toilet can propel **small drops of aerosolized fecal matter** through the air as far as twenty feet, potentially landing on every surface in your bathroom. Studies have found feces on faucets, sinks, counters, combs, brushes and toothbrushes. *Reminds me of the time I ate some of those fat-free potato chips with olestra. Propel is not even close to describing what my ass did.*

❯ Philip M. Tierno, *The Secret Life of Germs: What They Are, Why We Need Them, and How We Can Protect Ourselves Against Them* (Simon & Schuster, 2004), 92.

FACT: Some intestinal viruses can remain in the air **after you defecate and flush the toilet**, and can cause infection if inhaled or swallowed. *Why are you inhaling anyway? You like that smell? I hold my breath until I can get the hell out of Dodge.*

❯ J. Barker and M.V. Jones, "The Potential Spread of Infection Caused by Aerosol Contamination of Surfaces after Flushing a Domestic Toilet," Department of Pharmaceutical and Biological Sciences, School of Life and Health Sciences, Aston University, *www.ncbi .nlm.nih.gov.*

FACT: In a humid environment like a bathroom, **a single bacterial cell can multiply into 1 billion cells** overnight. *I imagine all that floating, flying feces doesn't help, either.*

❯ Philip M. Tierno, *The Secret Life of Germs: What They Are, Why We Need Them, and How We Can Protect Ourselves Against Them* (Simon & Schuster, 2004), 92.

FACT: **Forty percent** of the world's people have no toilet, and must use the bathroom in any public place they can find: bushes, roadsides, alleys, etc. *Roadsides sound especially fun. "Dad, can I borrow the car? I wanna go out to U.S.-1 and take a shit."*

❯ Rose George, *The Big Necessity: The Unmentionable World of Human Waste and Why It Matters* (St. Martin's Press, 2008).

FACT: Lack of sanitation and access to a toilet isn't just a Third World problem: 1.7 million people in the United States have **inadequate or no means of safe disposal of waste**. *Inadequate? There's no place inadequate for a quick potty break when you really gotta go.*

❯ Rose George, *The Big Necessity: The Unmentionable World of Human Waste and Why It Matters* (St. Martin's Press, 2008).

358

FACT: **Feces in the water supply** cause 10 percent of the world's communicable diseases. *On a moonless night, a well can easily be mistaken for a latrine.*

❯ Rose George, *The Big Necessity: The Unmentionable World of Human Waste and Why It Matters* (St. Martin's Press, 2008).

 359

FACT: People often **fart shortly after they die**. *Is this what they mean by a "death rattle"?*

❯ "Facts On Farts," SmellyPoop.com, *www.smellypoop.com.*

 360

FACT: Lack of clean water and improper disposal of human waste contribute to the spread of numerous preventable diseases, **including typhoid, cholera, and dysentery**, which take the lives of thousands of children each day. *So please stop crapping on playgrounds and in the foam ball cage at Chuck E. Cheese's.*

❯ "Poo Facts," Poo Productions Advocacy Group, *www.poo productions.org.*

FACT: Safe disposal of children's feces can reduce childhood diarrhea by **as much as 40 percent**. *A few years back I took my dogs for a hike. One of them went off the trail to sniff around and started wallowing in something on the ground. When the dog returned, he stank of what I assumed to be deer feces. We hiked on and the trail curved around by the spot where my dog had wallowed, so I glanced over . . . and saw a big pile of used toilet paper. That was not safe disposal of feces.*

> "Poo Facts," Poo Productions Advocacy Group, *www.poo productions.org.*

FACT: The most germ-laden place on your toilet isn't the seat or even the bowl: **it's the handle**. *The solution: don't flush. Let the next guy worry about it.*

> "The Truth about the Toilet," Clorox.com, *www.clorox.com.*

FACT: Some major world cities remain disturbingly behind the times **when it comes to sanitation**. Milan, Italy, one of the fashion centers of the world, continued to dump raw, dangerous sewage into the Lambro River until the city built its first treatment plant in 2005, spurred by the threat of a $15-million-a-day fine from the European Union. *And you thought Venice smelled bad.*

> Rose George, *The Big Necessity: The Unmentionable World of Human Waste and Why It Matters* (St. Martin's Press, 2008).

FACT: Brussels, Belgium, seat of the European Union, **dumped human waste into the Senne River** until completion of a water treatment plant in 2003. *All those Europeans were a–peein' directly into the Senne.*

> Rose George, *The Big Necessity: The Unmentionable World of Human Waste and Why It Matters* (St. Martin's Press, 2008).

365

FACT: When you pee, **a small amount of urine enters your mouth** through the saliva glands. *Which I suppose is better than urine entering your mouth any other way.*

❯ Greta Garbage, *That's Disgusting: An Adult Guide to What's Gross, Tasteless, Rude, Crude, and Lewd* (Ten Speed Press, 1999).

366

FACT: Urine with a sweet odor can indicate that blood sugar is being excreted, **a warning sign for diabetes**. The smell is also caused by starvation and ketonuria, a result of excessive dieting. *I don't think starving people are too concerned about the smell of their pee.*

❯ Sally Wadyka, "What Your Urine is Telling You About Your Health," MSN Health & Fitness, www.health.msn.com.

367

FACT: If you see **blood in your urine**, consult a doctor right away. It is most likely the sign of a urinary tract infection, but can also indicate bladder cancer. *Yes, see a doctor right away—after you regain consciousness, that is.*

❯ Sally Wadyka, "What Your Urine is Telling You About Your Health," MSN Health & Fitness, www.health.msn.com.

368

FACT: Holding in urine too long **puts you at risk of death from hyponatremia**, also called "water intoxication," the result of consuming more water than your body can regulate. In 2007, a twenty-eight-year-old woman died of hyponatremia during a "Hold Your Wee for a Wii" contest sponsored by a local radio station in Sacramento, California. *Well, her New Year's resolution was to drink more water.*

❯ Tom Zeller Jr., "Too High a Price for a Wii," The Lede—*New York Times*, January 15, 2007, http://thelede.blogs.nytimes.com.

FACT: Harvard researcher Dr. Marsha Moses is studying the **possibility of using a simple urine test to detect breast cancer** and predict its aggressiveness. Moses recommends that doctors look for the protein ADAM 12 in patients' urine, as increasing amounts indicate cancer growth. *Doctors should also check for the Dragnet protein and the CHiPs protein, an indicator of Poncharello's disease.*

❭ William J. Cromie, "Urine test tracks deadly birthmarks," *Harvard University Gazette*, February 24, 2005, *www.harvard science.harvard.edu*.

FACT: Red urine can indicate **diabetic nephropathy, papillary renal cell carcinoma, or aloe poisoning**. It can also be a sign that you ate too many beets, or a side effect of taking certain prescription drugs. *If you eat enough beets to turn your pee red, you might be a rabbit. Consult your local veterinarian.*

❭ "Causes of Red urine," Wrong-Diagnosis.com, March 17, 2009, *www.wrongdiagnosis.com*.

❭ Ruth Woodrow, *Essentials of Pharmacology for Health Occupations*, 4th ed. (Cengage Learning, 2001), 247.

❭ Joseph T. DiPiro and others, *Pharmacotherapy: A Pathophysiologic Approach*, 7th ed. (McGraw-Hill Professional, 2008), 84.

FACT: Black urine can be a sign that you have alkaptonuria, a rare hereditary condition that **causes pee to turn pitch black upon exposure to air**. Black urine disease can cause arthritis, and can inhibit cardiac, pulmonary, and renal function. *Black urine can also inhibit your "not-screaming-like-a-schoolgirl" function.*

❭ J. C. Segen, *The Dictionary of Modern Medicine* (Taylor & Francis, 1992).

372

FACT: Green urine can result from infections caused by *Pseudomonas aeruginosa*, **a bacteria found in soil and water**. Green urine disease can be fatal if it occurs in the lungs, urinary tract, or kidneys. *Exceptions: Kermit The Frog, The Incredible Hulk, leprechauns.*

> Samer Qarah, "*Pseudomonas aeruginosa* Infections," WrongDiagnosis.com, *www.wrongdiagnosis.com.*

> J. C. Segen, *The Dictionary of Modern Medicine* (Taylor & Francis, 1992).

 373

FACT: A gram of feces contains **up to a million bacteria**, ten times as many viruses, 100 worm eggs, and 1,000 parasitic cysts. *And corn.*

> Rose George, *The Big Necessity: The Unmentionable World of Human Waste and Why It Matters* (St. Martin's Press, 2008).

374

FACT: The average healthy adult expels between 100 and 200 grams—**almost half a pound**—of feces a day. *That sounds low. Did they include vegans? How about John Goodman?*

> The Merck Manuals Online Medical Library, Merck & Co., *www.merck.com.*

FACT: Some experts estimate that people who live without adequate sanitation **inadvertently consume ten grams of fecal matter every day**, potentially leading to infection, serious illness, and death. *So don't bother telling them to eat shit—they already do.*

> Rose George, *The Big Necessity: The Unmentionable World of Human Waste and Why It Matters* (St. Martin's Press, 2008).

FACT: The chemicals indole and skatole, **which cause the foul smell of human feces**, are used as ingredients in perfume. *White Diamonds and Jean Nate in particular.*

> Shayne C. Gad, *Toxicology of the Gastrointestinal Tract* (CRC Press, 2007).

> Richard Allen Miller and Iona Miller, *The Magical and Ritual Use of Perfumes* (Inner Traditions, 1990).

FACT: Thin stools can be an indicator of colon cancer or its precursor, polyps in the colon. *Or they can simply mean that you are a small dog, like a Chihuahua or a Dachshund.*

> Sally Wadyka, "What Your Bowel Movements Are Telling You About Your Health," MSN Health & Fitness, *www.health.msn.com.*

FACT: If your stool is pale or grayish, **you could have problems somewhere in your digestive tract**, such as a blockage in the liver or a pancreatic disorder. *Or maybe your stool just needs a little sun. Try shitting on the beach for a week or two and see if that helps.*

> Sally Wadyka, "What Your Bowel Movements Are Telling You About Your Health," MSN Health & Fitness, *www.health.msn.com.*

FACT: Stool that is black and tar-like can be the harmless result of taking an iron supplement, but **can also indicate dangerous bleeding** in a higher part of the GI tract, like the stomach or esophagus. *Stool that is black and tar-like can make you wish you had a bidet, because TP is powerless against it.*

> Sally Wadyka, "What Your Bowel Movements Are Telling You About Your Health," MSN Health & Fitness, *www.health .msn.com.*

FACT: Stools that have an extremely bad and unusual odor may be **indicators of a more serious condition**, such as cystic fibrosis, Crohn's disease, ulcerative colitis, and chronic pancreatitis. *They might also be an indicator of olestras eruptus—the volcanic ass explosion that often follows the consumption of olestra.*

> Christian Stone, "Stools—foul smelling," Medical Encyclopedia, Medline Plus, U.S. National Library of Medicine and National Institutes of Health, November 13, 2007, *www.nlm .nih.gov.*

FACT: Women are up to **five times more likely than men** to have urinary incontinence problems, primarily due to trauma the body experiences during pregnancy and childbirth. Of the 25 million Americans who suffer from incontinence, 75 to 80 percent are women. *Oh, great. Something to add to their "pregnancy ruined my body" bitch list.*

> "What Every Woman Should Know," National Association for Continence, March 27, 2009, *www.nafc.org.*

FACT: More than 6.5 million Americans have fecal incontinence—**the inability to control the passage of stool**—and most of them are women. More than 10 percent of adult women in this country suffer from fecal incontinence. *This is why they make cork.*

> "Fecal Incontinence," National Association for Continence, August 14, 2008, *www.nafc.org.*

FACT : During pregnancy, a woman can develop a fistula, or **a hole in the vaginal wall that allows urine to stream out constantly**. In the past, women with fistulas frequently became outcasts from their families and communities because of their odor. *My wife develops a fistula with her hand whenever I talk about old girlfriends.*

❯ Denise Grady, "After a Devastating Birth Injury, Hope," *New York Times,* February 23, 2009, *www.nytimes.com.*

FACT : A rectovaginal fistula is an abnormal connection between the rectum and the vagina that **can lead to passing gas or stool through the vagina.** The injury can be caused by childbirth, cancer, a complication from surgery, or an inflammatory bowel condition such as Crohn's disease. *Yes, passing stool through your vag is slightly abnormal.*

❯ Mayo Clinic staff, "Rectovaginal Fistula," May 30, 2008, *www.mayoclinic.com.*

FACT : Americans use **36.5 billion rolls of toilet paper** every year, which represents at least 15 million trees pulped. *Then my mother-in-law can wipe out an entire forest in just one trip to the can.*

❯ Justin Thomas, "Bidets: Eliminate Toilet Paper, Increase Your Hygiene," *www.treehugger.com.*

386

FACT: Steatorrhea is the presence of **excess quantities of fat in stools**, and is frequently a sign of a malabsorption syndrome such as celiac disease, cystic fibrosis, and chronic pancreatitis. *The first sign of steatorrhea? Floaters.*

❯ Richard Ravel, *Clinical Laboratory Medicine: Clinical Application of Laboratory Data,* 6th ed. (Elsevier Health Sciences, 1994).

387

FACT: Oliguria is extremely low urine output, similar to anuria, a condition in which the body stops making urine. **Both symptoms are classic signs of renal failure**, but can also indicate a urinary blockage or insufficient blood supply to the kidneys. *Old man: Doctor, I can't pee anymore. Doctor: How old are you? Old man: 97. Doctor: You've peed enough.*

❯ Prasad Devarajan and Louise M Williams, "Oliguria," December 3, 2008, eMedicine, *www .emedicine.medscape.com.*

388

FACT: Fecal transplant is becoming an increasingly popular option in the treatment of severe bacterial infections such as the Superbug (*Clostridium difficile*), which is resistant to many antibiotics. The transplant calls for **the use of disease-free feces from a patient's close relative**, whose bacteria somehow defeat the infection. *"Um, hi, Dad, how's it going? This is a little awkward, but I have a favor to ask . . . ."*

❯ Rose George, *The Big Necessity: The Unmentionable World of Human Waste and Why It Matters* (St. Martin's Press, 2008).

389

FACT : The Rashtriya Swayamsevak Sangh (RSS) is developing a **soft drink made from the urine of cows**. In parts of India, cow urine is considered sacred. *Names being considered for the drink include: Mr. Whizz, Cud-wine, and Holy Coly.*

> Matthias Williams, "They call it Mellow Yellow?" Reuters, February 12, 2009, *www.reuters.com*.

 390

FACT : Experts estimate that **more than 21 billion diapers are dumped into U.S. landfills each year**. Plastics used in many disposable diapers can take hundreds of years to degrade, and the byproducts of that breakdown can seep into the soil and create hazards to public water supplies. *It's hard to imagine any plastic lasting more than a few days against the noxious fury of hot steaming baby poop.*

> "Disposable Diaper Statistics," Hamptons Diaper Co., *www.hamptonsdiapers.com*.

 391

FACT : The largest water-contamination disease outbreak in U.S. history occurred in 1993, when the Milwaukee, Wisconsin water supply was infected with the parasite *Cryptospordium*. **The tainted water killed 100 people and made 400,000 others sick**. Many experts blamed the outbreak on sewage that is regularly dumped into Lake Michigan. *Most of the bad water was used to make Old Milwaukee beer, so no one noticed.*

> Rose George, *The Big Necessity: The Unmentionable World of Human Waste and Why It Matters* (St. Martin's Press, 2008).

> Centers For Disease Control and Prevention, *www.cdc.gov*.

 392

FACT : Most people produce one to four pints of gas and **pass it approximately fourteen times daily**. *Keep in mind that fourteen is an average. Some people fart more often, cutting a steady stream of smaller "fartettes" throughout the day, while others dispatch their gas with fewer but beefier blasts.*

> "Gas in the Digestive Tract," National Digestive Diseases Information Clearinghouse, National Institute of Diabetes and Digestive and Kidney Diseases, National Institutes of Health, January 2008, *www.digestive.niddk.nih.gov*.

FACT: The foul odor of flatulence comes from **intestinal bacteria as it releases gases** that contain sulfur and, in some cases, methane, one of the greenhouse gases responsible for global warming. *So please be aware of not only your carbon footprint, but your carbon ass–print.*

> "Gas in the Digestive Tract," National Digestive Diseases Information Clearinghouse, National Institute of Diabetes and Digestive and Kidney Diseases, National Institutes of Health, January 2008, *www .digestive.niddk.nih.gov.*

FACT: Flatulence can be caused by aerophagia, or swallowing air, something we all do as we eat and drink. Chewing gum, eating or drinking too rapidly, cigarette smoking, and wearing loose dentures causes increased aerophagia **leading to more flatulence in some people**. *Come to think of it, Grandma did cut a lot of cheese.*

> "Gas in the Digestive Tract," National Digestive Diseases Information Clearinghouse, National Institute of Diabetes and Digestive and Kidney Diseases, National Institutes of Health, January 2008, *www .digestive.niddk.nih.gov.*

FACT: Adolf Hitler suffered from chronic flatulence, for which he took anti-gas pills containing a mixture of belladonna and strychnine, both known poisons. One theory blames these and other "pernicious medications" prescribed for Hitler by a "diabolical quack" doctor for changes in his personality and temperament in the early 1940s. *Who says the universe has no sense of humor?*

> Robert G. L. Waite, *The Psychopathic God: Adolf Hitler* (Da Capo Press, 1993).

> Greta Garbage, *That's Disgusting: An Adult Guide to What's Gross, Tasteless, Rude, Crude, and Lewd* (Ten Speed Press, 1999).

FACT: Urolagnia—also known as "water sports" or "golden showers"—is a sexual fetish in which **partners derive pleasure from being urinated on**, urinating on others, or drinking urine. The practice is often classified by psychologists as a form of sexual sadomasochism. *Always discuss urolagnia with your partner before attempting it, as some people get pissed off when pissed on.*

> D. Richard Laws and William T. O'Donohue, *Sexual Deviance: Theory, Assessment, and Treatment*, 2nd ed. (Guilford Press, 2008).

397

FACT : Another waste-based fetish, coprophilia, focuses on **defecation for sexual satisfaction**, and can include eliminating on one's partner, and playing with or consuming fecal matter, which can have serious health risks. *Please come back when you're done puking. There are a lot more great facts in the book.*

❯ D. Richard Laws and William T. O'Donohue, *Sexual Deviance: Theory, Assessment, and Treatment*, 2nd ed. (Guilford Press, 2008).

398

FACT: The average human will spend **three years** on the toilet during his lifetime. *Lifetime? That's only about four visits for my old man.*

❯ David Boyle and Anita Roddick, *Numbers* (Anita Roddick Books, 2004).

399

FACT : Omorashi is a fetish subculture in Japan dedicated to arousal from the feeling of having a full bladder. Omorashi porn videos commonly feature schoolgirls, female professionals, and other women attempting to **appear dignified before succumbing to the urge to wet themselves**. *Really, who isn't turned on by incontinence? No wonder nonagenarians have so much sex.*

❯ "Top 10 Bizarre Fetishes," Listverse, September 24, 2007, *www.listverse.com*.

400

FACT : In March 2009, a New York restaurant owner was arrested for unlawful surveillance after a customer noticed **a video camera in the ladies' restroom**. The camera, connected to the man's office computer so he could observe females using the bathroom, was attached to the ceiling with regular cellophane tape. It had only been installed for a day before being spotted. *It took them a whole day to spot it?*

❯ Newsday, *www.newsday.com*.

CHAPTER 9

The Price Of Vice

Fifty More Reasons Not to Smoke, Drink, or Do Drugs

FACT: The U.S. has only 4 percent of the world's population, but consumes **65 percent of its supply of hard drugs**. *Except when Amy Winehouse is in the country; then it jumps to 95 percent.*

❯ "Drugs: America's Problem with Illicit Drugs," Narconon, *www.stopaddiction.com.*

FACT: The most abundant cash crop in the United States currently is marijuana. Growers in California's Mendocino County earn about **$1 billion in pot revenue each year.** *Frito-Lay and Hostess do well there, too.*

❯ Nitya Venkataraman, "Marijuana Called Top U.S. Cash Crop," ABCNews.com, December 18, 2006, *http://abcnews.go.com.*

❯ "Raw Data," *Playboy,* May 2009.

FACT: Smoking is the number one preventable cause of premature death in America. Though a difficult habit to break, a recent study suggests **smokers are more apt to quit if you bribe them**. A test group who was given an incentive to stop smoking had a significantly higher rate of completion of a cessation program than the comparable "information only" group, and more of them quit smoking within six months of enrollment. *Never underestimate the power of donuts.*

❯ "A Randomized, Controlled Trial of Financial Incentives for Smoking Cessation," *New England Journal of Medicine,* February 12, 2009, *www.content.nejm.org.*

FACT: About **14 million Americans** fit the criteria for alcoholism or alcohol abuse. *Those criteria include dancing badly, believing you are hilarious, telling people how much you love them even though you don't, screaming "show us your tits!" to female cops, and waking up face down in a puddle of your own vomit. In jail. Without pants.*

> Dennis M. Donovan and G. Alan Marlatt, *Assessment of Addictive Behaviors*, 2nd ed. (Guilford Press, 2007).

FACT: In rare instances, **someone's first use of cocaine can be fatal.** Deaths from cocaine often result from cardiac arrest or seizure followed by respiratory arrest. *That's one way to avoid addiction, though.*

> "Cocaine," *Psychology Today*, www.psychologytoday.com.

FACT: **Regularly snorting cocaine can lead to nasal problems**, such as nosebleeds, loss of sense of smell, hoarseness, problems with swallowing, and septum irritation which leads to a chronically inflamed, runny nose. *It can also rot your nose until it falls off your face. That's a nasal problem, too.*

> "Cocaine," *Psychology Today*, www.psychologytoday.com.

FACT: Binge cocaine use causes increased irritability, restlessness, and paranoia, and **can lead to full-blown paranoid psychosis** that causes the user to lose touch with reality. *This condition is also known as Republican Syndrome.*

> "Cocaine," *Psychology Today*, www.psychologytoday.com.
> "Cocaine: Facts," Alcoholism and Drug Addiction Research Foundation, *www.xs4all .nl/~4david/cocaine.html.*

408

FACT: Cocaine users who shoot the drug intravenously **may have allergic reactions to the drug or any of the additives** commonly found in street cocaine, which can result in death in severe cases. Users who inject the drug also risk acquiring HIV infection/AIDS and Hepatitis C if they share needles and injection equipment. *Sharing needles shows a serious lack of judgment. People who buy illicit drugs from strangers and shoot them directly into their veins should know better.*

> "Cocaine," *Psychology Today, www.psychologytoday.com.*

409

FACT: Cocaine suppresses the appetite which can lead to decreased food intake, making many chronic cocaine users **at risk for malnourishment and significant weight loss**. *Like when your nose falls off your face. That's gotta be a couple of ounces. Unless you're Barbra Streisand—then you're talking closer to a pound.*

> "Cocaine," *Psychology Today, www.psychologytoday.com.*

410

FACT: Potentially dangerous interactions can occur when taking cocaine and alcohol in any combination. Both drugs convert to cocaethylene in the body, which is more toxic and has a longer duration in the brain than either drug alone. The mixture creates **the most common fatal two-drug combination**. *I think more toxic and longer duration is the whole point.*

> "Cocaine," *Psychology Today, www.psychologytoday.com.*

411

FACT: Smoking is the cause of 90 percent of deaths from lung cancer in men and nearly 80 percent of deaths from lung cancer in women. The risk of death from lung cancer is **over twenty-three times greater** for male smokers and thirteen times greater for female smokers than for their counterparts who never smoked. *Even if you only thought about smoking, your risk of lung cancer triples.*

❯ "Fact Sheet—Health Effects of Cigarette Smoking," Centers for Disease Control and Prevention, National Center for Chronic Disease Prevention and Health Promotion, Office on Smoking and Health, January 2008, *www .cdc.gov.*

412

FACT: Smoking causes acute myeloid leukemia, **as well as cancer in other areas of the body**, including the bladder, mouth, larynx (voice box), cervix, kidneys, lungs, esophagus, pancreas, and stomach. *Bladder cancer sounds like fun.*

❯ "Fact Sheet—Health Effects of Cigarette Smoking," Centers for Disease Control and Prevention, National Center for Chronic Disease Prevention and Health Promotion, Office on Smoking and Health, January 2008, *www .cdc.gov.*

413

FACT: Smoking contributes to heart disease, **the number one cause of death in the United States**. Cigarette smokers quadruple their risk for developing coronary heart disease. *I think it would be fun to put on a Grim Reaper costume and go stand in the corner of the smoking room at the airport. Just stand there. With my sickle.*

❯ "Fact Sheet - Health Effects of Cigarette Smoking," Centers for Disease Control and Prevention, National Center for Chronic Disease Prevention and Health Promotion, Office on Smoking and Health, January 2008, *www .cdc.gov.*

414

FACT: Smoking cigarettes **nearly doubles** a person's risk of having a stroke. *And triples his risk of being asked, "Can I bum a cigarette?"*

❯ "Fact Sheet - Health Effects of Cigarette Smoking," Centers for Disease Control and Prevention, National Center for Chronic Disease Prevention and Health Promotion, Office on Smoking and Health, January 2008, *www.cdc.gov.*

FACT: Smoking can cause abdominal aortic aneurysm, **when a bulge forms in the wall of the aorta near the stomach**. About 15,000 Americans die of an abdominal aortic aneurysm each year, making it the thirteenth leading cause of death in the country. *If you think "abdominal aortic aneurysm" is hard to say, try having one.*

❯ Larry A. Weinrauch, "Abdominal aortic aneurysm," Medline Plus, U.S. National Library of Medicine and the National Institutes of Health, August 28, 2008, www.nlm.nih.gov.

❯ "Abdominal Aortic Aneurysm," MedicineNet.com, www.medicinenet.com.

FACT: Women who smoke **increase their risk** for infertility, stillbirth, preterm delivery, low birth weight, and sudden infant death syndrome (SIDS). *Some pregnant women wouldn't object to preterm delivery.*

❯ "The Health Consequences of Involuntary Exposure to Tobacco Smoke: A Report of the Surgeon General," U.S. Department of Health and Human Services, Centers for Disease Control and Prevention, National Center for Chronic Disease Prevention and Health Promotion, Office on Smoking and Health, 2006, www.surgeongeneral.gov.

FACT: About 18 percent of women aged fifteen to forty-four **smoke cigarettes while pregnant**. *You'd think a fifteen-year-old pregnant girl would have better judgment.*

❯ "The Health Consequences of Involuntary Exposure to Tobacco Smoke: A Report of the Surgeon General," U.S. Department of Health and Human Services, Centers for Disease Control and Prevention, National Center for Chronic Disease Prevention and Health Promotion, Office on Smoking and Health, 2006, www.surgeongeneral.gov.

FACT: Almost **one in five adult American women smoke cigarettes**, including: 20.7 percent of eighteen- to twenty-four-year-olds, 21.4 percent of twenty-five- to forty-four-year-olds, 18.8 percent of forty-five- to sixty-four-year-olds, and 8.3 percent of women sixty-five years or older smoke. *The sixty-five+ statistic is a bit misleading, however, because most long-term smokers are already dead by then.*

> "The Health Consequences of Involuntary Exposure to Tobacco Smoke: A Report of the Surgeon General," U.S. Department of Health and Human Services, Centers for Disease Control and Prevention, National Center for Chronic Disease Prevention and Health Promotion, Office on Smoking and Health, 2006, *www.surgeongeneral.gov.*

FACT: Cigarette smoking is most prevalent **among American Indian or Alaska Native women**. *So if you're in a crowded bar and need to bum a smoke, look for the gal in a feather headdress or a parka.*

> "The Health Consequences of Involuntary Exposure to Tobacco Smoke: A Report of the Surgeon General," U.S. Department of Health and Human Services, Centers for Disease Control and Prevention, National Center for Chronic Disease Prevention and Health Promotion, Office on Smoking and Health, 2006, *www.surgeongeneral.gov.*

FACT: Among women, **cigarette use correlates with level of education**. Smoking estimates are highest for women without traditional high-school diplomas and lowest for women with college degrees. *Shocking, I know.*

> "The Health Consequences of Involuntary Exposure to Tobacco Smoke: A Report of the Surgeon General," U.S. Department of Health and Human Services, Centers for Disease Control and Prevention, National Center for Chronic Disease Prevention and Health Promotion, Office on Smoking and Health, 2006, *www.surgeongeneral.gov.*

FACT: Smoking is more prevalent **among women who live below the poverty level** than women living at or above it. *Hey, they gotta do something while they're filling out lottery tickets.*

> "The Health Consequences of Involuntary Exposure to Tobacco Smoke: A Report of the Surgeon General," U.S. Department of Health and Human Services, Centers for Disease Control and Prevention, National Center for Chronic Disease Prevention and Health Promotion, Office on Smoking and Health, 2006, *www.surgeongeneral.gov.*

FACT : Exposure to secondhand smoke **causes disease and premature death** in those who don't smoke, as cigarette smoke contains hundreds toxic or carcinogenic chemicals like formaldehyde, arsenic, ammonia, and hydrogen cyanide. *Seems like the formaldehyde would keep you preserved a few extra years.*

> "The Health Consequences of Involuntary Exposure to Tobacco Smoke: A Report of the Surgeon General," U.S. Department of Health and Human Services, Centers for Disease Control and Prevention, National Center for Chronic Disease Prevention and Health Promotion, Office on Smoking and Health, 2006, *www.surgeongeneral.gov.*

FACT : Exposure to secondhand smoke can produce **immediate adverse effects on the cardiovascular system**, interfering with the way the heart, blood, and vascular systems normally function, and increasing the risk of a heart attack. *Yes, but secondhand smokers get to smoke for free! Think of all the money they're saving.*

> "The Health Consequences of Involuntary Exposure to Tobacco Smoke: A Report of the Surgeon General," U.S. Department of Health and Human Services, Centers for Disease Control and Prevention, National Center for Chronic Disease Prevention and Health Promotion, Office on Smoking and Health, 2006, *www.surgeongeneral.gov.*

FACT: Nonsmokers exposed to secondhand smoke at home or in the workplace **face a 30 percent increase** in their risk of developing heart disease or lung cancer. *"Secondhand" is a bit pejorative. "Preowned" would be a nice way to say the same thing.*

> "The Health Consequences of Involuntary Exposure to Tobacco Smoke: A Report of the Surgeon General," U.S. Department of Health and Human Services, Centers for Disease Control and Prevention, National Center for Chronic Disease Prevention and Health Promotion, Office on Smoking and Health, 2006, *www.surgeongeneral.gov.*

FACT : About **60 percent of American children** aged three to eleven years—nearly 22 million youth—are exposed to secondhand smoke. *Hey, nobody told them to inhale.*

> "The Health Consequences of Involuntary Exposure to Tobacco Smoke: A Report of the Surgeon General," U.S. Department of Health and Human Services, Centers for Disease Control and Prevention, National Center for Chronic Disease Prevention and Health Promotion, Office on Smoking and Health, 2006, *www.surgeongeneral.gov.*

FACT: Recent national surveys show that more than half of the American adult population drank in the past month, while 5 percent drank heavily (two drinks per day on average for men or one drink per day or more for women) and **15 percent of the population binge drank** (five drinks or greater in one night for men or four or greater for women). *Three days of consecutive binge drinking is defined as a "bender."*

> "Alcohol and Public Health," Centers for Disease Control and Prevention, Division of Adult and Community Health, National Center for Chronic Disease Prevention and Health Promotion, September 3, 2008, *www.cdc.gov.*

FACT: Long-term **excessive alcohol use** can lead to cancer of the mouth, throat, esophagus, liver, colon, and breast; dementia; stroke; neuropathy; myocardial infarction; cardiomyopathy; atrial fibrillation; hypertension; depression; anxiety; suicide; unemployment; lost productivity; and family crisis. *Is that all? So what's the big deal?*

> "Alcohol and Public Health," Centers for Disease Control and Prevention, Division of Adult and Community Health, National Center for Chronic Disease Prevention and Health Promotion, September 3, 2008, *www.cdc.gov.*

> "Quick Stats: General Information on Alcohol Use and Health," Centers for Disease Control, Division of Adult and Community Health, National Center for Chronic Disease Prevention and Health Promotion, August 6, 2008, *www.cdc.gov.*

FACT: From 2001 to 2005, about 79,000 deaths occurred each year from excessive use of alcohol (heavy and/or binge drinking), **the third most prevalent lifestyle-related cause of death** each year in the United States. *The good news: whenever a heavy drinker dies, there's always someone willing to step in and pick up his slack.*

> "Alcohol and Public Health," Centers for Disease Control and Prevention, Division of Adult and Community Health, National Center for Chronic Disease Prevention and Health Promotion, September 3, 2008, *www.cdc.gov.*

429

FACT: Excessive alcohol use, either as heavy drinking or binge drinking, **can result in increased health problems**, like liver disease, psychological disorders, unintentional injuries, and more. *Death is another increased health problem caused by heavy drinking.*

❯ "Alcohol-Attributable Deaths Report, Average for United States 2001–2005," Centers for Disease Control and Prevention, National Center for Chronic Disease Prevention and Health Promotion, *https://apps.nccd .cdc.gov.*

430

FACT: More than half of alcohol-attributed deaths from 2001 to 2005 **were from acute causes**, including motor vehicle accidents (almost 14,000 deaths), homicide (7,787), suicides (7,235), and injuries from falls (5,532). *Alcohol-related injuries and deaths are often preceded by someone yelling, "Hey, everybody, watch this!"*

❯ "Alcohol-Attributable Deaths Report, Average for United States 2001–2005," Centers for Disease Control and Prevention, National Center for Chronic Disease Prevention and Health Promotion, *www.cdc.gov.*

431

FACT: From 1995 to 2002, new heroin users ranged from **121,000 to 164,000** each year, most of them males over eighteen. *The late '90s were hard on everyone.*

❯ "Research Report Series—Heroin Abuse and Addiction," National Institute on Drug Abuse, U.S. Department of Health and Human Services, July 22, 2008, *www.nida.nih.gov.*

FACT: The National Survey on Drug Use and Health in 2003 estimated that **3.7 million people** had used heroin at some point in their lifetime, 314,000 used it in the year leading up to the survey, and 119,000 used it within a month. *Not me, though. I'm working, and it's hard enough sober.*

❯ "Research Report Series—Heroin Abuse and Addiction," National Institute on Drug Abuse, U.S. Department of Health and Human Services, July 22, 2008, *www.nida.nih.gov.*

FACT: The National Institute on Drug Abuse's Community Epidemiology Work Group (CEWG) reported heroin as **the primary drug of abuse for those seeking treatment admissions** in Boston, Baltimore, Los Angeles, Detroit, Newark, New York, and San Francisco in December 2003. *If you lived in Detroit or Newark, you'd shoot up, too.*

❯ "Research Report Series—Heroin Abuse and Addiction," National Institute on Drug Abuse, U.S. Department of Health and Human Services, July 22, 2008, *www.nida.nih.gov.*

FACT: Heroin withdrawal symptoms include muscle and bone pain, restlessness, insomnia, vomiting, diarrhea, cold flashes with goose bumps (hence the term, "cold turkey"), and involuntary leg movements. *That's nine good reasons not to stop.*

❯ "Research Report Series—Heroin Abuse and Addiction," National Institute on Drug Abuse, U.S. Department of Health and Human Services, July 22, 2008, *www.nida.nih.gov.*

FACT: Withdrawal symptoms from heroin **peak twenty-four to forty-eight hours after last use** and usually subside within about a week, though some users endure them for many months. *The involuntary leg movements include kicking yourself repeatedly in the ass for ever trying the drug in the first place. But involuntarily.*

❯ "Research Report Series—Heroin Abuse and Addiction," National Institute on Drug Abuse, U.S. Department of Health and Human Services, July 22, 2008, *www.nida.nih.gov.*

436

FACT: A 2007 survey found that among young adults eighteen to twenty-five, **the nonmedical use of prescription pain killers** increased sharply (12 percent) from the previous year. *"Nonmedical" sounds like they used pills as slingshot ammo or something, but that's not what it means. In case you were wondering.*

❯ "New National Survey Reveals Cocaine, Methamphetamine Use Drop among Young Adults; Prescription Drug Abuse Increases," News Release, Substance Abuse and Mental Health Services Administration, September 4, 2008, *www.oas.samhsa.gov.*

437

FACT: The same survey found that levels of illicit drug use among the fifty-five- to fifty-nine-year-old set **more than doubled over the previous year,** confirming concerns that baby boomers have continued to use as they age. *This just in: getting old sucks. Grandma needs something to ease the pain.*

❯ "New National Survey Reveals Cocaine, Methamphetamine Use Drop among Young Adults; Prescription Drug Abuse Increases," News Release, Substance Abuse and Mental Health Services Administration, September 4, 2008, *www.oas.samhsa.gov.*

438

FACT: Caffeine is **more addictive than marijuana.** *But you can drink coffee in your office without turning off the lights and putting on "Dark Side Of The Moon."*

❯ "The Most Addictive Drugs," Teen Drug Rehab Treatment Centers—Alcohol and Drug Rehabs for Young Adults—Addiction Treatment, *www.drugrehabtreatment.com.*

439

FACT: Excessive caffeine intake can lead to nausea, heartburn, vomiting, increased heart rate, dehydration, depression, anxiety, difficulty sleeping, and tremors. *Child's play compared to the symptoms that lack of caffeine intake can cause.*

❯ "The Most Addictive Drugs," Teen Drug Rehab Treatment Centers—Alcohol and Drug Rehabs for Young Adults—Addiction Treatment, *www.drugrehabtreatment.com.*

FACT: In severe cases, caffeine overdose **can result in death** from convulsions or an irregular heartbeat. *Caffeine underdose—i.e., not getting your morning coffee—has similar results: anxiety, depression, convulsions. It can also result in a swift and severe death to anyone who pisses you off.*

❯ "Quick Facts: Caffeine," CNN Food Central, www.cnn.com.

❯ David Zieve, Greg Juhn, and David R. Eltz, "Caffeine Overdose," Medline Plus, U.S. National Library of Medicine and the National Institutes of Health, January 23, 2008, www.nlm.nih.gov.

FACT: Marijuana was **the most used illicit drug** in the United States, with 14.4 million users in the past month, according to the 2007 National Household Survey on Drug Use and Health. *And that was just at the Phish concert.*

❯ "Results from the 2007 National Survey on Drug Use and Health: National Findings," Department of Health and Human Services, Substance Abuse and Mental Health Services Administration (SAMHSA), Office of Applied Studies (OAS), www.oas.samhsa.gov.

❯ "Your Brain on Marijuana," Teen Drug Rehab Treatment Centers—Alcohol and Drug Rehabs for Young Adults—Addiction Treatment, www.drugrehabtreatment.com.

FACT: Heavy and chronic use of marijuana **damages short-term memory** and may impair the ability to form memories, recall events, and shift attention from one thing to another. *It can also lead to, uhh, it can lead to . . . wait . . . what?*

❯ "Your Brain on Marijuana," Teen Drug Rehab Treatment Centers—Alcohol and Drug Rehabs for Young Adults—Addiction Treatment, www.drugrehabtreatment.com.

443

FACT: According to a study conducted by the Archives of General Psychiatry, long-term marijuana use **can cause abnormalities in the brain** that lead to learning difficulties and psychotic symptoms like paranoia, delusions, and odd social behaviors. *How do they know? Because they are watching you. All the time. Right now, in fact.*

❯ "Your Brain on Marijuana," Teen Drug Rehab Treatment Centers—Alcohol and Drug Rehabs for Young Adults - Addiction Treatment, *www. drugrehabtreatment.com.*

❯ Jennifer Warner, "Marijuana Use May Shrink the Brain," WebMD Health News, June 2, 2008, *www.webmd.com.*

444

FACT: In a 2005 National Household Survey on Drug Use and Health, 46 percent of U.S. residents aged twelve and older **admitted that they have used marijuana** one or more times in their lives. *The other 54 percent are lying.*

❯ "Your Brain on Marijuana," Teen Drug Rehab Treatment Centers—Alcohol and Drug Rehabs for Young Adults—Addiction Treatment, *www.drugrehab treatment.com.*

445

FACT: In a study of reckless drivers conducted in Tennessee, a third of all subjects not under the influence of alcohol **tested positive for marijuana.** *One of those tested positive for being Willie Nelson.*

❯ "Marijuana Myths and Facts: The Truth Behind 10 Popular Misconceptions," Office of National Drug Control Policy, *www. whitehousedrugpolicy.gov.*

446

FACT: Swedish researchers have discovered a link between marijuana use and **heightened risk of developing schizophrenia**. *Sounds like the Swedes need to work on growing better weed.*

❯ "Marijuana Myths and Facts: The Truth Behind 10 Popular Misconceptions," Office of National Drug Control Policy, *www.whitehousedrugpolicy.gov.*

447

F A C T : Pseudoephedrine or ephedrine is the most common ingredient used in methamphetamine (crystal meth), **also found in cold medicine**. Other ingredients such as ether, paint thinner, Freon, acetone, drain cleaner, battery acid, and lithium are also used. *Which, coincidentally, is nearly identical to the recipe for hot dogs.*

> "Meth Awareness," U.S. Department Of Justice, *www.usdoj.gov.*

448

F A C T : The crank bug is a **hallucination commonly experienced by meth users**, where they feel as though insects are creeping on or underneath the skin, causing them to pick or scratch obsessively. This can lead to open sores that may then become infected. *If you're a meth-head reading this book, I recommend you avoid the chapter on insects.*

> "Meth Awareness, U.S. Department Of Justice, *www.usdoj.gov.*

449

F A C T : The synthetic drug MDMA, better known as Ecstasy, **interferes with the ability of the body to regulate temperature** and can cause liver, kidney, and cardiovascular failure, and death. In one notable case, a fifteen-year-old Seattle teenager died in 2002 after taking Ecstasy for the very first time. *They call Ecstasy the "party drug," but I bet it's hard to party when you're dead.*

> "NIDA InfoFacts: MDMA (Ecstasy)," National Institute on Drug Abuse, *www.drugabuse.gov.*

> Sam Skolnik, "Teen's Death Raises Awareness that Ecstasy Can Be a Killer," *Seattle Post-Intelligencer,* SeattlePI.com, May 10, 2002. *www.seattlepi.com.*

450

F A C T : Ecstasy is **often used in conjunction with other drugs** such as marijuana, methamphetamine, cocaine, ketamine, and other drugs, making it even more dangerous. *Drugs: they're not a salad bar.*

> "NIDA InfoFacts: MDMA (Ecstasy)," National Institute on Drug Abuse, *www.drugabuse.gov.*

CHAPTER 10

You Have the Right to Remain Shocked

Things You Shouldn't Know about Crime and Punishment

FACT: More than **one in 100 American adults** are incarcerated, an all-time high for this country. *The fractional ones are the hardest to keep locked up. They always slip between the bars and escape.*

> "New High In U.S. Prison Numbers," *Washington Post*, February 29, 2008, *www.washingtonpost.com.*

FACT: The United States has **2.3 million people** behind bars, making it the world leader in the number and percentage of residents we incarcerate. China is a distant second. *That's because China just executes its criminals instead.*

> "New High In U.S. Prison Numbers," *Washington Post*, February 29, 2008, *www.washingtonpost.com.*

FACT: Two-thirds of the world's executions occur in China. *Told ya. Two-thirds in China, one-third in Texas.*

> Tania Branigan, "China Proclaims Big Fall in Executions after Court Reforms," *The Guardian*, March 11, 2006, *www.guardian.co.uk.*

454

FACT: State corrections dollars (adjusted for inflation) have increased **127 percent in the past twenty years**; the amount spent on higher education has increased just 21 percent. *And nobody sees the connection?*

> "New High In U.S. Prison Numbers," *Washington Post,* February 29, 2008, *www .washingtonpost.com.*

455

FACT: Ten percent of U.S. states now spend **as much money or more** on corrections than on they do on higher education. *Maybe China is on to something.*

> "New High In U.S. Prison Numbers," *Washington Post,* February 29, 2008, *www .washingtonpost.com.*

456

FACT: Felons who are considered physically unattractive receive **50 percent longer jail sentences** on average than those deemed attractive. *You are warned, Lyle Lovett.*

> Kimberly Barrett and William George, *Race, Culture, Psychology, & Law* (Sage, 2005).

457

FACT: In 1986, Wisconsinite Stephen Avery was convicted for sexual assault, attempted murder, and false imprisonment, but **was exonerated eighteen years later by DNA evidence**. In 2007, just four years out of prison, Avery was convicted again, this time for the murder of a young woman, and sentenced to life in prison. *And they say you can't go home again.*

> Russ Kick, *Disinformation Book of Lists: Subversive Facts and Hidden Information in Rapid-fire Format* (The Disinformation Company, 2004).
> "The Murder of Teresa Halbach," TruTV, *www.trutv.com.*

458

FACT : DNA tests proved that convicted rapist Larry Maze spent **more than two decades in prison under false charges**. When new prosecutors contacted the victim twenty-one years later, she revealed she'd been hypnotized by police before improperly identifying Maze in a photo lineup. He was exonerated in 2001. *Oops. I hope she sent him a "Sorry I sent you to prison for half of your life" card. I bet Hallmark makes one.*

❯ Russ Kick, *Disinformation Book of Lists: Subversive Facts and Hidden Information in Rapid-fire Format* (The Disinformation Company, 2004).

459

FACT: It took **two jolts of electricity** to kill convicted murderer Frank J. Coppola when he was executed by electrocution in 1982, the second of which caused Coppola's head and leg to catch fire. A spectator later reported that the odor of burning flesh and smoke had filled the death chamber. *Replacing the usual delightful aroma of the death chamber.*

❯ Russ Kick, *Disinformation Book of Lists: Subversive Facts and Hidden Information in Rapid-fire Format* (The Disinformation Company, 2004).

460

FACT : During the 1983 electrocution of convicted killer John Evans in Alabama, **sparks emerged from his hood and leg electrodes**, one of which caught on fire. When physicians found Evans' heart still beating, he was given a second jolt. A third jolt of electricity finally did the job. The execution lasted a total of fourteen minutes. *Isn't everyone supposed to get fifteen minutes of flame? Evans got shorted.*

❯ Russ Kick, *Disinformation Book of Lists: Subversive Facts and Hidden Information in Rapid-fire Format* (The Disinformation Company, 2004).

461

FACT: When a Virginia woman was raped and murdered in 1982, suspect Earl Washington confessed to that crime and four others. Though he was shown to have an IQ of 69, and his confessions dubious, he was sentenced to death, but **was exonerated by DNA evidence in 2000** and released from prison. *The first seeds of doubt were planted when Washington claimed that he killed the radio star. That video was behind that.*

❯ Russ Kick, *Disinformation Book of Lists: Subversive Facts and Hidden Information in Rapid-fire Format* (The Disinformation Company, 2004).

462

FACT: When Jimmy Lee Gray was executed by asphyxiation in 1983 for murdering a three-year-old girl, **his gasps for air were so desperate**, authorities cleared the room of witnesses. Gray's lawyer said, "Gray died banging his head against a steel pole in the gas chamber while reporters counted his moans." His executioner was later revealed to have been drunk at the time. *Karma's a bitch, ain't it?*

❯ Russ Kick, *Disinformation Book of Lists: Subversive Facts and Hidden Information in Rapid-fire Format* (The Disinformation Company, 2004).

463

FACT: When Jesse Tafero was electrocuted in Florida in 1990 for the murder of two police officers, **his head burst into flames**. After three jolts, he eventually stopped breathing. Officials blamed the use of a synthetic sponge (in place of a natural one) for the botched execution. *Others blamed the botched execution on Tafero's murder of two police officers.*

❯ Russ Kick, *Disinformation Book of Lists: Subversive Facts and Hidden Information in Rapid-fire Format* (The Disinformation Company, 2004).

❯ "Sonia Jacobs," Northwestern Law: Center On Wrongful Convictions, *www.law.northwestern.edu*.

464

FACT: During the execution of serial killer John Wayne Gacy in 1994 in Illinois, **the lethal serum solidified and got clogged up** in the IV tube leading to Gacy's arm. Executioners had to start over, and the process took eighteen minutes to complete. *And this was before smartphones, so it's not like you could text anyone or check your e-mail while waiting for them to off the guy.*

❯ Russ Kick, *Disinformation Book of Lists: Subversive Facts and Hidden Information in Rapid-fire Format* (The Disinformation Company, 2004).

465

FACT: At the 1997 execution of convicted murderer Pedro Medina in Florida, **foot-high flames erupted from his head**, causing the execution chamber to fill with smoke and gagging the two-dozen witnesses in attendance. Electricity was shut off, but Medina's chest heaved until the flames subsided and he died. *After this incident, Florida put "No Smoking" signs on its electric chairs.*

❯ Russ Kick, *Disinformation Book of Lists: Subversive Facts and Hidden Information in Rapid-fire Format* (The Disinformation Company, 2004).

466

FACT: When Allen Lee Davis was executed in Florida in 1999 for the beating death of a pregnant woman and her two young daughters, **blood spewed from his mouth** and he suffered burns to his head, leg, and groin. This marked the debut of the state's new electric chair, built specifically to accommodate a man Davis' size (350 lbs.). *Hopefully it had wheels.*

❯ Russ Kick, *Disinformation Book of Lists: Subversive Facts and Hidden Information in Rapid-fire Format* (The Disinformation Company, 2004).

467

FACT: Misidentified eyewitness testimony was a factor in **77 percent of DNA exoneration cases**, making it the leading cause of wrongful convictions in the United States. In 40 percent of cases, cross-racial identification was a factor. Studies show that people are less likely to recognize faces of a different race, making race a factor in wrongful convictions. *"Can you point to the honky who did this to you?"*

❯ "Facts on Post-Conviction DNA Exonerations," Innocence Project, *www.innocenceproject.org.*

468

FACT: Approximately 25 percent of wrongful convictions are made **because of incriminating statements and false confessions**. In more than a third of these, defendants were developmentally disabled and under the age of eighteen. *Remember, kids: if you must make an incriminating statement, just be sure it incriminates someone else.*

❯ "Facts on Post-Conviction DNA Exonerations," Innocence Project, *www.innocenceproject .org.*

FACT: **Taser stun guns are not safe** according to Amnesty International. The group reports that more than 330 Americans have died as a result of Taser attacks. *Unlike their victims, officers are rarely charged in the accidental deaths. Shocking, I know.*

> "Tasers—Potentially Lethal and Easy to Abuse," Amnesty International, December 16 2008, *www.amnesty.org.*

FACT: 15 percent of cases that were later overturned by DNA evidence **relied on informants or "snitches."** Most snitch testimony is considered unreliable, since it is often offered in return for dropped charges and other deals. *Snitches are so roundly despised that rats, canaries, stool pigeons, and weasels have all filed suit to have their names dissociated from them.*

> "Facts on Post-Conviction DNA Exonerations," Innocence Project, *www.innocenceproject.org.*

FACT: According to Amnesty International, security forces in southern Thai provinces **engage in systematic torture and abuse** during regional conflicts. Prisoners are beaten, burned, buried in the ground up to their necks, given electric shocks, and nearly suffocated with plastic bags, leading to several deaths. *Human rights abuses in southeast Asia? Nuh uh!*

> "Thai Security Forces Systematically Torture in Southern Counter-Insurgency," Amnesty International, January 13, 2009, *www.amnesty.org.*

FACT: A police officer in Orange County, Florida **shocked an eleven-year-old child with a learning disability** with a Taser when she punched him in the face in March 2008. The Orange County, Florida school called the police after the child became agitated and assaulted staff. *They just need a lower setting on that thing, one for kids, animals, midgets, and the elderly.*

> "Tasers—Potentially Lethal and Easy to Abuse," Amnesty International, December 16 2008, *www.amnesty.org*.

FACT: In 1953, **CIA director Allen Dulles ordered secret experiments** to test the effects of biological and chemical agents on humans. Uninformed subjects were given drugs like LSD and heroin, and at least two subjects died as a result, while many others suffered health consequences. *If you think that's torture, visit the Washington, D.C.-area airport named after Dulles. You'll beg for drugs—or death.*

> George J. Annas and Michael A. Grodin, *The Nazi Doctors and the Nuremberg Code: Human Rights in Human Experimentation* (Oxford University Press, 1995).

FACT: Laws that prohibit convicted felons from casting a ballot deny an estimated **5.3 million Americans** the right to vote. *But there is good news. After nearly ten years of intense study and debate, a team of America's top thinkers has come up with an innovative solution to this problem: don't be a felon.*

> Marc Mauer and Ryan S. King, "Uneven Justice: State Rates of Incarceration by Race and Ethnicity," Sentencing Project Advocacy Group, July 2007, *www.sentencingproject.org*.

475

FACT: Hispanics are jailed at nearly **twice the rate** of whites. *But they don't mind. Most of them are used to sharing a room with five other people.*

> Marc Mauer and Ryan S. King, "Uneven Justice: State Rates of Incarceration by Race and Ethnicity," Sentencing Project Advocacy Group, July 2007, *www.sentencingproject.org.*

476

FACT: Currently, **one in nine African-American males** aged twenty-five to twenty-nine is incarcerated. *But he's already in contact with the Cincinnati Bengals about signing once he gets paroled.*

> Marc Mauer and Ryan S. King, "Uneven Justice: State Rates of Incarceration by Race and Ethnicity," Sentencing Project Advocacy Group, July 2007, *www.sentencingproject.org.*

477

FACT: Timothy Cole, an African-American student, was arrested in 1985 and accused of being the rapist who'd been terrorizing the Texas Tech University campus. Jerry Wayne Johnson, the attacker, began writing confessions to Texas courts in 1995 **after the statute of limitations had ended.** Cole died in prison in 1999. *Johnson says he came forward out of guilt, which surfaced after he was off the hook. Guilt's smart like that.*

> Christal Bennett, "Family of Dead Inmate Seeks Exoneration," Fox News Lubbock, June 30, 2008, *www.truthinjustice.org.*

478

FACT: Hanging originated about 2,500 years ago in Persia as a method of execution. It became the favored method in many countries because **it remained a visible deterrent to crime** but was less gory than beheading. *You might know Persia better as modern-day Iran, and, if you do, you can't be too surprised that they invented hanging.*

> "Hanged by the neck until dead," Capital Punishment U.K., *www.capitalpunishmentuk.org.*

479

FACT: Crucifixion was **the most common form of execution in ancient Rome**, but today is an official method of capital punishment in just one country: Sudan. *Modern-day crucifixion—from the fine folks who brought you Darfur.*

❯ Tom Head, "Death by Crucifixion: An Overview and History of Death by Crucifixion," About .com, *www.about.com*.

❯ Donald G. Kyle, *Spectacles of Death in Ancient Rome* (Routledge, 2001).

❯ "Sudan: Imminent Execution/ Torture/Unfair Trial," Amnesty International, *www.amnesty.org*.

480

FACT: Viktor Bout, known widely as the "Merchant of Death," is the most notorious arms dealer, and **has accumulated a private air force as large as that of NATO countries**. His client list is said to include Al-Qaeda, the Taliban, the U.S. military in Iraq, NATO forces in Afghanistan, and the United Nations in Sudan. *I'll take "Things That Might Be A Conflict Of Interest" for $600, Alex.*

❯ "Spider Men," Crimes and Punishments, *Lapham's Quarterly*, Spring 2009.

❯ Douglas Farah and Kathi Austin, "The New Republic: Viktor Bout And The Pentagon," 2006, *www.globalpolicy.org*.

481

FACT: Charles Taylor, one of West Africa's most bloodthirsty warlords, **drugged his legions of child soldiers**, called "Small Boy Units," with cocktails of cocaine, gunpowder, and amphetamines. He is presently defending himself in a court in The Hague, Netherlands against charges of killings, mutilations, rape, and sexual slavery. *They should try him in Iran. They invented hanging, you know.*

❯ "Spider Men," Crimes and Punishments, *Lapham's Quarterly*, Spring 2009.

482

FACT: **The Russian mob flourished after the Soviet Union fell** in 1991, deeply involving itself in prostitution, drug trafficking, sexual slavery, extortion, and political corruption. *For latecomers to capitalism, they got the hang of diversification in a hurry.*

❯ "Spider Men," Crimes and Punishments, *Lapham's Quarterly*, Spring 2009.

FACT : Yakuza, the Japanese mafia, **consider themselves descendents of samurai**. These gangsters dress kidnapped women in short, pleated skirts and knee socks to cater to a "school girl" sex market. They also sell unwanted Chinese boys on the Tokyo black market for as much as $5,000. *They also cut off Andy Garcia's head in* Black Rain. *I realize it was just a movie, but come on, that was just uncalled for.*

❯ "Spider Men," Crimes and Punishments, *Lapham's Quarterly*, Spring 2009.

FACT : Pirate attacks off the Horn of Africa **tripled in 2008**. Somali pirates assaulted more than a hundred ships and captured at least forty, extorting up to $150 million in ransom from ship owners around the world. Among crafts hijacked: a Ukrainian freighter carrying thirty-three Soviet tanks, and a supertanker delivering $100 million in Saudi crude oil to the U.S. *Worse, they always demand the ransom in gold doubloons and barrels of rum, which are hard to find nowadays.*

❯ Matthew Power, "Hostile Takeovers," Crimes and Punishments, *Lapham's Quarterly*, Spring 2009.

FACT : In 1977, convicted killer Jack Henry Abbott contacted Norman Mailer, offering to provide an account of life behind bars. Mailer helped Abbott publish *In the Belly of the Beast*, and fought for his parole, which Abbott was granted in 1981. Though he became a celebrity, **Abbott was later arrested for another murder**, and returned to prison. *Abbott was working on* I Need Another Sucker *when he died in prison in 2002.*

❯ Crimes and Punishments, *Lapham's Quarterly*, Spring 2009.

FACT: In 1991, Milwaukee police officers, responding to a 911 call, found a naked teenage boy attempting to flee from an older man. The soft-spoken thirty-year-old man explained to the police that he and the boy were merely lovers having a domestic dispute. The man was so polite and persuasive that **the police let him take the boy back to his apartment**, where the man, serial killer Jeffrey Dahmer, strangled the boy, had sex with his body, and dismembered him. Dahmer was arrested two months later and convicted of fifteen murders. He was killed by another inmate in prison in 1994. *Most Americans remember exactly where they were and what they were doing when they heard the news that Jeffrey Dahmer had been killed. Wait—no, I'm thinking of JFK. Never mind.*

❯ Harold Schechter and David Everitt, *The A to Z Encyclopedia of Serial Killers* (Simon & Schuster, 2006).

FACT: Dr. Henry Howard Holmes was **America's first serial killer**. Holmes built a Chicago mansion complete with trap doors, secret passageways, and rooms lined with asbestos that could be turned into gas chambers. Upon his capture in 1894, Holmes confessed to twenty-seven murders. He was hanged in 1896. *Holmes wouldn't confess to more of his murders because he didn't want people to think he was an animal.*

❯ "World's worst killers," BBC News, October 30, 1999, *www.news.bbc.co.uk.*

❯ Harold Schechter and David Everitt, *The A to Z Encyclopedia of Serial Killers* (Simon & Schuster, 2006).

FACT: Sisters Delfina and Maria de Jesus Gonzales owned a Mexican brothel called Rancho el Angel, **where they killed prostitutes and customers**. Upon the sisters' arrest in 1964, police found the bodies of eighty women, eleven men, and babies. *The Sisters Gonzales killed a lot more employees than clients. What they lacked in workplace morale, they made up for in business sense: employees are easier to replace than customers.*

❯ "World's worst killers," BBC News, October 30, 1999, *www.news.bbc.co.uk.*

❯ Amanda Howard and Martin Smith, *River of Blood: Serial Killers and Their Victims* (Universal-Publishers, 2004).

489

F A C T : In the sixteenth century, Hungarian **Erzebet (Elizabeth) Bathory tortured and murdered more than 600 peasant girls** employed in her service and daughters of gentry sent to her estate to learn courtly etiquette. *What is the proper etiquette when one is tortured? Should you send a thank-you note to your torturer? What if there was more than one? Can you thank them both with one card, or do you have to send a separate card to each?*

❯ "World's worst killers," BBC News, October 30, 1999, *www .news.bbc.co.uk.*

❯ Peter Vronsky, *Female Serial Killers: How and Why Women Become Monsters* (Berkley Books, 2007).

 490

F A C T : On August 11, 1892, Lizzie Borden was **arrested for the murder of her father and stepmother**, who were both killed by blows from a hatchet. The attack not only crushed the skull of Lizzie's father, but also cleanly split his left eyeball. Borden was acquitted for the crime. *"And when she saw what she had done / She crushed his skull and cleanly split his left eyeball in half." Nah, it doesn't really work.*

❯ Edwin H. Porter, *The Fall River Tragedy: A History of the Borden Murders* (The Lawbook Exchange, 2006).

 491

F A C T : In 1989, Erik and Lyle Menendez were charged with the murder of their wealthy parents. The boys were not considered suspects until six months after their parents' death, **when their lavish spending caught investigators' attention**. The Menendez brothers were convicted and sentenced in 1996 to life in prison without parole. *They were also given a copy of "Lying Low For Dummies."*

❯ S. L. Alexander, *Media and American Courts: A Reference Handbook* (ABC-CLIO, 2004).

 492

F A C T : Kidnappings have reached an all-time high in Mexico. According to 2008 statistics, **about sixty-five people are kidnapped each month**. Many families avoid reporting it to the police, whom they distrust. Not only the rich are targeted; kidnappers have demanded as little as $500. *I heard about a minor league baseball player who was traded for some bats and ten pounds of catfish. A $500 ransom isn't quite that insulting, but it's close.*

❯ Ken Ellingwood, "Fear of Kidnapping Grips Mexico," *Los Angeles Times*, September 1, 2008, *www.latimes.com.*

493

FACT : Richard Kuklinski was known as a diabolical contract killer. He committed his first murder at age fourteen, and later became a mob hitman, **using weapons like cyanide and chainsaws to commit brutal murders**. Kuklinski was nicknamed Iceman because he sometimes froze corpses to disguise the time of death. *At least he was doing something he enjoyed. They say that's important.*

❯ Charles Montaldo, "Profile of Richard Kuklinski: The Iceman," About.com: Crime/Punishment, *www.crime.about.com*.

❯ Douglas Martin, "Richard Kuklinski, 70, a Killer of Many People and Many Ways, Dies," *New York Times*, March 9, 2006.

494

FACT : In 1978, over 900 Americans died in a mass murder-suicide led by Reverend Jim Jones, a self-appointed minister and phony faith healer who had led disciples of his People's Church to create a "socialist paradise" in South America. After a visit from California Representative Leo Ryan—whom Jones' followers gunned down—**Jones ordered his followers to drink poisoned Flavor Aid**. *Some say they drank Kool-Aid, but I don't buy it. If they had, Kool-Aid Man would've burst through a wall, everyone would've said, "Hey, Kool-Aid!" and Kool-Aid Man would've yelled, "OH YEAH!!!" And then it would have been a big party, and everyone would be having too much fun to commit suicide.*

❯ "Inside the Jonestown Massacre," CNN.com, November 13, 2008, *www.cnn.com*.

❯ Richard Rapaport, "Jonestown and City Hall Slayings Eerily Linked in Time and Memory," *San Francisco Chronicle*, November 16, 2003, *www.sfgate.com*.

495

FACT: By law, **all citizens must take a bath** at least once a year in Kentucky. *Whether they need it or not.*

❯ "Ky Law Mandates Bathing Once A Year," redOrbit.com, November 23, 2003, *www.redorbit.com*.

496

FACT: After pleading guilty to theft and vandalism in 1994, Michael Fay, an American teenager living in Singapore, was caned—a punishment in which **criminals are given blows to the bare buttocks with a bamboo cane**. Americans were outraged, and the U.S. government tried to stop the punishment, but failed. *The only outrage is that they didn't put it on TV for everyone to see. Even pay-per-view. I would've paid.*

> Cyndi Banks, *Punishment in America: A Reference Handbook* (ABC-CLIO, 2005).

497

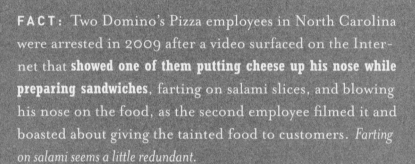

FACT: Two Domino's Pizza employees in North Carolina were arrested in 2009 after a video surfaced on the Internet that **showed one of them putting cheese up his nose while preparing sandwiches**, farting on salami slices, and blowing his nose on the food, as the second employee filmed it and boasted about giving the tainted food to customers. *Farting on salami seems a little redundant.*

> "Domino's Prankster A Sex Offender," The Smoking Gun, April 16, 2009, *www.thesmokinggun.com.*

498

FACT: In 2009, a mother in North Dakota faced child neglect charges for **drunkenly breast-feeding her infant**. Police witnessed the incident while responding to a domestic abuse call at her home, saying she was "extremely intoxicated." She was arrested because alcohol can pass from mother to child via breast milk. *Local headlines: "Loaded Boob Charged With Loaded Boob" and "Lit Twit Hit For Unfit Tit."*

> "Mother Faces BWI Charge," The Smoking Gun, April 28, 2009, *www.thesmokinggun.com.*

499

FACT: A fifty-one-year-old Cape Coral, Florida man was arrested in 2009 for having a "threesome" in his car in a grocery store parking lot—**with two inflatable sex dolls**. *"They just laid there,"* *the man later complained.*

❯ "Sex Doll Threesome Gets Man Off," MSNBC.com, May 4, 2009, *www.msnbc.msn.com.*

500

FACT: Two Florida women were arrested for theft in 2009 after taking nearly $200 worth of merchandise from a Wal-Mart in Port St. Lucie. They were caught a short time later after inadvertently **leaving behind a packet of recently developed pictures**—including some of themselves—in an envelope that listed one's name and phone number. *Like their photos, the two were finished in less than an hour.*

❯ "Shoplifting Suspects Caught After Forgetting Photos in Wal-Mart Cart," FoxNews.com, April 11, 2009, *www.foxnews.com.*

CHAPTER 11

When It Rains, It Pours

A S#*tstorm of Scary Facts about the Weather

FACT: New research predicts that the Earth's temperature could rise by 3°–6°C (37.4°–42.8°F) by the close of the twenty-first century, **enough to have a serious impact on human life** through rising sea levels, flooding, widespread drought, and more. *I plan to be long gone by then, so good luck with that, kids.*

> Michael D. Lemonick, "Global Warming: Beyond the Tipping Point," *Scientific American*, October 2008, *www.sciam.com*.

FACT: Scholars estimate that up **to 50 million people worldwide will be displaced by 2010** due to serious weather-related environmental changes caused by global warming. *I wonder how many of them ever said, "Change is good."*

> Larry West, "Scholars Predict 50 Million Environmental Refugees by 2010," About.com, *www.about.com*.

FACT: Ebola is a lethal virus in humans and has no cure. The source of the disease is unclear, but outbreaks usually occur after droughts and downpours in central Africa, **which will only increase as the planet warms**. *After droughts and downpours? So, it occurs whenever it's raining or not raining. At least it doesn't occur all the time.*

> David Biello, "Deadly by the Dozen: 12 Diseases Climate Change May Worsen," *Scientific American*, October 8, 2008, *www.sciam.com*.

FACT: Cholera bacteria thrives in warm waters and **causes diarrhea so severe that it can kill someone within a week**. With no improved sanitation, the rise in global temperatures will lead to deadly outbreaks. *After crapping your brains out for a week, death is probably a relief.*

> David Biello, "Deadly by the Dozen: 12 Diseases Climate Change May Worsen," *Scientific American*, October 8, 2008, *www.sciam.com*.

FACT: As **droughts caused by global warming** bring livestock and wildlife into closer proximity as they compete for water, tuberculosis among both humans and animals is likely to increase. *And the number of livestock is likely to decrease.*

> David Biello, "Deadly by the Dozen: 12 Diseases Climate Change May Worsen," *Scientific American,* October 8, 2008, *www.sciam.com.*

FACT: A malaria-like disease called babesiosis, which is carried by ticks and native to tropical climates, **is spreading to cooler climes** and has recently appeared in places like Italy and Long Island, New York. Babesiosis is rare in humans but that could change with increased global warming. *Babesiosis sounds like something that would turn a plain woman into a hottie, but I don't really think malaria has that ability.*

> David Biello, "Deadly by the Dozen: 12 Diseases Climate Change May Worsen," *Scientific American*, October 8, 2008, *www.sciam.com.*

FACT: One in four mammals is now threatened with extinction from deforestation, hunting, and climate change. *Do we get to pick which ones? Because armadilloes seem pretty pointless, but we're gonna need the cows.*

> "View: The Truth about Trash," *Scientific American*, January 9, 2009, *www.sciam.com.*

508

F A C T : Hurricane Ike lasted thirteen days, took 114 lives, and caused $10 billion in damage as it rolled through Cuba, Haiti, and the United States in September 2008. *That's a lot more damage than Ike Turner ever did.*

❯ "Terrifying Tornadoes, Wind Storms and Hurricanes," WebEcoist, October 22, 2008, *www .webecoist.com.*

509

FACT: In 2004, tens of thousands of people were displaced, injured, and made homeless when Hurricane Katrina hit the Gulf Coast. A combination of 175-mph winds, massive storm surge, lack of preparedness, and inadequate government response turned Katrina, **one of the most powerful hurricanes** in America's history, into an epic disaster. *In case you happened to miss it on the news. For a year.*

❯ "Terrifying Tornadoes, Wind Storms and Hurricanes," WebEcoist, October 22, 2008, *www.webecoist.com.*

510

F A C T : Hurricane Katrina decimated New Orleans, but also affected **90,000 square miles of Louisiana, Mississippi, and Alabama**, claiming more than 1,300 lives across the region. Dead bodies were still being found eight months after the hurricane. *It must be delightful to find a corpse after eight months. I might have to add that to my bucket list.*

❯ "Terrifying Tornadoes, Wind Storms and Hurricanes," WebEcoist, October 22, 2008, *www .webecoist.com.*

FACT : Tornadoes are the products of thunderstorms that **pop up suddenly and without warning**. They produce winds that can exceed 250 mph and can damage areas more than a mile wide and fifty miles long. *For once I will resist the urge to make a fart joke here. Why? Because you're probably expecting it, and I hate being predictable.*

> "Terrifying Tornadoes, Wind Storms and Hurricanes," Web-Ecoist, October 22, 2008, *www.webecoist.com.*

FACT : Approximately 800 tornadoes are reported in the United States each year, causing eighty fatalities and 1,500 injuries. **A tornado can happen in any season and at any hour**, from mountains to urban areas. *Even if you're a mile underground, a tornado will drill its way down through the Earth to get you. Even if you were on Mars, a tornado could fly up there and suck you up. Okay, not really, but they do sound pretty aggressive.*

> "Terrifying Tornadoes, Wind Storms and Hurricanes," Web-Ecoist, October 22, 2008, *www.webecoist.com.*

> "Tornadoes: Nature's Most Violent Storms," NOAA Severe Storms Laboratory, *www.nssl.noaa.gov.*

FACT : Think most tornado deaths occur in the Midwest? Think again. **Tennessee is the deadliest state for tornadoes**, killing 110 people over the last decade. *All of them related.*

> Adam Crisp, "Tennessee Tops for Tornado Deaths," *Chattanooga Times Free Press*, April 22, 2009, KnoxNews.com, *www.knoxnews.com.*

FACT : The Tri-State Tornado of 1925 was the deadliest in American history, **killing almost 700 people across Illinois, Indiana, and Missouri**. It also had the longest duration of any tornado before or since, taking almost 3½ hours to cut a record 219-mile path of destruction. *Sounds like my grandma driving to the beauty shop.*

> "1925 Tri-State Tornado," National Oceanic & Atmospheric Administration, National Weather Service, *www.crh.noaa.gov.*

> "Terrifying Tornadoes, Wind Storms and Hurricanes," Web-Ecoist, October 22, 2008, *www.webecoist.com.*

515

FACT: Lightning is a leading cause of weather-related injury and even death in the United States. Even when **a thunderstorm is ten miles away and skies are blue overhead, lightning can strike**, which most people do not realize and which puts them at risk. *They probably realize it after it happens, though.*

> "Flash Facts About Lightning," National Geographic News, June 24, 2005, *www.news .nationalgeographic.com.*

516

FACT: Lightning strikes the Earth **more than 5,000 times** every minute. *The trick is knowing where.*

> Kevin T. Pickering and Lewis A. Owen, *An Introduction to Global Environmental Issues,* 2nd ed. (Routledge, 1997).

517

FACT: Your odds of being struck by lightning in America are **1 in 700,000 in any given year**. *You have a 1 in 3,000 chance of being struck in your lifetime. The odds of it sucking are 1 in 1.*

> "Flash Facts About Lightning," National Geographic News, June 24, 2005, *www.news.nationalgeographic.com.*

518

FACT: Lightning **killed almost 4,000 Americans** between 1959 and 2003. *And scared the shit out of another 40 million.*

❯ "Flash Facts About Lightning," National Geographic News, June 24, 2005, *www.news.nationalgeographic.com.*

 519

FACT: About 10 percent of lightning-strike victims are killed. Of those who survive, 70 percent suffer **serious long-term effects from injuries** that include severe burns and can also lead to personality change, permanent brain damage, and memory loss. *I'm thinking death might be the way to go when it comes to lightning.*

❯ "Flash Facts About Lightning," National Geographic News, June 24, 2005, *www.news .nationalgeographic.com.*

 520

FACT: Most people associate lightning with thunderstorms, but **it can also occur in forest fires**, volcanic eruptions, heavy snowstorms, large hurricanes, and surface nuclear detonations. *Now that would suck. You narrowly escape a volcanic eruption and then: "Man, that was clo . . . ." BAM!*

❯ "Flash Facts About Lightning," National Geographic News, June 24, 2005, *www.news .nationalgeographic.com.*

 521

FACT: Take shelter when your hair stands on end in a storm: it often means that **positive charges are rising through you**, reaching up toward the negatively charged part of the storm and making you a target for lightning. *Or it just means that you are Phil Spector.*

❯ "Flash Facts About Lightning," National Geographic News, June 24, 2005, *www.news .nationalgeographic.com.*

522

FACT : The July 4th holiday is a **high-risk time of year for lightning strikes in America** as people across the country take to the outdoors for activities like swimming, boating, golfing, picnics, etc. *Hey, you wanted to see fireworks.*

> "Flash Facts About Lightning," National Geographic News, June 24, 2005, *www.news .nationalgeographic.com.*

 523

FACT : Once lightning enters a structure, **it may run through the electrical system, phone lines, plumbing, even TV and radio antennas and cables.** It is also possible for lightning to pass through metal in concrete walls or flooring. *Persistent little bastard, isn't it?*

> "Flash Facts About Lightning," National Geographic News, June 24, 2005, *www.news .nationalgeographic.com.*

 524

FACT : Talking on the telephone during a thunderstorm is **the leading cause of indoor lightning injuries** in the United States. *I pray for more thunderstorms over tele-marketing centers.*

> "Flash Facts About Lightning," National Geographic News, June 24, 2005, *www.news .nationalgeographic.com.*

 525

FACT : More deaths and injuries from lightning **have occurred in Florida** than all other states combined. *Carrot Top is from Florida. Call it karma.*

> Rachelle Oblack, "Top 10 of the Most Dangerous US States for Lightning Deaths," About .com, *www.weather.about.com.*

526

FACT: **Global warming is increasing the threat of wildfires in this country**, experts say, thanks to a continuing drying trend in the subtropics, including the American Southwest, and an increase in thunderstorms and lightning strikes, which are the primary cause of wildfires. *Have you ever grown tired of having to type the same two words over and over again? Words like—and this is just an example—global and warming?*

❯ Andrea Thompson, "Is Global Warming Fueling Forest Fires?" LiveScience, October 24, 2007, *www.livescience.com.*

527

FACT: Widespread drought conditions caused by global warming **resulted in thousands of wildfires across the United States** in 2008, with over 5.2 million acres burned and 1,000 homes and structures destroyed just in California. *Global warming. Global warming. Global warming.*

❯ Andrea Thompson, "Is Global Warming Fueling Forest Fires?" LiveScience, October 24, 2007, *www.livescience.com.*

❯ "Billion Dollar U.S. Weather Disasters: Narrative/Map," National Climatic Data Center, U.S. Department of Commerce, January 29, 2009, *www.ncdc.noaa.gov.*

528

FACT: In 2003 and 2005, **Portugal was ravaged by forest fires** that killed dozens of people and destroyed 10 percent of the country's forest land. The 2003 fire was attributed to global warming: higher overall temperatures in the region have lowered humidity, which has led to prolonged drought, hot winds, and dry air. *Global warming? No way!*

❯ "Six Worst Raging Fires and Explosive Volcanoes," Web-Ecoist, *www.webecoist.com.*

FACT: One of the worst storms of the last century was the Great New England Hurricane in 1938, when 120-mph winds and water surge pummeled New York, Connecticut, Massachusetts, Vermont, and Rhode Island, **killing 700 people and leaving 63,000 homeless.** *The cause was undetermined, but I'm going to go out on a limb here and say it had something to do with . . . yes . . . global warming.*

❯ "Terrifying Tornadoes, Wind Storms and Hurricanes," Web-Ecoist, October 22, 2008, *www .webecoist.com.*

FACT: Floods are one of the most severe weather events and **a leading cause of weather-related deaths.** Just six inches of fast-moving water is enough to knock an adult off his feet. *Unless that adult is Kirstie Alley or one of those contestants on* The Biggest Loser— *they require a little more.*

❯ Rachelle Oblack, "How to Stay Safe in a Flood," About.com, *www.weather.about.com.*

FACT: The deadliest type of flood is a flash flood, caused when heavy rain leads to sudden surges of water that can turn storm drains, river beds, creeks, and flood plains into raging torrents within minutes. **These waters can destroy buildings and make roads impassable,** preventing escape and assistance. *This is why everyone should own a surfboard.*

❯ Rachelle Oblack, "How to Stay Safe in a Flood," About.com, *www.weather.about.com.*

FACT: In 2007, flooding on the banks of the Huai River **displaced 2 billion rats in central China,** which destroyed over 6,000 square miles of cropland and caused an estimated $3.13 billion in damage. *Most of them relocated to New York City and are doing just fine.*

❯ "Chinese Floods Displace Billions of Rats, Mice; Raise Fears of Disease." USA Today, On Deadline, July 12, 2007, *http:// blogs.usatoday.com.*

FACT: The flood that plagued the United States in 1993 was the most costly and devastating in modern history, **lasting seven months and affecting 30,000 square miles of land** around the Mississippi and Missouri rivers and their tributaries, resulting in $15 to $20 billion in damages.

❯ "The Great Flood of 1993," USGS Missouri Water Science Center, *http://mo.water .usgs.gov.*

FACT: In March 1993, the U.S. East Coast was pummeled by what would be called the "Storm of the Century" because of **its fierce gales, deep snow, and widespread impact**. Record lows and wind gusts were recorded from Florida to Maine during the three-day storm, which caused $7 billion in damages and 270 deaths. *1993 was also the year that Mrs. Doubtfire came out. Bad things really do happen in threes, don't they?*

❯ "The Great Flood of 1993," USGS Missouri Water Science Center, *http://mo.water .usgs.gov.*
❯ "Six Chilling Ice Storms, Tsunamis and Floods," WebEcoist, *www.webecoist.com.*
❯ "BusinessWeek: Storm Watch," *BusinessWeek, www .images.businessweek.com.*

FACT: Heavy rains and flooding in India, Bangladesh, and Nepal in 1997 to 1998 **left thousands dead** and another 30 million injured or displaced. *All of them employed by Dell Tech Support.*

❯ "Six Chilling Ice Storms, Tsunamis and Floods," WebEcoist, *www.webecoist.com.*
❯ National Weather Service, Climate Prediction Center, Asia, *www.cpc.noaa.gov.*

FACT: A 1998 storm pelted Quebec, Canada with freezing rain and **enveloped the city in a layer of cement-like ice**, causing thirty deaths and weeks of electric power outages for millions of Canadians. *When did Canada get electricity?*

❯ "Six Chilling Ice Storms, Tsunamis and Floods," WebEcoist, *www.webecoist.com.*

FACT: The North American monsoon, also known as the Arizona monsoon or Mexican monsoon, can send **a daily deluge of thunderstorms** across parts of the southwestern United States and Mexico, causing flash floods, lightning strikes, and other potentially deadly conditions. *I blame identity problems. The storm is probably just pissed because no one can decide on its name.*

❯ "Monsoons Strike Again: Dam Break in the Grand Canyon," About.com Weather, August 17, 2008, *www.weather.about.com.*
❯ "Reports To The Nation: The North American Monsoon," National Weather Service, Climate Prediction Center, *www.cpc.noaa.gov.*

FACT: For the last fifteen years, Indonesia has been plagued by so many wildfires that breathing air near the burn sites is at times equivalent to **smoking eighty packs of cigarettes** a day. *But for Indonesians on a budget, it's a lot cheaper.*

❯ "Six Worst Raging Fires and Explosive Volcanoes," WebEcoist, *www.webecoist.com.*

FACT: The most destructive volcanic eruption of the twentieth century occurred in 1991 at Mount Pinatubo in the Philippines. The blast was so powerful that **it caused a global sulfuric haze and a temperature drop of almost one degree Fahrenheit** around the world. *But don't worry, global warming took care of that temperature drop within a day or two.*

> "Six Worst Raging Fires and Explosive Volcanoes," Web-Ecoist, *www.webecoist.com.*

FACT: Heat waves are one of the most lethal types of weather phenomena, claiming an average of 1,000 lives in America's fifteen largest cities each year. **Heat is especially deadly for senior citizens**, who are often too frail or afraid to leave their homes. *Or unwilling to miss the thrilling conclusion of Matlock. He's something else, that Matlock.*

> Lori Sharn and Carol J. Castaneda, "Human Nature Adds to Weather Death Toll," *USA Today*, July 8, 1999, *www.usa today.com.*

FACT: The 1988 heat wave and drought across the eastern United States cost the country **$61.6 billion in damages** and caused an estimated 5,000–10,000 deaths. *Luckily, we've gotten better at estimating death numbers since then.*

> Lori Sharn and Carol J. Castaneda, "Human Nature Adds to Weather Death Toll," *USA Today*, July 8, 1999, *www.usa today.com.*

FACT: A four-month heat wave in the summer of 1980 led to an estimated 10,000 deaths and **$48.4 billion in damages**. *Four months is not a heat wave—it's a heat tsunami.*

> Lori Sharn and Carol J. Castaneda, "Human Nature Adds to Weather Death Toll," *USA Today*, July 8, 1999, *www.usa today.com.*

FACT: In July 1995, a sudden and severe heat wave **killed over 700 people** in Chicago in just three days. *Come January, they'll be begging for that heat in Chicago.*

❭ Lori Sharn and Carol J. Castaneda, "Human Nature Adds to Weather Death Toll," *USA Today*, July 8, 1999, *www.usatoday.com.*

❭ "BusinessWeek: Storm Watch," *BusinessWeek, www.images.businessweek.com.*

❭ Paul Douglas, *Restless Skies: The Ultimate Weather Book* (Sterling Publishing Company, 2007).

FACT: Excessive heat causes not only physical stress, but psychological stress as well, to a degree that **causes an increase in violent crime**. *"My client pleads not guilty by reason of global warming, your honor."*

❭ Eric Klinenberg, *Heat Wave: A Social Autopsy of Disaster in Chicago* (University of Chicago Press, 2003).

FACT: Scientists have discovered evidence of an asteroid collision 3½ billion years ago that **likely created a massive tsunami** which swept around the Earth several times, flooding everything except the highest mountains and wiping out nearly all life on land. *So just about the time you get your cave dried out and recarve all those stick figures on the wall, here comes the fucker again.*

❭ "Tsunami Facts: How They Form, Warning Signs, and Safety Tips," National Geographic News, April 2, 2007, *www.news.nationalgeographic.com.*

FACT: Mount Washington, New Hampshire was the site of the **highest recorded wind velocity** in the United States clocking in at 231 miles per hour in 1934. *I'd heard that New Hampshire blows.*

❭ Sabrie Soloman, *Sensors Handbook* (McGraw-Hill Professional, 1998).

FACT: In February 1959 **a single storm dumped 189 inches of snow** on the Mount Shasta Ski Bowl, the greatest snowfall ever recorded. *The area is now known as the Mount Shasta Ski Dome.*

> "Sierra Snowfall Records," Sierra Nevada Virtual Museum, *www.sierranevadavirtual museum.com.*

FACT: **Tsunami waves can be as long as sixty miles**, occur as far apart as an hour, and be powerful enough to traverse entire oceans without losing significant energy. The Indian Ocean tsunami in 2004 traveled as far as 3,000 miles to Africa and still arrived with enough force to kill people and destroy property. *Who sticks around for an hour after the first tsunami hits?*

> "Tsunami Facts: How They Form, Warning Signs, and Safety Tips," National Geographic News, April 2, 2007, *www.news.nationalgeographic .com.*

FACT: Tsunamis **can travel unnoticed** in deep water as fast as 500 miles an hour, and cross an entire ocean in less than a day. *Sneaky bastards.*

> "Tsunami Facts: How They Form, Warning Signs, and Safety Tips," National Geographic News, April 2, 2007, *www.news.nationalgeographic.com.*

FACT: **The 2004 Indian Ocean tsunami could be the deadliest in history**, killing more than 200,000 people, many of them washed out to sea. *Hopefully they were already dead by the time they were taken to sea.*

> "Tsunami Facts: How They Form, Warning Signs, and Safety Tips," National Geographic News, April 2, 2007, *www.news.nationalgeographic .com.*

CHAPTER 12

You Animals!

Beastly Tales of Creatures That Outnumber Us

551

FACT : If you urinate when swimming in a South American river, you might encounter the candiru, a tiny fish that will follow a stream of urine to its source, enter the body, and flare its barbed fins, **keeping it firmly embedded in the flesh** until it can be surgically removed. *I need some of those in my pool.*

> Ross Piper, *Extraordinary Animals: An Encyclopedia of Curious and Unusual Animals* (Greenwood Publishing Group, 2007).

 552

FACT : Electric eel cells can generate and release pulses of **more than 500 volts**. *Scientists are hoping to use these cells to power medical equipment, which sounds to me like something out of "The Flintstones": your sleep apnea machine stops, you open a compartment on the side, and there's an eel with his feet up, having a smoke. "What? I'm on a break!" he says, and slams the door.*

> Eric Bland, "Electric Eel Cells Inspire Energy Source," Discovery Channel, *www.dsc .discovery.com.*

 553

FACT : The sea lizard is a type of sea slug that will eat venomous cnidarians like the Portuguese Man of War, **swallowing its stinging cells whole**, and collecting them in its outer extremities to act as a defense against predators. *Sea lizards are such users.*

> Edmund D. Brodie and John D. Dawson, *Poisonous Animals* (Macmillan, 2001).

 554

FACT : One of the most venomous marine creatures in the world is the box jellyfish. **It can kill a human within minutes** by uncoiling and firing its stinging tentacles into the victim, then pumping venom through the tentacles to paralyze him and cause cardiac arrest. *If I were a box jellyfish, I'd work on getting a more badass name. "Box jellyfish" sounds like something you get for lunch at summer camp.*

> "The 10 Most Dangerous Animals in the World," AOL Travel, *www.travel.aol.co.uk.*

555

FACT: The Australian blue-ringed octopus has **potent venomous saliva** that can cause numbness, paralysis, and death in humans. *I once saw a nature program on TV that described the octopus as "affectionate." I don't think they were talking about this one.*

❯ Edmund D. Brodie and John D. Dawson, *Poisonous Animals* (Macmillan, 2001).

556

FACT: Lampreys and hagfishes are jawless, eel-like creatures that **secrete toxic skin slime** and blood that has a bitter taste, and can irritate the eyes and cause death from internal bleeding if consumed. *The hagfish is a close relative of several other fish, including the Pimpled Fug and the Jersey Buttaface.*

❯ Edmund D. Brodie and John D. Dawson, *Poisonous Animals* (Macmillan, 2001).

557

FACT: The stingray uses a serrated spine on the upper surface of its tail to lash and cut into victims, **injecting them with venom**. Stings are intensely painful, and cause decreased blood pressure and erratic heart rate. *At least they don't bury themselves in the sand and wait for you to step on them so they can sting you. Oh, wait, yes they do.*

❯ Edmund D. Brodie and John D. Dawson, *Poisonous Animals* (Macmillan, 2001).

FACT: When threatened, **the sea cucumber ejects sticky, long threads** from its body to ensnare predators. Some species will contract their bodies, violently expelling internal organs that contain a deadly toxin. *The sea onion, on the other hand, just falls apart and cries.*

❯ "The Sea Cucumber," How Stuff Works, *www.animals .howstuffworks.com.*

❯ "Sea Cucumber," National Geographic, Animals, *http:// animals.nationalgeographic.com.*

FACT: Up to **30 percent** of Britain's rats carry Weil's disease, which can be fatal to humans. *They're the ones toting little boxes and acting suspiciously.*

❯ "The UK's Deadliest Creatures," AOL Travel, *www.travel.aol.co.uk*

FACT: A rat can compress its body to fit through an opening **as small as a half-inch in diameter**, making it almost impossible to rat-proof a building or home. *I once compressed a rat even smaller than that—with a shovel.*

❯ "The UK's Deadliest Creatures," AOL Travel, *www.travel .aol.co.uk.*

❯ "Norway Rats," Illinois Department of Public Health: Prevention & Control, *www .idph.state.il.us.*

561

FACT: Male desert rats can copulate **up to 150 times** in an afternoon. *God, I miss college.*

> Edward G. Long, *Chimpanzees Don't Wear Pants: A Retired Psychiatrist Takes a Second Look at Human Nature* (Buy Books On The Web, 2001).

562

FACT: Ursodiol, **a compound made from bear bile**, is used in Western medicine to dissolve gall stones and treat cirrhosis of the liver. *Getting the bile—that's the tricky part.*

> Constanza Villalba, "Ten Lessons Medicine Can Learn from Bears," *Scientific American,* January 6, 2009, *www.sciam .com.*

563

FACT: Of the world's numerous species of bears, **the most deadly are polar, black, and grizzly bears**. These species will attack, trample, and maul their prey until it is frightened off or dead, and will attack for a variety of reasons, including hunger. *Or simply to impress their bear friends. "Hey, guys—watch me scare the shit out of this tourist."*

> "The 10 Most Dangerous Animals in the World," AOL Travel, *www.travel.aol.co.uk.*

564

FACT: The world's longest snake, the reticulated python, **can reach almost forty feet in length**. *Its cousin, the matriculated python, is several feet shorter, but a lot smarter.*

> Mark O'Shea, *Boas and Pythons of the World* (New Holland Publishers, 2007).

565

FACT: Australia's Eastern Brown snake is one of the world's most deadly. Even baby Brown snakes have **enough venom to kill a human**. *What can Brown do to you?*

> Andrew Claridge and David Lindenmayer, *Wildlife on Farms: How to Conserve Native Animals* (CSIRO Publishing, 2003).

566

FACT: The **small but venomous saw-scaled viper causes more deaths** in North Africa and the Middle East than any other snake. When attacked, it can hurl its body at an aggressor and bite quickly. *That's exactly how I fight. They never expect the biting.*

> Ted Mertens and Helen Lucas, *Deadly & Dangerous Snakes* (Magic Bean, 1995).

567

FACT: If cornered, some **horned lizard species can shoot blood from their eye sockets up to six feet**. Though not toxic, the blood has a foul taste, particularly to canine predators like coyotes and foxes. *You know, if I corner something that wants to live so badly that it's willing to shoot blood from its eyes, I'd spare it just on principle.*

> Wade C. Sherbrooke, *Introduction to Horned Lizards of North America* (University of California Press, 2003).

568

FACT: Cone shells are a dangerous type of snail with **hollow, venom-filled teeth** that it can shoot like darts at its victims. Their deadly venom causes paralysis and can sometimes kill humans within minutes. *Killed by a snail—that would suck. I need to tell my wife to lie for me if that happens, tell people I ate it hang-gliding or climbing Mt. Everest or something cool. Not by a snail.*

> Edmund D. Brodie and John D. Dawson, *Poisonous Animals* (Macmillan, 2001).

569

FACT: To fight off predators, **poison dart frogs ooze a slimy neurotoxin** from their colorful skin. One frog produces enough toxin to kill ten humans. *"This season on Jon & Kate Plus 8, the kids get a pet frog and the entire family croaks."*

❯ "Top 10 Deadliest Animals," LIVEScience, *www.livescience .com.*

❯ "Ten of the Most Bizarre Animal Defense Mechanisms," WebEcoist, November 4, 2008, *www.webecoist.com.*

570

FACT: When threatened, the hairy frog, or "horror frog," **intentionally breaks its own bones** to produce claws that puncture through the frog's toe pads to become defensive weapons. *I liked frogs better when they just peed in your hand and gave you warts.*

❯ "Top 10 Deadliest Animals," LIVEScience, *www.livescience.com.*

❯ "Ten of the Most Bizarre Animal Defense Mechanisms," WebEcoist, November 4, 2008, *www.webecoist.com.*

571

FACT: A tiger shark's bite is powerful enough **to slice through a hard turtle shell**. *That doesn't mean they will. That's a lot of work for a little bit of meat—kinda like crab legs.*

❯ Mark Carwardine, *Shark* (Firefly Books, 2004).

572

FACT: Sharks can be dangerous even before they are born: while dissecting a sand tiger shark, one scientist was **bitten by a pup in its mother's womb**. *I'd bite him, too, if he killed my momma.*

> Walter Sullivan, "In Shark Womb, Fetus 'Cannibalizes' Rivals," *New York Times*, December 7, 1982, *www .nytimes.com.*

573

FACT: In some species of sharks, **embryos are cannibalistic**, feeding on each other in the womb until only the strongest shark remains. *Sibling rivalry starts early. "Where's your brother? And what's that in your mouth?"*

> Walter Sullivan, "In Shark Womb, Fetus 'Cannibalizes' Rivals," *New York Times*, December 7, 1982, *www .nytimes.com.*

574

FACT: If you swim in ocean areas known to contain sharks, avoid wearing yellow or orange: sharks have very good eyesight and **find these colors particularly irritating**. *Which makes felons' day out at the beach even more fun to watch.*

> "The 10 Most Dangerous Animals in the World," AOL Travel, *www.travel.aol.co.uk.*

575

FACT : A zorilla, or striped polecat, is a type of weasel that resembles a skunk, and is arguably **the world's smelliest animal**. If threatened, the zorilla ejects a powerful, foul-smelling fluid from its anus into the face of its assailant with impressive accuracy. *Babies can do that, too.*

❭ Robert Burton, *International Wildlife Encyclopedia*, 3rd ed. (Marshall Cavendish, 2002).

❭ "Ictonyx Striatus," University Of Michigan Museum Of Zoology, *www.animaldiversity.ummz .umich.edu.*

576

FACT : An adult tiger can kill its prey **with a single bite**, and can eat a large amounts of food—up to 180 lbs—in just a few days. *Whew. I'm safe.*

❭ Valmik Thapar, *Land of the Tiger: A Natural History of the Indian Subcontinent* (University of California Press, 1997).

577

FACT : A giraffe has twelve-inch hooves and legs that **can kick in all four directions** with incredible power. Giraffe kicks have been known to decapitate lions. *I bet lions hate that.*

❭ Lynn Sherr, *Tall Blondes: A Book about Giraffes* (Andrews McMeel, 1997).

578

FACT : Female marsupials have three vaginal openings, and males have a bifurcated, or forked, penis. *There's a limerick in there somewhere.*

❭ Luis P. Villarreal, *Viruses and the Evolution of Life* (ASM Press, 2005).

579

FACT: In 2009, **a 200-pound chimpanzee attacked an elderly Connecticut woman**, crushing her hands and ripping large chunks from her scalp, face, jaw, and eyes. Medics at first had trouble determining if the victim was a man or a woman. *Did it really matter at that point?*

> "Some Injuries Too Much Even for Doctors to Handle Alone," ABCNews.com, February 24, 2009, *www.abcnews.go.com.*

580

FACT: Elephants may appear friendly and approachable, but don't be fooled: these unpredictable giants cause **an estimated 300–500 fatalities a year**. Even tame, trained elephants have been known to attack without provocation and kill zookeepers who have been with them for as long as fifteen years. *Elephant to her shrink: "I tried to forget all the hurtful things he said to me over the years, but I couldn't."*

> "The 10 Most Dangerous Animals in the World," AOL Travel, *www.travel.aol.co.uk.*

581

FACT: In 1972, the Chandka Forest area in India was hit by a heat wave so brutal, it caused elephant herds **to stampede through five villages**, leaving a trail of devastation and twenty-four fatalities. *And nobody heard them coming?*

> David Wallechinsky, *The New Book of Lists: The Original Compendium of Curious Information* (Canongate U.S., 2005), 397.

582

FACT: The hippopotamus is a highly aggressive animal, and one of Africa's most deadly. **Hippos will charge, trample, and gore victims** with alarming ferocity, and have upended boats and canoes to feast on victims inside, despite being herbivores. *They are sensitive about their weight, and the whole "hungry, hungry hippo" thing makes them furious.*

> "The 10 Most Dangerous Animals in the World," AOL Travel, *www.travel.aol.co.uk.*

583

FACT: Crocodiles are ferocious killers that cause 600–800 human deaths every year. Crocs attack with terrifying speed, **launching themselves out of the water to snare prey**, which they drag underwater and spin repeatedly in a death roll until the victim is drowned or too disoriented to fight back. *Death roll—sounds like something a croc orders at a sushi bar.*

❯ "The 10 Most Dangerous Animals in the World," AOL Travel, *www.travel.aol.co.uk.*

584

FACT: Big cat attacks on humans cause an estimated 800 fatalities a year—and they are increasing, particularly attacks by tigers in Africa and India, and mountain lions in North America. Experts blame the increase on **destruction of the animals' natural habitats** and a decline in prey species. *I think we got the better end of that deal. Tigers are bad news. So are mountain lions, but the news is worse with tigers.*

❯ "The 10 Most Dangerous Animals in the World," AOL Travel, *www.travel.aol.co.uk.*

585

FACT: If a swan hisses at you, take heed. **Swans have been known to capsize boats**, attack humans on jet skis, and strangle dogs to death. They kill by holding their victim's head under the water until it drowns. *I think I just found a new prey species for big cats.*

❯ "The 10 Most Dangerous Animals in the World," AOL Travel, *www.travel.aol.co.uk.*

❯ "The UK's Deadliest Creatures," AOL Travel, *www.travel.aol.co.uk.*

FACT : Because of deadly attacks, the United Kingdom's **1991 Dangerous Dogs Act forbids ownership of aggressive breeds**—Pit bulls, Dogo Argentino, Japanese Tosa, and Fila Brasileira—without a special permit, which is only issued after a dog has been insured, neutered, given a special tattoo, and fitted with an identity chip. *Pit bulls are only aggressive if you raise them that way. At least that's what the lady on the news said. The one who was being interviewed after her dog mauled a four-year-old child.*

❯ "The UK's Deadliest Creatures," AOL Travel, *www.travel.aol.co.uk.*

FACT : At 1,500 pounds and wielding two large, sharp horns, the cape buffalo is not an animal to cross. **These unpredictable creatures will charge head-on when threatened**, sometimes in groups, and can reach a top speed of 35 mph. *The top speed of a human is less than 30 mph—and that's a professional sprinter, not you—so you can't outrun the buffalo. But as long as you can outrun at least one person in your safari group, you're good.*

❯ "Top 10 Deadliest Animals," LIVEScience, *www.livescience .com.*

❯ "The Cape Buffalo: A Very Dangerous Animal," Africa On The Matrix, *www.on-the-matrix.com.*

❯ "Buffalo," African Wildlife Federation, *www.awf.org.*

❯ Matthew Herper, "What's The Human Speed Limit?" Forbes.com, May 14, 2004, *www.forbes.com.*

FACT : A polar bear can rip the head off a human **with one swipe of its paw**. *Ha, my mom could do that with just a look.*

❯ "Top 10 Deadliest Animals," LIVEScience, *www.livescience.com.*

589

FACT: Almost **4 million cats and dogs are euthanized** every year in U.S. animal shelters. *Hopefully more cats than dogs. Cats are buttholes.*

❯ "Introducing PETA's ABC Campaign," PETA, *www.peta.org*.

 590

FACT: The skunk's anal musk is so powerful that **it can cause temporary blindness** if sprayed directly into the eyes. *Sounds a lot like my Uncle Phil. His anal musk could make your hair bleed.*

❯ "Ten of the Most Bizarre Animal Defense Mechanisms," WebEcoist, November 4, 2008, *www.webecoist.com*.

 591

FACT: If cornered, an opossum can foam at the mouth to convince a predator that it is toxic or sick, or **discharge an anal fluid** that smells almost as bad as a skunk's spray. *Unfortunately, neither of these works on a speeding car.*

❯ "Ten of the Most Bizarre Animal Defense Mechanisms," WebEcoist, November 4, 2008, *www.webecoist.com*.

 592

FACT: A dead whale spontaneously exploded while in transit on a truck in 2004. Internal pressure caused by methane gas build up within the body was the cause. *I'm sure that smelled wonderful.*

❯ "A Brief History of Actual Exploding Animals," WebEcoist, September 5th, 2008, *www .webecoist.com*.

FACT: A resurgent wild turkey population caused problems in Boston in 2008, **chasing joggers and schoolchildren,** often in large mobs of birds. *Note to Boston: wild turkey is edible.*

❯ Tim Dowling, "A Beginner's Guide to Beating off these Vicious Predators," *The Guardian,* May 13, 2008, *www.guardian.co.uk.*

FACT: The largest predatory fish in the world is the great white shark. They average fifteen feet in length, though great whites as long as twenty feet have been documented. **Over 100 shark attacks occur worldwide each year** and 30–50 percent of them are caused by great whites. *The great white can also swim up to 15 mph. Know what cannot? You.*

❯ "Great White Shark Profile," National Geographic, *www .animals.nationalgeographic .com.*

FACT: The largest lizard native to the United States is the venomous Gila monster, which can grow up to two feet long. Though rarely fatal, the Gila's bite is extremely painful; unlike snakes, which inject venom, the lizard will latch onto victims and chew, **allowing neurotoxins to move through its teeth and into the open wound.** *Fatal actually sounds better in this case.*

❯ "Gila Monster Profile," National Geographic, *www .animals.nationalgeographic .com.*

FACT: The black mamba is widely considered the world's deadliest snake. Territorial and aggressive, **the black mamba strikes repeatedly to kill its prey with powerful venom.** One of Africa's longest venomous snakes, the mamba can grow up to fourteen feet long, and is also among the fastest snakes in the world, moving at up to twelve and a half miles per hour. *What, no wings?*

❯ "Snakes," National Geographic, *www.animals .nationalgeographic.com.*
❯ "Snakebit: Surviving The Black Mamba," ABC News, *www .abcnews.go.com.*

FACT: The Western diamondback is among the largest and most aggressive rattlesnake species, **biting more people in the United States every year** than any other venomous snake. *The Western is almost identical to his cousin, the Eastern diamondback, except for the little cowboy hat.*

❯ "Snakes," Photo Gallery, National Geographic, *www .animals.nationalgeographic .com.*

❯ "Western Diamondback Rattlesnake," Washington Nature Mapping Program, *www.depts .washington.edu.*

FACT: Pigs can **become alcoholics.** *No. Too easy.*

❯ FactLib.com, *www.factlib.com.*

FACT: Two snakes cause more human deaths than any others in the world: the Russell's viper and the spectacled cobra, named for the eyeglass design on its flared hood. **Both are extremely venomous** and found in highly populated areas in Southeast Asia. *Highly populated for now, that is.*

❯ "Snakes," Photo Gallery, National Geographic, *www .animals.nationalgeographic .com.*

FACT: The cassowary is the world's most dangerous bird: it weighs over a hundred pounds, can run thirty miles per hour, and jump over three feet high. New Guinea tribesmen use the cassowary's sharp claws as spearheads. Attacks on humans have **resulted in broken bones and even death**. *Why aren't we eating these things?*

❯ Brendan Borrell, "Invasion of the Cassowaries," *Smithsonian Magazine*, October 2008, *www .smithsonianmag.com.*

CHAPTER 13

The Fruited Plain

Frightening Facts about America and Americans

601

FACT: It is illegal in Alabama to operate a vehicle **while you are blindfolded**. *It is also illegal in Alabama to marry your sister, but that doesn't stop anybody.*

❯ Alex Wade, "The World's Strangest Laws," Times Online, August 15, 2007, *www.business timesonline.co.uk.*

 602

FACT: It is illegal **to get a fish intoxicated** in the state of Ohio. *And not really necessary if you buy it a nice dinner and sweet talk it a little.*

❯ Alex Wade, "The World's Strangest Laws," Times Online, August 15, 2007, *www.business.timesonline.co.uk.*

 603

FACT: It is illegal for unmarried women **to parachute in Florida on Sundays**; violators can be arrested. *As they should be. From that altitude, Florida looks like a giant penis, and no unmarried woman should be looking at that, especially on the Lord's day.*

❯ Alex Wade, "The World's Strangest Laws," Times Online, August 15, 2007, *www.business .timesonline.co.uk.*

FACT: You should never carry concealed weapons **longer than six feet** in the state of Kentucky—the offense is punishable by law. *Is that a howitzer in your pants or are you just glad to see me?*

❯ Alex Wade, "The World's Strangest Laws," Times Online, August 15, 2007, *www.business .timesonline.co.uk.*

FACT: It is **not legal to own pets** in Boulder, Colorado—locals are considered "pet minders" only. It is also illegal to kill a bird. *Two good laws, because anyone who owns a bird usually wants to kill it after a day or two.*

❯ Alex Wade, "The World's Strangest Laws," Times Online, August 15, 2007, *www.business .timesonline.co.uk.*

FACT: Vermont women must get **written permission from their husbands** before they get false teeth. *Some men prefer their women toothless, if you know what I mean (wink wink).*

❯ Alex Wade, "The World's Strangest Laws," Times Online, August 15, 2007, *www.business .timesonline.co.uk.*

FACT: Famed American comedian **Groucho Marx took LSD and smoked pot** in the late 1960s. *That explains the elephant in his pajamas.*

❯ Russell Kick, *Disinformation Book of Lists: Subversive Facts and Hidden Information in Rapid-Fire Format* (The Disinformation Company, 2004).

608

FACT: Average Americans watch over four hours of TV per day: that's twenty-eight hours each week, two months each year. That accounts for nine years for the average sixty-five-year-old person. *And he still won't finish Ken Burns' Baseball.*

❯ "Television & Health: Television Statistics," Compiled by TV-Free America, *www.csun.edu.*

609

FACT: Collectively, Americans spend **250 billion hours watching television every year**. If spent working for a $5 per hour wage, this time would be worth $1.25 trillion. *I don't think five bucks an hour is enough to pull anybody away from the TV.*

❯ "Television & Health: Television Statistics," Compiled by TV-Free America, *www.csun.edu.*

610

FACT: When polled, more than half of four- to six-year-olds pick **watching television over spending time** with their fathers. *Probably because spending time with your dad usually involves being put to work in some way.*

❯ "Television & Health: Television Statistics," Compiled by TV-Free America, *www.csun.edu.*

611

FACT: By the time they finish elementary school, **American children have seen 8,000 murders on TV**. By the time they graduate high school, they witness 200,000 violent acts and 40,000 murders. *Or you can just save him some time and let him watch the movie* 300.

❯ "Television & Health: Television Statistics," Compiled by TV-Free America, *www.csun .edu.*

FACT: One-third of American adults are over-weight. According to a study by the *American Journal of Public Health*, adults who watch three hours of TV a day are **more likely to be obese** than those who watch less than sixty minutes a day. *Who can watch TV without a few chips? I know I can't.*

> L. A. Tucker and G. M. Friedman, "Television Viewing and Obesity in Adult Males," *American Journal of Public Health*, April 1989, 516–518.

FACT: Almost 60 percent of Americans know the Three Stooges by name, but **just 17 percent** are able to name three U.S. Supreme Court justices. *Luckily, three of the justices are the Stooges.*

> "Television & Health: Television Statistics," Compiled by TV-Free America, *www.csun.edu*.

FACT: 75 percent of American women think they are fat, perhaps owing to the fact that American actresses and models are **thinner than 95 percent** of the female population. *Which is why they are models and actresses. If we wanted to see fat people, we'd go to a family reunion, not the movies.*

> "Television & Health: Television Statistics," Compiled by TV-Free America, *www.csun .edu*.

615

FACT: In a poll conducted by *Newsweek* in 2007, **41 percent of Americans** continued to believe that Saddam Hussein's Iraqi regime planned, financed, or carried out the September 11th, 2001 terrorist attacks. The majority of people polled did not know most of the 9/11 hijackers hailed from Saudi Arabia. *I would expect no less from people who believe that pork is the "other white meat" and Budweiser is "premium" beer.*

> Joerg Wolf, "More Americans Believe that Saddam Was Directly Involved in 9/11," *Atlantic Review,* June 27, 2007, www.atlanticreview.org.

616

FACT: The United States government first became debt-free in 1835—which was also **the last time** the government was debt-free. *"Debt-free"? What is that?*

> "Weird, Wacky and Wonderful Facts about Our Amazing America—Did you Know?" Travel America, FindArticles.com, March 5, 2009, *www.findarticles.com.*

617

FACT: It is **against the law** in several states to dance to the "Star Spangled Banner." *Shame, because it's such a great dance song.*

> "Weird, Wacky and Wonderful Facts about Our Amazing America—Did you Know?" Travel America, FindArticles.com, March 5, 2009, *www.findarticles.com.*

FACT: In 1992, Nike paid Michael Jordan $2 million to promote their shoes, as much money as **the combined wages of all the workers** in the factories that made them. *But they all got free Nike "swoosh" headbands, which really help control the sweat on that three-hour walk to and from work every day.*

❯ Diana Elizabeth Kendall and others, *Sociology in Our Times*, 2nd ed. (Nelson Thomson Learning, 1999).

FACT: In 2005, the American Nazi Party erected two signs **using taxpayers' money** on roads outside Salem, Oregon. The racist group had adopted a stretch of highway, and their right of free speech guaranteed by the Constitution prohibited the Adopt-A-Highway program from censoring them. *Whenever they clean up their stretch of road, it's called, "White Trash Day."*

❯ Niki Sullivan, "'Nazi Party' Adopts Highway Near Salem in Rural Oregon," *Spokesman Review*, January 28, 2005, *www.spokesmanreview.com*.

FACT: As of September 15, 2009, there are **103,516 Americans on waiting lists** for organ transplants. *I wonder how many of those are waiting on brains. Because I know a lot of people who aren't using theirs.*

❯ Organ Procurement and Transplantation Network, U.S. Department of Health and Human Services and the Health Resources and Services Administration, *http://optn.transplant.hrsa.gov*.

FACT: Eight of every ten e-mails sent worldwide are spam. **American companies lose an estimated $22 billion annually** in time spent deleting junk e-mail. *The other two of ten are hoaxes, chain mail, urban myths, and other crap with little flashing hearts and teddy bears, sent by your mom.*

❯ Swartz, Nikki, "Deleting Spam Costs Businesses Billions," *Information Management Journal*, May/Jun 2005, *www.findarticles.com*.

622

FACT: **35 percent of Americans** eat at a fast food restaurant at least once a week. *And then 99 percent of them race home to take a dump. The other 1 percent can't wait that long and have the added delight of going right there in Burger King. Or crapping their pants, which might actually be preferable.*

❭ "Consumers in Europe—Our Fast Food/Take Away Consumption Habits," AC Nielsen, 2004, www.ie.nielsen.com.

623

FACT: In its first year at sea, dozens of seats on the newly launched luxury cruise liner, the *Queen Mary 2*, collapsed **when obese American passengers sat down on them**. *They weren't obese when the cruise started.*

❭ Olinka Koster, "QM2 Chairs Buckle Under Weighty Cruisers," *Daily Mail*, www.dailymail.co.uk.

624

FACT: In 2004, students at Alexandria Country Day School, a private elementary school in Virginia, got a surprise with their lunch: **cafeteria workers accidentally served them pre-mixed margaritas** left over from a staff party, mistaking it for limeade. *Unlike the staff, the students kept their clothes on. Like the staff, several of them barfed.*

❭ Valerie Strauss, "'Limeade' Packs a Punch," *Washington Post*, September 29, 2004, www.washingtonpost.com.

625

FACT: A 1999 Gallup poll revealed that one in five Americans believes that **the sun orbits Earth**. *Wait—it doesn't?*

> Steve Crabtree, "New Poll Gauges Americans' General Knowledge Levels," Gallup, www.gallup.com.

 626

FACT: Less than 50 percent of American adults comprehend that **the Earth revolves around the sun on a yearly basis**. *These are the same folks who think that Elvis is alive and Bigfoot is real, so you can't really be surprised.*

> Steve Crabtree, "New Poll Gauges Americans' General Knowledge Levels," Gallup, www.gallup.com.
> Peter Strupp and Alan Dingman, *Fat, Dumb, and Ugly: The Decline of the Average American* (Simon & Schuster, 2004).

 627

FACT: More Americans choke on toothpicks than any other object. Toothpicks injure almost 9,000 people every year. *You have to chew them first, people.*

> Noel Botham, *The Book of Useless Information* (Perigee, 2006).

628

FACT: Soft drinks represent the **largest single source of added sugars** in the American diet. The average American will drink fifty-four gallons of soft drinks in a year. *Know what I love? Restaurants that charge for a soft drink refill. I just paid $2.39 for three cents' worth of cola syrup and some soda water, and they want another fifty cents for a refill.*

> William D. McArdle, Frank I. Katch and Victor L. Katch, *Exercise Physiology: Energy, Nutrition, and Human Performance*, 6th ed. (Lippincott Williams & Wilkins, 2006).

629

FACT: The obesity rate in the United States doubled from 1988 to 2002. Approximately **65 percent of adult Americans** are either obese or overweight. *But they all intend to lose it. No, really. They're getting a treadmill.*

> "Prevalence of Overweight and Obesity Among Adults: United States, 1999–2002," National Center for Health Statistics, Centers for Disease Control and Prevention, *www.cdc.gov.*

630

FACT:. The newborn mortality rate in America is **more than twice that of Finland, Iceland, or Norway.** The only developed country in the world where the newborn death rate surpasses the United States is Latvia. *You can't really blame anyone for not wanting to be Latvian.*

> Jeff Green, "U.S. Has Second Worst Newborn Death Rate in Modern World, Report Says," CNN, May 10, 2006, *www.cnn.com.*

631

FACT: Can you find Iraq on a map? About **14 percent of Americans** between eighteen and twenty-four cannot, and 18 percent can't find Afghanistan. *Which is why the Army recruits from that age group.*

> Peter Strupp and Alan Dingman, *Fat, Dumb, and Ugly: The Decline of the Average American* (Simon & Schuster, 2004).

632

FACT: Ten percent of Americans between eighteen and twenty-four can't **find the United States on a blank world map.** *Shhh, I'm watching* The Hills!

> Peter Strupp and Alan Dingman *Fat, Dumb, and Ugly: The Decline of the Average American* (Simon & Schuster, 2004).

FACT: In 1976, only 16 percent of Americans said they believed in ghosts. By 2000, **that number had risen to 33 percent**. *In related news, idiots are breeding faster than nonidiots.*

❯ Peter Strupp and Alan Dingman, *Fat, Dumb, and Ugly: The Decline of the Average American* (Simon & Schuster, 2004).

FACT: Research shows that the average American has one more hour of free time every day than he did in 1965, but spends **40 percent less time** with his children now. *That's why they call it free time.*

❯ Peter Strupp and Alan Dingman. *Fat, Dumb, and Ugly: The Decline of the Average American* (Simon & Schuster, 2004).

FACT: **Seventy percent of Americans** cannot identify the source of the phrase, "life, liberty, and the pursuit of happiness." *But then, not everyone watches Superman.*

❯ Peter Strupp and Alan Dingman, *Fat, Dumb, and Ugly: The Decline of the Average American* (Simon & Schuster, 2004).

FACT: Twenty-eight million Americans use indoor tanning booths every year. Perhaps it is no coincidence, then, that the **per capita rate for melanoma has increased** by 100 percent in the last thirty years. *Well, tanning beds do look a lot like coffins.*

❯ Peter Strupp and Alan Dingman, *Fat, Dumb, and Ugly: The Decline of the Average American* (Simon & Schuster, 2004).

FACT: Thanks to technology like TV screens in grocery stores and airports, cell phone videos, and digital movie libraries, the average American sees **sixty-one minutes of ads and promotions** on television every day. *That's still not enough to make me want to eat at McDonald's or drive a Ford.*

❯ Brian Stelter, "Eight Hours a Day Spent on Screens, Study Finds," *New York Times,* March 26, 2009, www.nytimes.com.

FACT: From 1997 to 1998, the The National Rifle Association, America's largest gun rights lobby, **gave $1.3 million to Republican candidates** for federal offices and $285,700 to Democrat candidates. Handgun Control, Inc., the largest gun-control lobby in the United States, gave about $137,000 to Democrats and $9,500 to Republicans. *Guns don't kill people. Gun lobbies kill people.*

❯ "Gun Control," Just Facts, www.justfacts.com.

FACT: The Brady Bill and Assault Weapons Ban were enacted in 1993. In the five years that followed, **nine school shooting massacres occurred**. *I guess the "ban" is still a work in progress.*

❯ "Gun Control," Just Facts, www.justfacts.com.

FACT: Studies show that American presidential speeches today are geared to **the comprehension level of an average seventh grader**. Fifty years ago, presidents spoke to Americans at a twelfth-grade level. *From 2001 to 2008, former president George W. Bush spoke to Americans at a first-grade level.*

> Rick Shenkman, *Just How Stupid Are We?: Facing the Truth About the American Voter* (PublicAffairs, 2009).

FACT: Just five days before the 2008 election, **23 percent of Texans** still believed—erroneously—that Barack Obama was Muslim. *I could make an entire chapter on screwy things that Texans believe.*

> Richard S. Dunham, "UT Poll Shows McCain, Cornyn with Comfortable Margins," *Houston Chronicle*, October 29, 2008, www.chron.com.

FACT: Only a quarter of Americans know **two or more of the five freedoms** set forth by the First Amendment. More than 50 percent of Americans can name two or more members of the cartoon Simpsons family. *Yes, well,* The Simpsons *haven't disappeared for years at a time.*

> Rick Shenkman, *Just How Stupid Are We?: Facing the Truth About the American Voter* (PublicAffairs, 2009).

643

FACT : A majority of Americans don't know that **we are the only country** that has used nuclear weapons in war. *Many Americans can't even pronounce "nuclear," so, once again, not surprising.*

Rick Shenkman, *Just How Stupid Are We?: Facing the Truth About the American Voter* (PublicAffairs, 2009).

 644

FACT : Half of Americans believe that **the president has the power to suspend** the Constitution. *Some of them were presidents themselves. Isn't that right, Mr. Bush?*

› Rick Shenkman, *Just How Stupid Are We?: Facing the Truth About the American Voter* (PublicAffairs, 2009).

 645

FACT : The Strategic Task Force on Education Abroad assessed Americans' knowledge of world affairs in 2003, concluding that "America's ignorance of the outside world" is **a "national liability" that creates a threat** to our security. *Not to be confused with The Strategic Ass Force on Educatin' A Broad.*

› Rick Shenkman, *Just How Stupid Are We?: Facing the Truth About the American Voter* (PublicAffairs, 2009).
› Burton Bollag, "Report Urges Federal Effort to Triple Number of Students Studying Abroad," Institute Of International Education, Chronicle of Higher Education, November 21, 2003, *www.opendoors.iienetwork.org.*

 646

FACT : More than 50 percent of U.S. workers don't **use all of their paid vacation time**; 30 percent say they don't even take half. *For some Americans, every day at work is a paid vacation.*

› "Do Us A Favor, Take A Vacation," *BusinessWeek*, May 21, 2007, *www.businessweek.com.*

FACT: Forty-two percent of American professionals say **they are "regularly" forced** to cancel vacation plans. *The only way you'll force me to cancel a vacation is with a gun to my head, and even then I'll lie about canceling it.*

> "Do Us A Favor, Take A Vacation," *BusinessWeek*, May 21, 2007, www.businessweek.com.

FACT: *Karoshi*—the phenomenon of **being worked to death**—is a Japanese phenomenon. Even the Japanese take more vacation than Americans. *Karoshi—because karaoke wasn't enough punishment already.*

> "Do Us A Favor, Take A Vacation," *BusinessWeek*, May 21, 2007, www.businessweek.com.

FACT: **Seven percent of Americans believe that Elvis Presley is still alive**, even though the singer died in 1977. Interestingly, the percentage is even higher (11 percent) among people under age thirty, the group least likely to be Elvis fans. *Elvis is dead, trust me. If he were alive, he would deny the story that he died on the crapper. That's just embarrassing.*

> "The King's Popularity Contest," CBS News Polls, August 11, 2002, www.cbsnews.com.

FACT: In a 2008 poll, 41 percent of respondents said **they believe that creatures like Bigfoot exist**. *I didn't—until I got a good look at Rosie O'Donnell.*

> "CNN Poll," BigfootForums. com, www.bigfootforums.com.

CHAPTER 14

Open Wide and Say, "Oh, S#*t"

Bad Medicine. Really, Really, Really Bad

651

FACT: A recent report from the National Academy of Sciences, Institute of Medicine estimates that **hospitals make preventable medical errors** that kill as many as 98,000 people each year—more than cancer, AIDS, and auto accidents. *And not nearly as fun.*

❯ Tamar Nordenberg, "Make No Mistake: Medical Errors Can Be Deadly Serious," *FDA Consumer,* U.S. Food and Drug Administration, September-October 2000, *www.fda.gov.*

 652

FACT: Patients who endure errors in treatment while in hospital care typically face a **one in four chance of death** from the mistake. *Which means the staff who make the mistakes face a three in four chance of getting their asses kicked.*

❯ Tamar Nordenberg, "Make No Mistake: Medical Errors Can Be Deadly Serious," *FDA Consumer,* U.S. Food and Drug Administration, September-October 2000, *www.fda.gov.*

 653

FACT: Almost 250,000 patients studied by independent research group Health-Grades from 2003 and 2005 were **killed by preventable problems.** *The medical professionals at fault have kindly agreed to apologize to any of the patients they accidentally killed.*

❯ Tamar Nordenberg, "Make No Mistake: Medical Errors Can Be Deadly Serious," *FDA Consumer,* U.S. Food and Drug Administration, September-October 2000, *www.fda.gov.*

❯ Dan Childs, "Medical Errors, Past and Present," ABC News, November 27, 2007, *www .abcnews.com.*

FACT: In 2007, a New York fertility doctor made headlines for **accidentally using the wrong man's sperm** to inseminate a woman's eggs. The Hispanic woman and her white husband realized the mistake upon giving birth to an African-American baby. Subsequent DNA tests confirmed that the baby was indeed another man's. *Thank goodness they got those DNA tests. They might never have known for sure.*

❭ Todd Venezia, "Black Baby Is Born to White Pair," *New York Post*, March 22, 2007.

❭ Naomi Cahn, *Test Tube Families: Why the Fertility Market Needs Legal Regulation* (NYU Press, 2009), 68.

FACT: According to Institute of Medicine (IOM) estimates, 1.5 million patients suffer each year because of **mistakes made with medicine they are given in hospitals**. *Yeah, like the time my doctor gave me Flomax instead of Flovent. For a week, every time I coughed, I peed my pants.*

❭ Dan Childs, "Medical Errors, Past and Present," ABC News, November 27, 2007, www.abcnews.com.

❭ Tamar Nordenberg, "Make No Mistake: Medical Errors Can Be Deadly Serious," *FDA Consumer*, U.S. Food and Drug Administration, September-October 2000, www.fda.gov.

FACT: The IOM also estimates that 50 percent of bad reactions to medicine result from **errors in how they are administered**. Common causes are "environmental factors such as lighting, heat, noise, and interruptions that can distract health professionals from their medical tasks," says The American Hospital Association. *Lighting? Heat? Noise? At least they aren't easily distracted.*

❭ Dan Childs, "Medical Errors, Past and Present," ABC News, November 27, 2007, www.abcnews.com.

❭ Tamar Nordenberg, "Make No Mistake: Medical Errors Can Be Deadly Serious," *FDA Consumer*, U.S. Food and Drug Administration, September-October 2000, www.fda.gov.

FACT: A leading cause of **drug-related errors is name confusion**. For example, the arthritis drug Celebrex is often confused with the anticonvulsant Cerebyx and the antidepressant Celexa. Prescribing the wrong drug based on name confusion can be fatal. *So if you or someone you know takes the prescription drugs Nyacide or Larsenic, you might want to double check your medicine before taking it.*

❭ Tamar Nordenberg, "Make No Mistake: Medical Errors Can Be Deadly Serious," *FDA Consumer*, U.S. Food and Drug Administration, September-October 2000, www.fda.gov.

658

FACT: A seventeen-year-old girl named Jésica Santillán died in 2003 after she received a heart and lung transplant from **a patient whose blood type was not a match**. Doctors at the Duke University Medical Center did not check compatibility, and transplanted organs from a type-A donor to Santillán, whose blood was type-O. *"On the bright side," said one Duke official, "she wasn't on the basketball team."*

❯ Carol Kopp, "Anatomy Of A Mistake," *60 Minutes,* CBSNews.com, September 7, 2003, *www.cbsnews.com.*

❯ Tom Baker, *The Medical Malpractice Myth* (University of Chicago Press, 2007), 4.

659

FACT: Doctors from Rhode Island Hospital in Providence performed **brain surgery on the incorrect side of three patients' heads** in 2007. Two of the mistakes caused no serious damage, but one led to the patient's death. The hospital paid $50,000 in fines and faced reprimand by the state Department of Health. *Okay then, as long as they were reprimanded.*

❯ Associated Press, "Third Wrong-Sided Brain Surgery at R.I. Hospital," MSNBC.com, November 27, 2007, *www.msnbc.msn.com.*

660

FACT: In 2006, **surgeons at a Los Angeles V.A. hospital removed the healthy right testicle** of a forty-seven-year-old man by mistake. There were several botched steps leading to the surgery which resulted in the error, including a mistake on the consent form and forgetting to mark the surgical site before the procedure. *That's just nuts.*

❯ Julia Hallisy, *The Empowered Patient: Hundreds of Life-Saving Facts, Action Steps and Strategies You Need to Know* (The Empowered Patient, 2007), 119.

❯ "SoCal Vet Claims Wrong Testicle Removed In Surgery," CBS5.com, April 5, 2007, *www.cbs5.com.*

661

FACT: A Tampa, Florida **surgeon removed the incorrect leg** of a fifty-two-year-old patient by mistake during amputation in 1995. The team realized their error mid-procedure, but too late in the process to save the leg. *Wanna get away?*

❯ "Florida Hospital Surgeons Mistakenly Amputate Wrong Leg of Patient," *Jet,* March 20, 1995, *www.findarticles.com.*

❯ Robert M. Wachter, *Understanding Patient Safety* (McGraw-Hill Professional, 2007), 58.

FACT: In a 2002 case, a woman was admitted to a teaching hospital for a cerebral angiography procedure. After, the hospital transferred her to another floor. The next morning she was **mistakenly taken in for open-heart surgery**. *"Students, today we're going to learn about malpractice suits."*

> Robert M. Wachter, Lee Goldman, and Harry Hollander, *Hospital Medicine*, 2nd ed. (Lippincott Williams & Wilkins, 2005), 152.

> Mark R. Chassin and Elise C. Becher, "The Wrong Patient," *Annals of Internal Medicine*, June 4, 2002, 826–833, www.annals.org.

663

FACT: A laboratory mix-up prompted a thirty-five-year-old woman on Long Island, New York **to have both of her healthy breasts removed unnecessarily** in 2006. Her doctor told her the diagnoses. She sought a second opinion, but the next doctor relied on the same set of erroneous records as the first and reiterated her cancer diagnosis. *The two boobs were removed. From the hospital staff, that is.*

> Dan Childs, "Medical Errors, Past and Present," November 27, 2007, ABC News, www.abcnews.com.

664

FACT: In June 2000, a man was admitted to the University of Washington Medical Center in Seattle to have a tumor removed. Doctors removed the growth, but **left a 13" retractor** in the patient's abdomen when they sewed him up—the fifth documented case of University of Washington surgeons leaving a medical instrument inside a patient after surgery. *Free parting gift for all surgery patients!*

> Carol Smith, "Surgical Tools Left in Five Patients," *Seattle Post-Intelligencer*, www.seattlepi.nwsource.com.

665

FACT: A minister was admitted to a hospital in West Virginia in 2006 for exploratory abdominal surgery to diagnose the cause of pain. An anesthesiologist gave him drugs to prevent his muscles from twitching during surgery, **but not general anesthesia until after the first incision**. The patient felt excruciating pain but was unable to move or communicate. *I bet he communicated once the anesthesia wore off.*

> Associated Press, "Family Sues after Man Gets Wide-Awake Surgery," MSNBC.com, *www.msnbc.msn.com.*

666

FACT: In 2007, actor Dennis Quaid's newborn twins nearly died after receiving **an overdose of a blood-thinning drug**, Heparin, at a Los Angeles hospital. Three premature babies were killed in Indianapolis in 2006 due to a similar mistake, where nurses administered Heparin for adults instead of Hep-lock for children. The medications were stocked in the wrong cabinet. *I bet no one at the hospital got his autograph after that.*

> Dan Childs, "Medical Errors, Past and Present," November 27, 2007, ABC News, *www.abcnews.com.*

667

FACT: While being treated for breast cancer at Dana-Farber Cancer Institute in Boston in 1994, **two women received poisonous quantities of chemotherapy**. Instead of receiving a daily dose of a powerful anticancer drug for four days, the doctor incorrectly prescribed four days worth of the drug to be administered each day. One patient, a thirty-nine-year-old medical reporter for the *Boston Globe* named Betsy Lehman died; the second endured irrevocable heart damage and died from cancer several months later. *The formerly prestigious Dana-Farber Cancer Institute.*

> Tamar Nordenberg, "Make No Mistake: Medical Errors Can Be Deadly Serious," *FDA Consumer*, U.S. Food and Drug Administration, September-October 2000, *www.fda.gov.*

FACT: The drug Mirapex (pramipexole), developed in 1997 to treat Parkinson's disease, also works in treating patients with Restless Leg Syndrome (RLS), **but it can cause amnesia.** Amnesia is also a possible side effect of taking some cholesterol-lowering medications like Lipitor. *I get RLS at school board meetings when some parent launches into a rant. My leg starts twitching because it wants to get up and kick that person in the ass.*

FACT: Some researchers and physicians believe that **Mirapex leads to compulsive behaviors** in some patients, turning occasional drinkers into alcoholics, casual card gamers or sports fans into compulsive gamblers, and otherwise normal people into hypersexuals, shopaholics, and binge eaters. *I don't know, that sounds kind of fun. I should ask my doctor if Mirapex is right for me.*

FACT: Patients who use Lipitor (atorvastatin) can be **plagued by pain and weakness in their muscles,** even to the point of loss of muscle control and coordination. Some patients have filed lawsuits against Lipitor's maker, Pfizer, stating the drug causes permanent muscle damage, nerve damage, and memory loss. *The suit was dropped when the patients forgot they were suing Pfizer and failed to show up for court.*

FACT: The drug Vasotec (enalapril) was developed to lower high blood pressure and treat congestive heart failure, but **it can also have a detrimental effect on almost all of your senses,** including loss of smell and taste, ringing in the ears (tinnitus), blurred vision, and dry eyes. *Dying has a detrimental effect on the senses, too, so take your pick.*

❯ Diane S. Aschenbrenner and Samantha J. Venable, *Drug Therapy in Nursing*, 3rd ed. (Lippincott Williams & Wilkins, 2008).

❯ Allyson T. Collins, "Strange Side Effects Surprise Patients," ABC News, July 15, 2008, *www.abcnews.com.*

❯ *The PDR Pocket Guide to Prescription Drugs*, 6th ed. (Simon & Schuster, 2003), 76.

❯ Aaron Smith, "Pfizer Sued Over Alleged Lipitor Side Effects," June 8, 2006, CNNmoney, *www.cnnmoney.com.*

❯ "Vasotec: Drug Description," RxList, *www.rxlist.com.*

FACT: Viagra (sildenafil), a treatment for erectile dysfunction, can cause blurred vision and problems distinguishing between green and blue. Researchers suspect that **Viagra users are at risk for permanent loss of vision** because the drug cuts off the flow of blood from the optic nerve, a condition called nonarteritic ischemic optic neuropathy (NAION). *I wonder where all that blood goes instead?*

❯ "About Viagra," Viagra.com, *www.viagra.com.*

❯ "Viagra Can Cause Permanent Vision Loss in Some Men, University of Minnesota Researchers Say," Medical News Today, March 31, 2005, *www.medicalnewstoday.com.*

FACT: Xenical (orlistat) prevents the body from absorbing fat, decreasing the caloric intake of users. Test trials showed that up to 30 percent of ingested fat was excreted unabsorbed by subjects. Side effects of the drug include "**gas with oily discharge**, an increased number of bowel movements, an urgent need to have them, and an inability to control them." *Which is why Xenical's street name is "White Castle."*

❯ "Important Safety Information," Xenical.com, *www.xenical.com.*

FACT: Lariam (mefloquine), a malaria drug administered to American servicemen overseas, is believed **to be the cause of some soldiers' suicidal tendencies**. It is known to cause "neuropsychiatric adverse events." Even Lariam's maker, Roche Pharmaceuticals, warns, "Some patients taking Lariam think about killing themselves." *Other patients taking Lariam think about killing people at Roche Pharmaceuticals.*

❯ David Kohn, "The Dark Side Of Lariam," CBS News, January 29, 2003, *www.cbsnews.com.*

❯ Associated Press, "Hallucinations Linked to Drug Given to Troops," MSNBC.com, February 14, 2005, *www.msnbc.msn.com.*

FACT: Many patients have reported suicidal thoughts while taking the antidepressant Paxil (paroxetine). Lawsuits allege Paxil has severe withdrawal symptoms that, in some, resulted in suicide and attempted suicide. Evidence in one lawsuit shows GlaxoSmithKline, the drug's manufacturer, might have concealed data linking the drug to these effects. *"Paxil. I'd rather die than switch."*

❯ "FDA Statement Regarding the Anti-Depressant Paxil for Pediatric Population," FDA Talk Paper, U.S. Food and Drug Administration, June 19, 2003, *www.fda.gov.*

❯ "Glaxo Sued for 'Drug Claim Fraud'," BBCNews.com, June 2, 2004, *www.howstuffworks.com.*

676

FACT: Over 40 suicides and 400 suicide attempts are linked to Chantix (varenicline), an anti-smoking drug. The U.S. Department of Veterans Affairs has come under attack for recruiting soldiers who served in Iraq and Afghanistan **as subjects in tests on Chantix** after the FDA issued warnings about the drug's possible violent side effects. *They never said how Chantix stopped people from smoking, just that it could.*

❯ Maddy Sauer and Vic Walter, "Tough Questions for VA on Suicide-Linked Chantix," ABC News, July 8, 2008, *www.abc news.com*.

677

FACT: The drug thalidomide is infamous for its link to birth defects. **Though never proven to be safe**, the drug was a popular sleeping aid and anti-nausea pill in the 1950s, taken by thousands of pregnant women around the world. From 1956 to 1962, almost 10,000 women who were administered thalidomide delivered babies with phocomelia, a congenital disorder that causes children to be born with extremely short or missing limbs. *I'm guessing their nausea and insomnia returned after those births.*

❯ Michael J. O'Dowd, *The History of Medications for Women: Materia Medica Woman* (Informa Health Care, 2001), 249.

678

FACT: Accutane (isotretinoin), a drug used to treat severe acne, also has been **linked to phocomelia**. Women taking the drug have to adhere to a strict regimen to prevent becoming pregnant, including two methods of birth control and a required monthly blood test for pregnancy before a prescription refill is approved. *It's actually three methods of birth control, including the acne.*

❯ Michael J. O'Dowd, *The History of Medications for Women: Materia Medica Woman* (Informa Health Care, 2001), 249.

❯ Paula Begoun, *The Complete Beauty Bible: The Ultimate Guide to Smart Beauty* (Rodale, 2004).

FACT: Half of all psychotherapists are **threatened, harassed, or physically attacked** by a patient, and up to 15 percent of them have been stalked by former clients. *If they were better therapists, they wouldn't have this problem.*

❯ Bryce Nelson, "Acts of Violence Against Therapists Pose Lurking Threat," *New York Times*, June 14, 1983.

❯ John C. Norcross and James D. Guy, Jr., *Leaving It at the Office: A Guide to Psychotherapist Self-Care* (Guilford Press, 2007), 44.

FACT: Some psychotherapists have been murdered by patients, though exact figures are unobtainable. In a six-week period in 1981, four psychiatrists, one each in Massachusetts, Florida, California, and Michigan, were murdered by patients. *"Sorry, doc, our time is up for today."*

❯ Bryce Nelson, "Acts of Violence Against Therapists Pose Lurking Threat, *New York Times*, June 14, 1983.

❯ John C. Norcross and James D. Guy, Jr., *Leaving It at the Office: A Guide to Psychotherapist Self-Care* (Guilford Press, 2007), 44.

FACT: For centuries **processed cockroaches have been used to cure ailments** and physical disorders: cockroach tea has been used to treat dropsy (edema), an accumulation of fluid beneath the skin; fried cockroaches were used in African American folk medicine as a cure for indigestion; and cockroach poultice has been used to cure wounds and stingray burns. *Eh, I'll just stick with the dropsy and Tums, thanks.*

❯ Darrell Addison Posey and Kristina Plenderleith, *Indigenous Knowledge and Ethics: A Darrell Posey Reader* (Routledge, 2004), 29.

❯ Marion Copeland, *Cockroach* (Reaktion Books, 2003).

682

FACT: Urine therapy is the application of urine to the body through the skin or oral ingestion. **Advocates drink a cup of their own urine every morning**, which is to be sipped, not guzzled, and taken from "midstream urine" collected in the morning. The treatment has been prescribed to stop chronic itching, soothe throat aches, and prevent cancer. *I'll just stick with scratching and Ricola, thanks.*

❯ Flora Peschek-Böhmer and Gisela Schreiber, *Urine Therapy: Nature's Elixir for Good Health* (Inner Traditions / Bear & Company, 1999).

683

FACT: One seventeenth-century treatment for acne: chop the heads off two puppies, hang them by their heels to bleed, **mix the collected blood with white wine**, and apply the concoction to the face. A similar serum of "Dog's Blood" was also once considered an effective treatment for tuberculosis. *Who came up with that treatment, a cat?*

❯ Herbert P. Goodheart, *Acne For Dummies* (For Dummies, 2005).

❯ *Boston Medical and Surgical Journal* (Massachusetts Medical Society, 1892).

684

FACT: Another folk remedy recommends **rubbing earwax on cold sores** or severely cracked lips to heal them. *Your own earwax, not someone else's. That would be disgusting.*

❯ Elisabeth Janos, *Country Folk Medicine: Tales of Skunk Oil, Sassafras Tea and Other Old-Time Remedies* (Globe Pequot, 2004).

685

FACT: Spiders were once thought to be an effective cure for malaria and were **eaten alive in a pat of butter** or in a spoonful of syrup. In India, spider webs were considered more effective, and were rolled into pellets and ingested orally. *As opposed to being ingested in some other way, which I prefer not to think about.*

❯ Charles M. Poser and G. W. Bruyn, *An Illustrated History of Malaria* (Informa Health Care, 1999).

FACT: Dr. Cecil B. Jacobson, a fertility specialist in the Washington D.C. area, was sentenced in 1992 to five years in prison for **using his own sperm to inseminate female patients** rather than that of anonymous donors. He made some patients believe they had become fertile under his care but had suffered miscarriages when, in fact, they had never been pregnant. *He must pack 'em in on visiting day at the prison.*

❯ "Fertility Doctor Gets Five Years," *New York Times*, May 9, 1992.

FACT: In 2002, orthopedist David Arndt left the operating room seven hours into surgery so that **he could cash his paycheck before the bank closed.** Arndt was gone for thirty-five minutes while the hospital paged him repeatedly. His medical license was later suspended in Massachusetts. *Two words for you, Arndt: "direct" and "deposit."*

❯ Neil Swidey, "What Went Wrong?," *Boston Globe*, March 21, 2004, www.boston.com.

FACT: Manhattan obstetrician Dr. Allan Zarkin made headlines in 2000 by **carving his initials with a scalpel into a patient's stomach** after delivering her baby by Caesarean section. Said Zarkin at the time, "I did such a beautiful job, I'll initial it." Zarkin was charged with assault and sued for malpractice by the patient. *Wow, a doctor did something obscenely arrogant. I'll alert the press.*

❯ Jennifer Steinhauer, "Patient Settles Case Of Initials Cut in Skin," *New York Times*, February 12, 2000.

❯ Barbara Ross and Dave Goldiner, "Doctor Carved His Initials on New Mom," *New York Daily News*, January 21, 2000.

FACT: An episiotomy is a surgical incision made below the vagina to assist childbirth. This common procedure is believed to lessen trauma to vaginal tissue, but **it also carries a risk of numerous complications**, including tearing of the rectum, bleeding, infection, extreme pain, and more. Some studies show that episiotomies cause more postpartum pain than not performing the procedure. *Imagine that.*

❯ Melissa Conrad Stöppler and William C. Shiel, Jr., "Episiotomy," Medicinenet.com, December 9, 2008, www.medicinenet.com.

690

FACT: Though relatively common, Caesarean sections (C-sections) are major surgeries that deliver a baby through a mother's abdomen. A horizontal incision is made through the skin to the uterus. Though almost a third of American births are done by C-section, **it poses risk to the health of the mother**, including infection, injury to other organs, hemorrhage, complications from anesthesia, and a mortality rate for the mother that is twice to four times that of vaginal birth. *Other than that, it's a relatively simple and safe procedure.*

❯ "Delivery Settings and Caesarean Section Rates in China," World Health Organization Bulletin, *www.who.int.*
❯ Rita Rubin, "Answers Prove Elusive as C-Section Rate Rises," *USA Today*, January 8, 2008, *www.usatoday.com.*
❯ "Cesarean Fact Sheet," Childbirth.org, *www.childbirth.org.*
❯ Robin Elise Weiss, "Cesarean Section Photos: Step-by-Step," About.com, *www.pregnancy.about.com.*
❯ Gerard M. DiLeo, "Your C-Section: A Step-by-Step Guide," Babyzone.com, *www.babyzone.com.*

 691

FACT: In 1990, a sixty-three-year old Tennessee woman went in for exploratory surgery on what doctors thought was a tumor on her buttock. They were wrong: **the "tumor" was a four-inch pork chop bone**, which doctors estimated had been in place for five to ten years, but had not caused the woman any pain due to her obesity. *I like pork chops, too, but not enough to eat the bone.*

❯ *Worlds Most Incredible Stories* (Barnes & Noble Publishing).

 692

FACT: American women undergo **twice as many hysterectomies** as British women, and four times as many as Swedish women. By some estimates, 76–85 percent of these procedures are unnecessary, studies saying that removing the ovaries will raise, not lower, her health risks unless a woman is highly at risk for ovarian cancer. *In most cases a woman is willing to take that chance if it means not having any more goddamn kids.*

❯ Curt Pesmen, "Five Surgeries to Avoid," *Health*, July 2007, updated September 18, 2008, *www.living.health.com.*

FACT: Decompressive cranioplasty is an emergency surgery in which **part of the cranium or skull is removed** to reduce swelling of the brain. In some cases the removed bone fragment is stored in tissue of the abdominal wall and then reinserted into the skull several months later. *That bone fragment must be hell to swallow.*

> T. Flannery and R. S. McConnell, "Cranioplasty: Why Throw the Bone Flap Out?" *British Journal of Neurosurgery*, December 2001, 518–520, www.informaworld.com.

FACT: Blepharoplasty, or eye lift, is a surgical procedure that removes excess tissue to reshape the upper or lower eyelid. Risks of the surgery include asymmetry, cyst formation, and **an inability to close the eye(s)** due to excess skin removal. *Um, yeah, not being able to close your eyes? That's a problem.*

> Neil Sadick and others, *Concise Manual of Cosmetic Dermatologic Surgery* (McGraw Hill Professional, 2007.
> John L. Wobig and Roger A. Dailey, *Oculofacial Plastic Surgery: Face, Lacrimal System, and Orbit* (Thieme, 2004).

FACT: A bezoar is **a ball of swallowed fiber or hair that gathers in the stomach** and gets stuck in the intestines. Chewing on hair, fuzzy things, or indigestible items like plastic bags, can lead to bezoars, which, if large enough, require surgery for removal. *You say bezoar. I say hairball. And if you like to eat fuzz and plastic bags, you've got bigger problems than hairballs. For starters, you might be part goat.*

> Daniel Rauch, "Bezoar," Medline Plus, U.S. National Library of Medicine, July 26, 2007, www.nlm.nih.gov.

FACT : Gastric bypass surgery is a popular but risky procedure. Studies have shown that the health risks that make morbidly obese patients eligible for the procedure in the first place can also lead **to complications during and after the surgery**, such as pulmonary embolism, suture tears and leaks, pneumonia, and infection. An estimated 1,000 Americans died in 2006 from complications related to gastric bypass surgery. *If I'm "morbidly obese," death is a risk I'm willing to take. But can I finish this pork roast first?*

❯ Eileen Korey, "Gastric Bypass Surgery Riskiest for Those Who Need It Most," news release, Medical News Today, December 2, 2003, *www.medicalnewstoday.com.*

❯ J. Eric Oliver, *Fat Politics: The Real Story Behind America's Obesity Epidemic* (Oxford University Press, 2006).

FACT : Surgical tools found in most operating rooms are **similar to items you might find in a wood shop**, including saws, drills, chisels, and clamps. Other tools are the rongeur—French for "gnawer"—a type of bone chisel, and retractors like the rib spreader, which uses a rack-and-pinion system to force apart ribs and tissue for surgical access to the internal cavity. *I apologize for this chapter. It wasn't my idea, I swear.*

❯ Cynthia Spry, *Essentials of Perioperative Nursing*, 3rd ed. (Jones & Bartlett Publishers, 2005).

❯ "The Rib Spreader: A Chapter in the History of Thoracic Surgery," *Chest*, May 1972, 469–474.

FACT : According to 2001 U.S. Justice Department statistics, though 90 percent of medical malpractice trials alleged that the error had caused death or permanent injury, **the win rate for malpractice plaintiffs was only 27 percent**. From 2000 to 2004, most malpractice suits in seven states resulted in no compensation for plaintiffs. *This must be why medical insurance costs rarely go up.*

❯ "Medical Malpractice Trials and Verdicts in Large Counties, 2001," U.S. Department Of Justice, Bureau Of Justice Statistics, *www.ojp.usdoj.gov.*

❯ "Majority of Medical Malpractice Claims in Seven States Closed Without Compensation Payments," U.S. Department Of Justice, Office Of Justice Programs, March 25, 2007, *www.ojp.usdoj.gov.*

FACT: England's Queen Victoria (1837–1901) eased the discomfort of her menstrual cramps with **marijuana supplied by her doctor**. *Even after menopause. Oops—she forgot to tell him.*

> "Medical Marijuana," Canadian Foundation For Drug Policy, *www.cfdp.ca.*

FACT: In the early 1900s, aspirin-maker **Bayer also commercially developed and sold heroin** for several medicinal uses, including cough suppression. *I'm sure heroin suppresses many things.*

> "Before Prohibition: Images from the Preprohibition Era when Many Psychotropic Substances Were Legally Available in America and Europe," University at Buffalo Department of Psychology, Addiction Research Unit, September 2001, *www.wings.buffalo.edu.*

CHAPTER 15

They Did What?

Not-So-Proud Moments in World History

F A C T : **Ancient Romans used human urine** as an ingredient in their toothpaste. *At least it wasn't pig urine. That would be disgusting.*

❯ Joel Levy, *Really Useful: The Origins of Everyday Things* (Firefly Books, 2003).

F A C T : Cruel treatment of slaves was forbidden in ancient Babylon by the Code of Hammurabi, but the code also commanded that **slaves be branded on the forehead** and forbidden to hide their mark. *That's why the Dress Code Of Hammurabi forbade headbands and 'do-rags.*

❯ Isaac Asimov, ed., *Isaac Asimov's Book of Facts* (Hastings House, 1979).

F A C T : When a body was mummified in Ancient Egypt, **the brain was removed through the nostrils**, and other organs were stored in jars. Only the heart was left in the corpse. *I don't want to know how they got the other organs out. But I can guess. Hint: not through the nostrils.*

❯ A. Lucas and John Richard Harris, *Ancient Egyptian Materials and Industries*, 4th ed. (Courier Dover Publications, 1999).

FACT: Ancient Egyptians stuffed moldy bread inside wounds to treat infections. *I bet that's how yeast infections started.*

❯ Walter H. Lewis and Memory P. F. Elvin-Lewis, *Medical Botany: Plants Affecting Human Health*, 2nd ed. (John Wiley & Sons, 2003), 557.

705

FACT: A father in early Rome could **legally sell** any family member into slavery. *My dad would've loved early Rome.*

> G. D. A. Sharpley, *Essential Latin: The Language and Life of Ancient Rome*, 2nd ed. (Routledge, 2000), 62.

706

FACT: In early Rome, a father could **legally execute** any member of his household. *I'm glad I didn't grow up in early Rome.*

> G. D. A. Sharpley, *Essential Latin: The Language and Life of Ancient Rome*, 2nd ed. (Routledge, 2000), 62.

707

FACT: When blonde hair became fashionable in ancient Rome, **thousands of Nordic blondes were captured or slain** by Roman soldiers so that their hair could be used for wigs. *I guess this was before blondes started having more fun.*

> Joanna Pitman, *On Blondes* (Bloomsbury, 2003), 26.

708

FACT: In 336 B.C., **King Philip II of Macedonia was murdered by a servant** just as he was about to launch an invasion of Persia. Some historians suspect that the assassination was a conspiracy orchestrated by Philip's own son, Alexander The Great, so he could lead the Macedonians to victory instead of his father. *And so he could change his name from "Alexander The Just Average," which was given to him by his father.*

> Thom Burnett, *Conspiracy Encyclopedia: The Encyclopedia of Conspiracy Theories* (Franz Steiner Verlag, 2006).

709

FACT: Ancient Egyptian court records dating to 1500 B.C. include **the world's oldest recorded death sentence**. A teenaged male convicted of "magic" was ordered to kill himself by either poison or stabbing. *Good. Magicians should be killed. Jugglers and mimes, too. And clowns for sure.*

❯ Charles Panati, *Panati's Extraordinary Endings of Practically Everything and Everybody* (New York: Harper & Row, 1989).

 710

FACT: The Classic Mayan civilization thrived for over 600 years before collapsing abruptly in the ninth century. **The cause of their extinction is unknown**, and still debated today, more than 1,100 years later. *By nerds with nothing better to do.*

❯ Frank Joseph, ed., *Unearthing Ancient America: The Lost Sagas of Conquerors, Castaways, and Scoundrels* (Franklin Lakes, NJ: New Page Books, 2009).

 711

FACT: Poor Aztec peasants picked lice from their bodies and offered that to the king when they had no gold to give. *Even the Aztecs knew that gifts that you make are so much more thoughtful than others.*

❯ Bruce Felton and Mark Fowler, *Felton & Fowler's More Best, Worst, and Most Unusual* (New York: Thomas Y. Crowell Company, 1976).

 712

FACT: Russia was founded in the ninth century by Vikings traveling between Scandinavia and the Byzantine Empire; **the nation began as essentially a by-product of their slave raids**. *The United States began as a by-product of Christopher Columbus not knowing where the hell he was going.*

❯ "Slavery," *Encyclopædia Britannica*, 15th ed.

713

FACT: Every day, **Martin Luther ate a spoonful of his own excrement**. He wrote praises to God for his generosity in giving man such an important and useful remedy. *CUT TO: God, laughing His ass off.*

> Rose George, *The Big Necessity: The Unmentionable World of Human Waste and Why It Matters* (St. Martin's Press, 2008).

 714

FACT: **Vikings sent eighty "dragon ships"** outfitted with 100 soldiers each, in a single raid on Britain around the year 1000. *The King of England usually asked for a red shirt when he saw an enemy ship approaching, so that if he was wounded in battle and bled, his men would not notice. When he saw the eighty Vikings ships coming, however, the King asked for his brown pants.*

> Isaac Asimov, ed., *Isaac Asimov's Book of Facts* (Hastings House, 1979).

 715

FACT: In 1014, **the original London Bridge was destroyed by Saxons**, who rowed warships up the river Thames, attached cables to the bridge, and pulled it down as they rowed away. *It took awhile. They started pulling in 1012.*

> Jack Mingo and Erin Barrett, *Just Curious, Jeeves: What Are the 1001 Most Intriguing Questions Asked on the Internet?* (Emeryville, CA: Ask Jeeves Inc., 2000).

FACT: King John of England died in 1216 **from overeating.** *There wasn't much else to do in 1216.*

> Geoff Tibballs, ed., *The Ultimate Lists Book* (Carlton Books, Bristol, 1998).

FACT: During the bloody thirty-eight-year reign of Henry VIII (1509–1547), an estimated **57,000 to 72,000 English subjects lost their heads.** *They never found them, either.*

> Julia Layton, "Top 10 Heads That Rolled During the Reign of Henry VIII," HowStuffWorks. com, *www.howstuffworks.com.*

FACT: In 1517, Spanish missionary Bartolomé de Las Casas, disgusted by the enslavement of Native Americans by Spanish colonizers, suggested **bringing Africans to the New World as slaves instead.** *De Las Casas also suggested that Spain start its own Inquisition and send its Armada to invade England. Then they shot him before he could make any other suggestions.*

> David Wallechinsky and Irving Wallace, *The People's Almanac #2* (New York: Bantam Books, 1978).

FACT: Roughly **7–10 million slaves** were kidnapped from Africa and brought to the Americas. *Oops. Our bad.*

> David Wallechinsky and Irving Wallace, The People's Almanac #2 (New York: Bantam Books, 1978).

> "Slavery," Encyclopædia Britannica, 15th ed.

FACT: In the process of divorcing Catherine of Aragon and marrying Anne Boleyn, his mistress, **Henry VIII ordered the beheadings of many who questioned his motives**, including political leaders, high-ranking church officials, two of his six wives, and countless members of his royal court. *Know what would have been funny? If all the lopped-off heads woke up and started right back to bitching at Henry about his divorce.*

❯ Julia Layton, "Top 10 Heads That Rolled During the Reign of Henry VIII," HowStuffWorks.com, *www.howstuffworks.com.*

FACT: St. Edmund the Martyr, King of East Anglia, was killed by the Vikings in 869 after they defeated his army. According to legend, Edmund's executioners either "spread-eagled" him, **prying open his ribs and exposing his still-breathing lungs**, or whipped him, shot him with arrows, and eventually chopped off his head. *"Hmm," said Edmund, upon hearing his choices, "is there by chance a third option?"*

❯ Ian Crofton, *Brewer's Cabinet of Curiosities* (Cassell, 2006).

❯ "St. Edmund The Martyr," *Catholic Encyclopedia, www.newadvent.org.*

FACT: After victory in battle, **Vikings drank the blood** of vanquished enemies from human skulls, hence the Scandinavian toast, "Skol!" *Is there really any other way to drink blood?*

❯ Bruce Felton and Mark Fowler, *Felton & Fowler's More Best, Worst, and Most Unusual* (New York: Thomas Y. Crowell Company, 1976).

FACT: Pope John XII was deposed by Roman Emperor Otto I in 963 for **raping female pilgrims to St. Peter's**, stealing church offerings, drinking toasts to the devil, and invoking the aid of pagan gods when playing dice. John XII reportedly died from a stroke while in bed with a married woman. *Pope John XII: "What?! You're firing me? What'd I do?" That's what fired people always say. Like it's a surprise.*

❯ Simon Adams and Lesley Riley, eds., *Reader's Digest Facts & Fallacies* (Pleasantville, NY: Reader's Digest Association 1988).

❯ Eamon Duffy, *Saints & Sinners: A History of the Popes*, 3rd ed. (Yale University Press, 2006).

724

FACT: After the French town of Beziers fell during the bloody Albigensian Crusade in 1209, the victorious Church-sanctioned army was faced with the problem of how to distinguish the town's heretics from Christians. One of their leaders reportedly said, "Kill them all, for the Lord will know his own," and **thousands of citizens were slaughtered**. *And you thought the Marines came up with that saying.*

> Isaac Asimov, ed., *Isaac Asimov's Book of Facts* (Hastings House, 1979).

> "Beziers," France And Beyond, *www.franceandbeyond.co.uk.*

725

FACT: When red precipitation fell on Paris on Easter Sunday in 582, **terrified French believed that it was raining blood**, a sign of divine displeasure. Theories suggest that the "rain" was red sand particles stirred by strong windstorms in the Sahara and blown across the Mediterranean Sea into Europe. *At least it wasn't raining men. That would have been worse.*

> Randy Cerveny, *Freaks of the Storm: From Flying Cows to Stealing Thunder, the World's Strangest True Weather Stories* (Thunder's Mouth Press, 2005).

726

FACT: George Washington and Thomas Jefferson grew **marijuana on their plantations**. *George called his "Mt. Burnin'" and Tom's was known as "Monticello Mellow."*

> North American Industrial Hemp Council, *www.naihc.org.*

FACT: Patrick Henry, the colonial American leader famous for saying, "Give me liberty, or give me death," owned **sixty-five slaves** when he died in 1799. *"Or give me just a second to come up with a new line."*

❯ David Wallechinsky, Irving Wallace, and Amy Wallace, *The Book of Lists* (New York: Bantam Books, 1977).

FACT: In 1732, England's King George II gave General James Oglethorpe a charter to create a new colony in America where **imprisoned British debtors could be relocated** so that they might start new lives and become self-sufficient. That colony became the state of Georgia. *They should've stayed in prison.*

❯ Alexander Hewatt, *An Historical Account of the Rise and Progress of the Colonies of South Carolina and Georgia* (BiblioBazaar, 2007), 24.

FACT: By 1837, **the Andrew Jackson administration removed 46,000 Native Americans** from the Eastern United States, freeing up to 25 million acres for white settlement. *The whiteys immediately built an Olive Garden, a Crate & Barrel, three golf courses, and eighteen Starbucks.*

❯ "Indian removal," PBS.org, www.pbs.org.

FACT: The Indian removal put in place by President Andrew Jackson forced the Cherokee nation to vacate the southern U.S. and move west to what is now Oklahoma. Their long journey in 1838–1839 was dubbed the "Trail Of Tears" after it claimed the lives of 4,000 Cherokee—**almost a third of their population**—from hunger, disease, and exhaustion. *I'd rather die than live in Oklahoma, too.*

❯ "Indian removal," PBS.org, www.pbs.org.
❯ "The Trail of Tears," PBS.org, www.pbs.org.

FACT: Roman Emperor Gaius (Caligula) was so proud of his horse that **he gave the animal a position in the Senate**. *This practice continues today in America, but we only let the horse's ass in the Senate, not the entire animal.*

> Facts Library, *www.factlib .com.*

FACT: By the Civil War's end in 1865, victorious Union general Ulysses S. Grant owned four slaves, whom **he refused to free**. Confederate General Robert E. Lee had freed his slaves in the late 1840s. *Grant: "Wait. We were fighting for what?"*

> Jack Mingo and Erin Barrett, *Just Curious, Jeeves: What Are the 1001 Most Intriguing Questions Asked on the Internet?* (Emeryville, CA: Ask Jeeves Inc., 2000).

FACT: In 1898, the American battleship *USS Maine* blew up in Havana harbor, Cuba, killing 266 American servicemen. The American media blamed Spanish forces and helped create a frenzy that ultimately led to the Spanish-American war. Yet, **no terrorist activity was ever proven**, and today, many researchers believe the explosion was accidental. *Oops.*

> Alan Axelrod, *Profiles in Folly: History's Worst Decisions and Why They Went Wrong* (Sterling Publishing Company, 2008), 72.

> "The Destruction of USS Maine," Department Of The Navy, Naval Historical Center, *www.history.navy.mil.*

> "Yellow Journalism," PBS.org, *www.pbs.org.*

FACT: In May 1902, volcanic activity on the Caribbean island of Martinique drove **more than a hundred fer-de-lance snakes into the town of St. Pierre**, where the large, venomous reptiles killed fifty people and hundreds of animals. *Fer-de-love of God, do they not have cats on that island?*

> David Wallechinsky, *The New Book of Lists: The Original Compendium of Curious Information* (Canongate U.S., 2005).

FACT : In 1919, a large tank of molasses burst in Boston's North End, **causing a deadly wave of molasses to flow through the streets** at an estimated 35 mph, killing 21 people and injuring 150 more. *The victims knew the wave was coming, but probably figured they had plenty of time to escape. I mean, come on, it's molasses.*

❯ Stephen Puleo, *Dark Tide* (Beacon Press, 2004).

FACT: India tested its **first nuclear bomb** in 1974. *Indian food sets off a few bombs of its own.*

❯ "Nuclear Proliferation," U.S. Department Of Energy, Office Of History & Heritage, *www.doe.gov.*

FACT : From 1915 to 1918, 2 million Armenians in Turkey were slaughtered or deported from their historic Asia Minor homeland by the Turkish government, which also demolished ancient cities, architecture, and records, **removing nearly all traces of the 3,000-year-old civilization**. *"Would you like to be slaughtered or deported?" "Hmm, let me think. I guess I'll go with deported."*

❯ "Armenian Genocide," The Armenian Genocide Museum-Institute, *www .genocide-museum.am.*

FACT : The German luxury ship *St. Louis* sailed to North America in 1939, carrying more than 900 European Jews seeking safe refuge from Germany's Nazi government. **The ship was turned away by both Cuba and the United States** and returned to Europe, where many of the fleeing Jews were later captured and executed by the Nazis. *You've heard of FDR's New Deal. This was the Raw Deal.*

❯ "The Tragedy Of The *St. Louis*," Chapter 113, The American Jewish Historical Society, *www .ajhs.org.*

FACT: An estimated 7 million people died during the Ukraine famine of 1932–1933, **about 25,000 a day** at its peak. The famine was engineered by Joseph Stalin to destroy the region's drive for independence.

> "Ukrainian Genocide of 1932–1933," Ukrainian Genocide Famine Foundation-USA, Inc., www.ukrainiangenocide.com.
> "Ukranian Famine," Ibiblio.org, www.ibiblio.org.

FACT: By the end of World War II in 1945, **nearly all of Europe's Jewish population** had been wiped out by the Holocaust: 4 million in Adolf Hitler's death camps, and 2 million in ghettos in Warsaw, Theresienstadt, and other cities.

> "The Holocaust," United States Holocaust Memorial Museum, www.ushmm.org.

FACT: China's Chairman Mao Zedong was a ruthless leader whose policies wiped out millions of Chinese. In the 1950s, Mao's so-called "Great Leap Forward" of collective farming and rapid industrialization led **to famine throughout China**, killing as many as 35 million people.

> "1976: Chairman Mao Dies," On This Day, BBC News, http://news.bbc.co.uk.

FACT: China's Cultural Revolution, started by Chairman Mao Zedong in 1966 to purge opponents, dragged on for 10 years and **slaughtered tens of thousands** of Chinese citizens. *And that concludes this episode of "History's Biggest Buttholes."*

> "China's Communist Revolution: A Glossary," BBC News, http://news.bbc.co.uk.

739 ... 740

743

FACT: Illinois passed a law in 1853 that levied a $50 fine on any black person from another state who **spent more than ten days there**. If the person was unable to pay the fine, he could be sold into slavery. *The law was moot. Most people got bored within a day and split. I mean, it's Illinois.*

> Isaac Asimov, ed., *Isaac Asimov's Book of Facts* (Hastings House, 1979).

744

FACT: Fourteen years before the Titanic sank, a novel titled *Futility* told the story of an ocean liner named Titan that met its demise one April night when **it collided with an iceberg**. *A novel that didn't sell a lot of copies, I'm guessing.*

> Facts Library, *www.factlib.com*.

745

FACT: In July 1945, a B-25 crashed into the Empire State Building in New York, **engulfing six floors in flames**. Amazingly, only fourteen people died: the crash happened on a Saturday and the building was all but empty. *Hopefully they were stockbrokers.*

> David Wallechinsky, *The New Book of Lists: The Original Compendium of Curious Information* (Canongate U.S., 2005), 397.

746

FACT: Since the 1950s, several of the most notorious dictators, mass murderers, and state terrorists of Latin America have **trained at the Western Hemisphere Institute for Security Cooperation** (formerly the School of the Americas) run by the CIA at Fort Benning, Georgia. *Yes, but they pay out-of-state tuition, and we need the money.*

> Thom Burnett, *Conspiracy Encyclopedia: The Encyclopedia of Conspiracy Theories* (Franz Steiner Verlag, 2006), 172.

FACT: In 1981, President Ronald Reagan approved nutrition guidelines that **qualified ketchup as a vegetable** in school lunches, saving the U.S. government millions of dollars. *That's preposterous. Everyone knows the tomato is a fruit, not a vegetable.*

❯ Susan Levine, *School Lunch Politics: The Surprising History of America's Favorite Welfare Program* (Princeton University Press, 2008), 177.

FACT: One week prior to his assassination, President Abraham Lincoln had a dream about someone crying in the White House. He followed the sound to a room where he found a man by a coffin. When Lincoln asked who had died, **the man replied, "The President."** *But the man by the coffin was Bill Clinton, so Lincoln didn't believe him.*

❯ "Facts About Abraham Lincoln," Abraham Lincoln Library, www.alincoln-library.com.

FACT: Napoleon used a sandbox to construct his battle plans. *He was too short to reach the map tables.*

❯ Facts Library, www.factlib.com.

FACT: St. Lawrence of Rome was martyred by order of Roman emperor Valerian in the year 258, reportedly **by being grilled over an open flame**. *Legend also claims that while being cooked, Lawrence told his torturers, "This side is well roasted; turn me over." If that's true, then they should change his name to St. Bad-Ass.*

❯ "The Martyrdom of St. Laurence," Free Republic, www.freerepublic.com.

CHAPTER 16

Buggin' Out

Insect Facts That Will Give You the Creepy-Crawlies

751

F A C T : A cockroach carries **more than forty different pathogens** that can be transferred to humans, including pneumonia, hepatitis, and typhoid. *I have a pathogen that can be transferred to cockroaches. It's called the bottom of my shoe, and it is fatal 100 percent of the time.*

❯ Greta Garbage, *That's Disgusting!: An Adult Guide to What's Gross, Tasteless, Rude, Crude, and Lewd* (Ten Speed Press, 1999).

752

F A C T : Because of its high food intake, **a housefly deposits feces constantly**—about every five minutes—which makes it a carrier of more than 100 disease-causing agents. *And you thought babies crapped a lot.*

❯ Yiu H. Hui, *Handbook of Food Science, Technology, and Engineering* (CRC Press, 2006).

753

F A C T : The color of a head louse tends **to mimic the color of the person's hair** in which it lives, making it more difficult to detect. *After years of lousy service, Bob was named Head Louse of his department.*

❯ May R. Berenbaum, *Bugs in the System: Insects and Their Impact on Human Affairs* (Basic Books, 1996).

754

F A C T : Aphids are born impregnated, do not require sex to procreate, and can **give birth within a week of being born themselves**, making them quite prolific. In large numbers, aphids can cause serious damage to crops. *Probably because they aren't getting any sex.*

❯ Jerry Baker, *Jerry Baker's Bug Off!: 2,193 Super Secrets for Battling Bad Bugs, Outfoxing Crafty Critters, Evicting Voracious Varmints and Much More!* (American Master Products, 2005).

❯ Denny Schrock, *Home Gardener's Problem Solver: Symptoms and Solutions for More Than 1,500 Garden Pests and Plant Ailments,* 3rd ed. (Ortho Books, 2004).

755

FACT: There are about **10 quintillion insects on Earth** at any given moment; that's 1.5 billion bugs for every human on the planet. *One and a half billion bugs? Sounds like Windows Vista.*

> Jerry Baker, *Jerry Baker's Bug Off!: 2,193 Super Secrets for Battling Bad Bugs, Outfoxing Crafty Critters, Evicting Voracious Varmints and Much More!* (American Master Products, 2005).

 756

FACT: The *Vespa mandarinia* japonica, or Japanese giant hornet, is the size of your thumb, has a painful sting, and can **spray flesh-melting poison into your eyes**. Its poison also contains a pheromone that can summon every hornet in the hive to attack. *At least they don't overdo it.*

> Ross Piper, *Extraordinary Animals: An Encyclopedia of Curious and Unusual Animals* (Greenwood Publishing Group, 2007).

 757

FACT: As the world's most venomous insect per sting, **the Japanese giant hornet kills forty people every year**, all of them excruciatingly painful deaths. *What, all that stinging and flesh-melting and hive-summoning, and they only manage forty kills a year?*

> Ross Piper, *Extraordinary Animals: An Encyclopedia of Curious and Unusual Animals* (Greenwood Publishing Group, 2007).

FACT: The bullet ant earned its name because of **a sting that feels like getting shot with a gun.** Some consider the bullet ant's sting the most painful of all insects, and pain can persist for up to twenty-four hours after contact. *How would they know? Do they shoot a guy and let a bullet ant sting him at the same time and then ask him if the two feel the same?*

❯ John L. Capinera, *Encyclopedia of Entomology*, 2nd ed. (Springer, 2008).

FACT: Africanized honey bees, better known as "killer bees," hail from South and Central America, and as of 2006, were established in the American South and Southwest. **Killer bees are extremely aggressive** and prone to potentially deadly attacks when disturbed. *I'm the same way when I'm on the can and my kid tries to come into the bathroom.*

❯ John L. Capinera, *Encyclopedia of Entomology*, 2nd ed. (Springer, 2008).

FACT: Killer bees are extremely territorial and have **a propensity for mass stinging attacks** on both humans and animals. Swarms can kill any number of humans from a few dozen people in Mexico to several hundred in Venezuela. *I'd like to see killer bees and Japanese hornets fight it out. That would make a great pay-per-view event. I'd pay to see it.*

❯ John L. Capinera, *Encyclopedia of Entomology*, 2nd ed. (Springer, 2008).

FACT: Africanized bees have only been around since the 1950s, when Brazilian scientist **Warwick E. Kerr bred a European bee with an African bee** in hopes of propagating the positive qualities of the former with a tolerance for tropical climates. The bees swarmed accidentally during quarantine and have been successfully invading the Americas ever since. *Thanks for that, Kerr. Ass.*

❯ John L. Capinera, *Encyclopedia of Entomology*, 2nd ed. (Springer, 2008).

762

FACT: There is no physical way to determine the difference between an Africanized honey bee and the less harmful European bee—**even a specialist must examine several bees together** to differentiate them. *Can't you just ask them?*

> John L. Capinera, *Encyclopedia of Entomology*, 2nd ed. (Springer, 2008).

763

FACT: Army ants are a half-inch in length and **notorious for dismantling any living thing in their path**, regardless of its size, thanks to massive, machete-like jaws that are half the size of their own bodies. *Army ants are also known as Hilary Swank ants.*

> Ken Preston-Mafham, *The Encyclopedia of Land Invertebrate Behaviour* (MIT Press, 1993).

764

FACT: Army ants earned their name because the entire colony—anywhere from 300,000 to 700,000—is **a mobile battalion.** They don't make permanent hives like other ants, but bivouac in frequently changing locations. *I bet ants would be thrilled to know that they "bivouac."*

> Ken Preston-Mafham, *The Encyclopedia of Land Invertebrate Behaviour* (MIT Press, 1993).

765

FACT: Army ants attack cows and horses by swarming up their legs and **attacking the soft tissue of the eyes and nose**. If assaulted while penned, these animals can become so hysterical they will beat themselves to death trying to escape. *I feel the same way at my in-laws'.*

> Ken Preston-Mafham, *The Encyclopedia of Land Invertebrate Behaviour* (MIT Press, 1993).

> Alzada Carlisle Kistner, *An Affair with Africa: Expeditions and Adventures Across a Continent* (Island Press, 1998).

766

FACT : There are dozens of varieties of botfly, each highly adapted to target a specific animal. Examples include the horse stomach botfly, deer nose botfly and the human botfly. Each breed has a different and elaborate reproductive cycle that **includes a fat, half-inch maggot** embedded in the host creature's living flesh.

> ❯ Jerome Goddard, *Physician's Guide to Arthropods of Medical Importance,* 5th ed. (CRC Press, 2007).

767

FACT : The human botfly lays its eggs on a blood-sucking host—like a horsefly or a mosquito—and when this carrier lands on a human, **the botfly maggot emerges and burrows into the human skin**, where it feeds and grows in a sub-dermal cavity for 5–10 weeks.

> ❯ Jerome Goddard, *Physician's Guide to Arthropods of Medical Importance,* 5th ed. (CRC Press, 2007).

768

FACT : Human botfly larva can grow anywhere in the body, and have been removed from the head, arms, back, abdomen, buttocks, thighs, and armpits of humans. **They can even penetrate the incompletely ossified skull of a young child** and burrow into the brain. *There had better not be a human scrotum botfly.*

> ❯ Jerome Goddard, *Physician's Guide to Arthropods of Medical Importance,* 5th ed. (CRC Press, 2007).

769

FACT : One of the largest terrestrial insects in North America, the wheel bug attacks by piercing the prey's skin with a large beak and **injecting it with a flesh-dissolving poison**. Being bitten by a wheel bug is excruciating for humans, and the wound can take weeks to heal. *That's just how wheel bugs roll, yo.*

> ❯ Stephen Welton Taber and Scott B. Fleenor, *Insects of the Texas Lost Pines* (Texas A&M University Press, 2003).

FACT: Bee assassin bugs have hairs on their legs that allow them to catch and hold onto their prey. Though named for their penchant for killing bees, assassins are opportunistic and attack many other insects, **immobilizing prey with a powerful, fast-acting toxin.** Their bite is more painful to humans than bee and wasp stings. *You've probably heard of would-be assassins, but not bee assassins. Don't confuse would-be assassins with insects aspiring to become bee assassins; those are called would-be bee assassins.*

❯ Maurice Burton and Robert Burton, *International Wildlife Encyclopedia*, 3rd ed. (Marshall Cavendish, 2002).

FACT: The bite of some assassin bugs found in the Sinai and Negev deserts of Israel is **more toxic than the bite of venomous snakes** in the region. *Hopefully this doesn't ruin anyone's vacation plans.*

❯ Lance A. Durden, *Medical and Veterinary Entomology*, 3rd ed. (Academic Press, 2002).

FACT: Kissing bugs usually prey on bed bugs but will suck blood from humans, too. They earn their sweet name in a not-so-sweet way: **by biting the lips, eyelids, and ears of sleeping human victims**, causing intense pain that can last weeks or even months. *Kissing bugs are not the same as Ass-Kissing bugs, which do not bite but will continuously lick and nibble the hindquarters of anyone in authority.*

❯ Howard Garrett and C. Malcolm Beck, *Texas Bug Book: The Good, the Bad, and the Ugly*, 2nd ed. (University of Texas Press, 2005).

FACT: Kissing bugs carry a deadly sleeping sickness, Chagas disease, which infects 11 million people in Latin America, **many of whom do not know they are infected**. Without treatment the condition is lifelong and can be fatal. *Similar to Chagas disease is Jag-Ass disease, which affects millions of people all over the world, most of whom are aware of their infection but don't give a damn. If untreated, the condition is lifelong and can be fatal.*

❯ Howard Garrett and C. Malcolm Beck, *Texas Bug Book: The Good, the Bad, and the Ugly*, 2nd ed. (University of Texas Press, 2005).

FACT: The most dangerous insect in the world is the mosquito, responsible for the spread of malaria, which infects 350–500 million people each year, killing as many as a million. There are **2,500 species** of mosquitoes throughout the world; about 200 of them occur in the United States. *All of them in my backyard.*

❯ Eric R. Eaton and Kenn Kaufman, *Kaufman Field Guide to Insects of North America* (Houghton Mifflin Harcourt, 2007).
❯ "Malaria," Centers for Disease Control and Prevention, *www.cdc.gov*.
❯ American Mosquito Control Association, *www.mosquito.org*.

FACT: When biting prey, **Brazilian wandering spiders inject up to .003 ounces of powerful venom**, an amount strong enough to kill 300 mice. *What do you call 300 dead mice on the jungle floor? A good start.*

❯ Robert S. Anderson, Richard Beatty, and Stuart Church, *Insects and Spiders of the World* (Marshall Cavendish, 2003).

FACT: Jumping spiders hunt by stalking and leaping on victims while trailing a safety line of silk behind them. **Their eight eyes give them almost 180-degree vision**, and they can jump up to twenty times their own length. *Because regular old walking spiders weren't creepy enough.*

> Paul Hillyard, *The Private Life of Spiders* (New Holland Publishers, 2007).

FACT: The Sydney funnel-web spider is Australia's most dangerous arachnid, with a bite capable of **causing death in as little as fifteen minutes**. *Just try not to get bitten until the end of your trip, because Sydney is a great city and I recommend seeing as much of it as you can before you die. Especially since you probably won't be returning.*

> Jerome Goddard, *Physician's Guide to Arthropods of Medical Importance*, 5th ed. (CRC Press, 2007).

FACT: It has no bite, but the common housefly is one of the world's most deadly insects, thanks **to the long list of diseases that it carries and spreads**: typhoid, cholera, gangrene, tuberculosis, smallpox, bubonic plague, diptheria, dysentery, and more. *Bubonic plague? That shit's still around?!*

> Leland Ossian Howard, *The House Fly, Disease Carrier: An Account of Its Dangerous Activities and of the Means of Destroying It*, 3rd ed. (Frederick A. Stokes, 1911).

FACT: An individual housefly can carry **up to 33 million bacteria** on the outer surface of its body, 6 million on its feet alone. *For this reason, you should always insist that a housefly wipe its feet before entering your home.*

> Leland Ossian Howard, *The House Fly, Disease Carrier: An Account of Its Dangerous Activities and of the Means of Destroying It*, 3rd ed. (Frederick A. Stokes, 1911).

> Julie J. Shaffner, Kasey Jo Warner, and W. Wyatt Hoback, *Filth Flies: Experiments to Test Flies as Vectors of Bacterial Disease* (The American Biology Teacher Online, Feb 2007).

FACT: Houseflies can also carry microbes of conjunctivitis (pinkeye) from diseased eyes to healthy eyes, including trachoma, **a highly contagious cause of blindness** throughout the world. *Which ranks trachoma ahead of other causes of blindness such as science and the light.*

❯ Mitchell H. Friedlaender, "Conjunctivitis," The Merck Manuals Online Medical Library, June 2008, *www.merck.com.*

FACT: Flies typically transmit their harmful microorganisms **to humans through our mouths**, when we eat food on which they have landed and deposited their feces and bacteria. *I suppose that's better than letting them crap right into your mouth. But not by much.*

❯ Julie J. Shaffner, Kasey Jo Warner, and W. Wyatt Hoback, *Filth Flies: Experiments to Test Flies as Vectors of Bacterial Disease* (The American Biology Teacher Online, Feb 2007).

FACT: In 1979, the Linondoll Pest Control Company of Schenectady, New York had the honor of treating **the world's largest cockroach infestation**: 3 million roaches inhabited the walls, ceilings, floors, attic, and basement of a two-family dwelling. *Sounds more like two families inhabited a 3-million-roach dwelling.*

❯ Mark L. Winston, *Nature Wars: People Vs. Pests* (Harvard University Press, 1999).

783

FACT : There are 4,000 species of cockroach in the world, **95 percent of them** able to survive completely independent of humans. *We'd get along just fine without them, too.*

❯ Jerome Goddard, *Physician's Guide to Arthropods of Medical Importance*, 5th ed. (CRC Press, 2007).

 784

FACT : A cockroach can survive **for several weeks with no head**. *Yes, but it spends those weeks bumping into walls and screaming, "Where the FUCK is my head?!"*

❯ Jerome Goddard, *Physician's Guide to Arthropods of Medical Importance*, 5th ed. (CRC Press, 2007).

 785

FACT : Cockroaches can crawl through astonishingly small spaces. Young cockroaches need just **a dime-sized crevice** while adults males can squeeze into a space the width of a quarter. Pregnant females require the width of two nickels. *If they all try to squeeze through at the same time, they'll need a space about the size of a half-dollar coin. Those are pretty hard to find these days, which is why roaches usually just go through holes one at a time.*

❯ Jerome Goddard, *Physician's Guide to Arthropods of Medical Importance*, 5th ed. (CRC Press, 2007).

 786

FACT : In Africa, cattle bitten by the *O. savignyi* breed of tick may die of toxicosis **in just one day**. *Right before the animal dies, it makes a horrible grimace that researchers call the "O. savignyi Face," or "O Face" for short.*

❯ Jerome Goddard, *Physician's Guide to Arthropods of Medical Importance*, 5th ed. (CRC Press, 2007).

787

FACT: Hundreds of pets and livestock are injured or killed by tick paralysis, **a result of bites from certain breeds of ticks**. The severity of the paralysis depends on the number of female tick bites received by the host. *Of course it does. Weaker sex, my ass.*

❯ Jerome Goddard, *Physician's Guide to Arthropods of Medical Importance*, 5th ed. (CRC Press, 2007).

788

FACT: There are **1,250 species of scorpions** in the world, on every continent but Antarctica. Their toxic stings can result in abdominal cramps, blurred vision, partial paralysis, abnormal eye movements, priapism (persistent erection), hypertension, tachycardia, convulsions, and death from respiratory paralysis. *Aside from the priapism, scorpion bites sound like a drag.*

❯ Jerome Goddard, *Physician's Guide to Arthropods of Medical Importance*, 5th ed. (CRC Press, 2007).

❯ "Priapism," Merriam-Webster Online Dictionary, *www .merriam-webster.com.*

789

FACT: **The United States is home to just one dangerous species of scorpion**, *C. exilacauda*, or the Arizona Bark scorpion, but beware: its sting can cause respiratory failure, metabolic acidosis, and death. *Other scorpion species exist here, but the Bark is much worse than their bites.*

❯ Jerome Goddard, *Physician's Guide to Arthropods of Medical Importance*, 5th ed. (CRC Press, 2007).

❯ "The Scorpion Files, *Centruroides exilicauda*," Norwegian University of Science and Technology, *www.ub.ntnu.no.*

790

FACT: There are an estimated **40,000 scorpion stings** every year in Morocco. *Hopefully not all on the same guy.*

❯ Jerome Goddard, *Physician's Guide to Arthropods of Medical Importance*, 5th ed. (CRC Press, 2007).

791

FACT: The seemingly harmless ladybug has been known **to inflict unprovoked bites** and release a defensive secretion that causes a stinging sensation on human skin. *Not very ladylike, if you ask me.*

> Jerome Goddard, *Physician's Guide to Arthropods of Medical Importance*, 5th ed. (CRC Press, 2007).

 792

FACT: Many parasitic worms use beetles as intermediate hosts to get to humans. One case from the Mississippi Department of Health reported **an eight-centimeter worm** found in a baby's diaper; the infant had presumably ingested an infected beetle via contaminated flour or bread products. *If you've ever changed a poopy diaper, there's really nothing you could find in there that would surprise you—a worm, a frog, Jimmy Hoffa, whatever.*

> Jerome Goddard, *Physician's Guide to Arthropods of Medical Importance*, 5th ed. (CRC Press, 2007).

 793

FACT: When threatened, blister beetles secrete **a chemical that will produce a sore within a few hours** of penetrating the skin. This chemical agent is poisonous to some animal species, and, when ingested, can lead to abdominal pain, kidney damage, and even death. *The blister beetle will also secrete some chemicals when stamped into smithereens by my foot, which is what will happen to any beetle that gives me a blister.*

> Jerome Goddard, *Physician's Guide to Arthropods of Medical Importance*, 5th ed. (CRC Press, 2007).

794

FACT : Marketed as a sexual stimulant for thousands of years, **the Spanish fly is a European blister beetle** that has been dried, crushed, and consumed, but doing so can cause painful urination, fever, and permanent damage to the kidneys and genitals. *Proving once again that being a sucker has always been painful.*

> Jerome Goddard, *Physician's Guide to Arthropods of Medical Importance*, 5th ed. (CRC Press, 2007).

> John L. Capinera, *Encyclopedia of Entomology*, 2nd ed. (Springer, 2008).

795

FACT : It would take **500–800 honey bee stings** to kill a human based on the toxic effects of the venom alone, but to someone with a bee allergy, one sting can cause a deadly anaphylactic reaction. *If you get stung 500–800 times by bees, you need better sneakers.*

> Jerome Goddard, *Physician's Guide to Arthropods of Medical Importance*, 5th ed. (CRC Press, 2007).

796

FACT : Long-term lice infection of humans can result in what's known as secondary sensitization, or **a feeling of apathy, pessimism, or irritability**, hence the term, "feeling lousy." *Long-term lice infection of a human can also result in what's known as never having a date, ever. This also creates a feeling of apathy, irritability, pessimism, and chronic virginity.*

> Jerome Goddard, *Physician's Guide to Arthropods of Medical Importance*, 5th ed. (CRC Press, 2007).

797

FACT : The skin of people who continually harbor body lice **hardens and becomes darkly pigmented**, and is commonly known as vagabond's syndrome. *I always thought vagabond's syndrome was roaming the country with all your stuff tied up in a kerchief at the end of a stick and singing songs like "Jimmy Crack Corn."*

> Jerome Goddard, *Physician's Guide to Arthropods of Medical Importance*, 5th ed. (CRC Press, 2007).

798

FACT: The praying mantis is a formidable predator with a large head, numerous eyes, powerful front legs, and **quick reflexes that are difficult to notice with the naked eye**. Their prey includes flies, grasshoppers, moths, and other insects. *I once saw a praying mantis kill a mouse. You don't forget something like that.*

> "Praying Mantis," Animals, National Geographic, *http:// animals.nationalgeographic.com.*

 799

FACT: The praying mantis will eat its own kind. The most famous example of this is the female's notorious mating behavior where **she sometimes eats the male just after—or even during—mating**. *Whether it's after or during depends largely on how good he is in the sack.*

> "Praying Mantis," Animals, National Geographic, *http:// animals.nationalgeographic.com.*

 800

FACT: Some caterpillars possess **poison-filled spines** that break off and release venom-like substances into human skin upon contact. *Some caterpillars need to be introduced to Mrs. Praying Mantis.*

> Jerome Goddard, *Physician's Guide to Arthropods of Medical Importance*, 5th ed. (CRC Press, 2007).

> "Praying Mantis," Animals, National Geographic, *http://animals.nationalgeographic.com.*

> "Stomach bots in horses," Cooperative Extension System, *www.extension.org.*

> "Killer Insects: 6 Natural Born Anthropod Assassins," WebEcoist, September 21, 2008, *www.webecoist.com.*

> Alex Levinton, "The 5 Most Horrifying Bugs in the World," Cracked.com, *www.cracked.com.*

CHAPTER 17

Foreign Objects

Strange Facts about Faraway Places Where People Talk Funny

FACT: A mummified hand has been on display in city hall in Münster, Germany for 400 years. It belonged to a notary who falsely certified a document, and had **his hand chopped off as punishment**, then displayed as a warning. *You should see the warning to flashers.*

❯ Andrea Schulte-Peevers and others, *Lonely Planet Germany*, 5th ed. (Lonely Planet, 2007), 583.

FACT: Flamingo tongue was **a common delicacy** at Roman feasts. *You can still find it today in vienna sausages and deviled ham.*

❯ Noel Botham, *The Book of Useless Information* (Perigee, 2006).

FACT: In the Satere-Mawe tribe in South America, a boy being initiated into manhood is forced to wear gloves woven with hundreds of bullet ants, whose **sting is considered the most painful of any insect**. The ants sting the boy until he passes out from pain; if he can be revived, he is considered a true man. *Is he disqualified if he craps himself?*

❯ Alex Levinton, "The 5 Most Horrifying Bugs in the World," Cracked.com, *www.cracked.com*.

❯ Steve Backshall, *Venom: Poisonous Animals in the Natural World* (New Holland Publishers, 2007).

FACT: In Britain, placing a postage stamp **bearing the British monarch upside down** is considered treason. *Even if she looks better that way?*

❯ Alex Wade, "The World's Strangest Laws," Times Online, August 15, 2007, *www.business.timesonline.co.uk*.

FACT: In France, you are forbidden **to name a pig "Napoleon."** *The French hate redundancy.*

> Alex Wade, "The World's Strangest Laws," Times Online, August 15, 2007, *www.business.timesonline.co.uk.*

FACT: By law, **a pregnant woman can urinate anywhere** she wants in Britain— even, if she so chooses, in a police officer's helmet. *But if she has to go number two, she'll need to find a Queen's Guard with the big furry hat. Gotta wipe, you know.*

> Alex Wade, "The World's Strangest Laws," Times Online, August 15, 2007, *www.business .timesonline.co.uk.*

FACT: Masturbation is **an offense punishable by decapitation** in Indonesia. *Tell me they at least let you finish.*

> Alex Wade, "The World's Strangest Laws," Times Online, August 15, 2007, *www.business.timesonline.co.uk.*

FACT: Drunk driving is handled seriously in El Salvador. In San Salvador, **offenders may be sentenced to death by** firing squad. *Except that the firing squad soldiers are usually drunk, too, and tend to miss.*

> Alex Wade, "The World's Strangest Laws," Times Online, August 15, 2007, *www.business .timesonline.co.uk.*

809

FACT: Male doctors in Bahrain are not legally permitted **to look directly at a woman's genitals**: they may only examine them with a mirror. *I bet that makes childbirth fun.*

❯ Alex Wade, "The World's Strangest Laws," Times Online, August 15, 2007, *www.business .timesonline.co.uk.*

810

FACT: It is illegal for a cab in London **to carry rabid dogs or corpses**. *I hope Keith Richards has his own car.*

❯ Alex Wade, "The World's Strangest Laws," Times Online, August 15, 2007, *www.business.timesonline.co.uk.*

811

FACT: All males fourteen years or older are **to perform longbow practice for two hours** each day in England. *Is that what the kids call that now? We called it "beating the bishop."*

❯ Alex Wade, "The World's Strangest Laws," Times Online, August 15, 2007, *www.business .timesonline.co.uk.*

812

FACT: An Australian writer was sentenced to three years in a Thai prison and experienced "unspeakable suffering" because of **a few lines in his self-published novel** that were deemed insulting to the monarchy. The book sold only seven copies. *The "unspeakable suffering" occurred when they read his book aloud to him.*

❯ Grant Peck, "Australian Convicted of Insulting Thai Monarchy," ABC News, January 19, 2009, *www.abcnews .go.com.*

FACT: In Lebanon, men are permitted **to have sexual intercourse with an animal**, but only if it is female. Sex with a male animal is punishable by death. *If you survive the attempt, that is.*

> Eve Marx, *What's Your Sexual IQ?* (Citadel Press, 2004), 175.

FACT: It is against the law in France to sell a doll with **a face that is not human**. *Which is why no one makes a Sarah Jessica Parker Barbie in France.*

> Noel Botham, *The Best Book of Useless Information Ever: A Few Thousand Other Things You Probably Don't Need to Know (but Might as Well Find Out)* (Perigee, 2007).

FACT: Donald Duck was once banned in Finland because **he doesn't wear any pants**. *Finns, you didn't miss anything.*

> Noel Botham, *The Best Book of Useless Information Ever: A Few Thousand Other Things You Probably Don't Need to Know (but Might as Well Find Out)* (Perigee, 2007), 46.

FACT: One of Taiwan's most successful theme restaurant chains is Modern Toilet, where **customers sit on commodes** and enjoy chocolate ice cream and curry chicken served in dishes shaped like small toilets to resemble feces. *The closest thing we have is to that is Chili's, but their food only tastes like it came from the toilet.*

> Jonathan Adams, "Waiter, There's a Toilet in My Soup," Globalpost.com, *www.global post.com.*

817

FACT: Hindus believe **cow urine is medicinal**; it is often drunk in religious festivals. *They'll never run out, that's for sure.*

> Matthias Williams, "They Call it Mellow Yellow?" Reuters, February 12, 2009, *www.reuters.com.*

818

FACT: A fifth of Ireland's towns are at **high risk for cryptosporidium infection**, a disease spread through drinking water contaminated by human feces. *But no one ever gets it because it's not found in booze.*

> Rose George, *The Big Necessity: The Unmentionable World of Human Waste and Why It Matters* (St. Martin's Press, 2008).

819

FACT: The drive-through line on opening day of a new McDonald's in Kuwait City, Kuwait reached **seven miles long at times**. *That's a lot of disappointed people.*

> "The McDonald's History— 1994 to Today," McDonald's Corporation, *www.mcdonalds .com.*

820

FACT: In South Korea in 2005, a twenty-eight-year-old man was killed by a heart attack brought on by exhaustion from **playing a video game online for fifty straight hours**. *PWN3D!!!*

> "S Korean dies after games session," BBC News, August 10, 2005, *www.news.bbc.co.uk.*

FACT: On average, a Chinese person takes his or her own life **every two minutes**, adding up to 250,000 to 300,000 suicides a year. *Some Chinese like to save the government the trouble.*

> Pascale Trouillaud, "Chinese Committing Suicide Every Two Minutes," news.com.au, December 9, 2008, *www.news.com.au*.

FACT: In 2005, as many as twelve Iraqi barbers were executed by militant Islamic gangs for **shaving men's beards** and giving Western-style haircuts. *The ones who gave mullet cuts were executed twice.*

> Robert F. Worth, "A Haircut in Iraq Can Be the Death of the Barber," *New York Times*, March 18, 2005, *www.nytimes.com*.

FACT: Malawi president Bingu wa Mutharika vacated his home, a 300-bedroom mansion, in 2005 believing it **to be haunted**. *It wasn't ghosts he heard in the night, but Madonna, sneaking around looking for more kids to steal.*

> "Ghosts Scare off Malawi Leader," BBC News, March, 2005, *www.news.bbc.co.uk*.

FACT: More than a dozen Nigerian Muslims were sentenced to death by stoning in 2007 for "sexual offenses" **such as adultery and homosexuality**. Many others were flogged by horsewhip for drinking alcohol. *Hopefully they drank enough not to feel anything.*

> "Gay Nigerians Face Sharia Death," BBC News, August 10, 2007, *www.news.bbc.co.uk*.

FACT: Afghanistan passed a new law this year allowing husbands to refuse food **to wives who refuse sex**. *Brilliant! Either men get laid or their wives lose weight. A win-win.*

❯ "New Afghan Law Does Not Allow Marital Rape . . . But Lets Men Refuse to Feed Wives Who Deny Them Sex, Says Cleric," MailOnline, April 17, 2009, www.dailymail.co.uk.

FACT: In Saudi Arabia, sodomy is considered a legal offense for which you can be **sentenced to death**. *I'm guessing there are a lot of things punishable by death in Saudi Arabia.*

❯ Nadya Labi, "The Kingdom in the Closet," *The Atlantic Monthly*, May 2007, www.theatlantic.com.

FACT: Despite the fact that **fourteen women a day die** because of domestic violence in Mexico, eight states have no laws against it. *Wait. Mexico has laws?*

❯ Laura Carlsen, "Women's Rights Eroding in Latin America," CounterPunch, March 12/13, 2005, www.counterpunch.org.

828

FACT: An eleven-year-old schoolgirl in New Delhi, India died at the hands of her teacher in 2009. **The student was beaten and forced to stand outside in the hot sun** for nearly two hours for her inability to say the English alphabet. *I hope that guy was fired.*

❯ "Delhi Girl in Coma after School Punishment Dies," *Times of India*, April 18, 2009, *www .timesofindia.indiatimes.com.*

829

FACT: When a flash flood swept a bus into a river near New Delhi, India in 1973, seventy-eight passengers drowned because they belonged to two separate castes and refused **to share a rope that would have saved their lives.** *India sounds fun. Let's go there.*

❯ Bruce Felton and Mark Fowler, *Felton & Fowler's More Best, Worst, and Most Unusual* (New York: Thomas Y. Crowell Company, 1976).

830

FACT: In 1974, the Public Works Minister for the state of Karnataka, India, informed the state legislature that **his political enemies had hired witches and sorcerers** to kill him. The state's chief minister ordered police to find the sorcerers. *"Round up the usual suspects!"*

❯ Chuck Shepherd, John J. Kohut, and Roland Sweet, *More News of the Weird* (New York: Plume Books, 1990).

831

FACT: The land that later became the country of Liberia was purchased by the American Colonization Society in 1822. They bought it for **a box of beads, several pairs of shoes, soap, some rum, and several spoons**, among other things. *They overpaid.*

❯ David Wallechinsky and Irving Wallace, *The People's Almanac* (Garden City, NY: Doubleday & Company, 1975).

FACT: Newborns in parts of northern Spain participate in an annual "baby-jumping" festival each spring, where a man dressed as the devil leaps over **as many as five or six infants on a mattress** at a time. The ancient rite is meant to drive away evil spirits. *Because evil spirits might traumatize babies, not unlike a man dressed as the devil leaping over them.*

> Editors Of Mental Floss, *Mental Floss Presents Instant Knowledge* (HarperCollins, 2005).

> "Spanish Village Holds Baby Jump," BBC News, May 25, 2008, *www.news.bbc.co.uk.*

FACT: Gloucestershire, England's annual cheese-rolling contest, where **contestants chase a seven-pound circular block of cheese** down a steep, bumpy hill, is a dangerous event. Contestants fall, break bones, and have even split their heads open. *Gloucestershire must be really boring.*

> Editors of Mental Floss, *Mental Floss Presents Instant Knowledge* (HarperCollins, 2005).

FACT: In 2007, a British teacher working in Sudan was arrested and charged with blasphemy for **letting a student call their teddy bear "Mohammed."** The teacher spent fifteen days in jail, but, under Sudanese law, could have been given forty lashes and three months in prison. *There go my vacation plans. I need somewhere a little less intense. I wonder if North Korea is nice this time of year?*

> "Reports: Sudan Arrests UK Teacher for Teddy Bear Blasphemy," CNN.com, November 26, 2007, *www.cnn.com.*

> "Mohamed Teddy Bear Teacher, Gillian Gibbons, Is Spared Lash but Gets 15 Days in Jail," Times Online, November 30, 2007, *www.timesonline .co.uk.*

FACT: In the 1800s, the Chinese considered strangling a less severe punishment than other forms of execution, since **the body would not be permanently disfigured**. *Because it's important to look your best for the worms.*

> Isaac Asimov, ed., *Isaac Asimov's Book of Facts* (Hastings House, 1979).

836

FACT: Dogs are considered food in some regions of East and Southeast Asia. 1 million dogs, 6,000 restaurants, and 10 percent of the population are involved in the dog meat industry in South Korea. *I wish some dog-eating South Koreans would move to my neighborhood.*

> William Saletan, "Wok the Dog," Slate.com, January 16, 2002, *www.slate.com.*

837

FACT: During famines that ravaged North Korea from 1995 to 1997, starving people commonly dug up bodies from fresh graves **to eat the meat**. *If I ever get that hungry, please shoot me. Thanks in advance.*

> Doug Struck, "Opening a Window on North Korea's Horrors," *Washington Post*, October 4, 2003, *www.washingtonpost.com.*

838

FACT: In 2008, Tanzanian witch doctors sanctioned a series of murders in which at least **twenty-nine albino children were hacked to death** for their body parts, believed by local customs to bring good luck. *Because being an albino didn't suck enough already.*

> Alex Duval Smith, "Albino Africans Live in Fear after Witch-Doctor Butchery," *The Observer*, November 16, 2008, *www.guardian.co.uk.*

FACT : The Parsee, a Zoroastrian sect in India, practice the ancient ritual of "sky-burial," where the dead bodies of loved ones are **placed on a high stone platform, stripped naked, and left for vultures**. Once picked clean, the bones are swept into a deep well. *As delightful as that sounds, I think I'll stick with cremation.*

❯ Tim McGirk, "Shortage of Vultures Threatens Ancient Culture: Many Parsees Are Questioning the Tradition of Sky Burial," *The Independent*, September 16, 1992, www.independent.co.uk.

FACT : Every year on the eve of December 5th, St. Nicholas Day, Austrians celebrate Krampus Night, when people dress up as Krampus, a demon, and roam the streets **looking for incorrigible children to beat with a stick**. The tradition is meant to encourage good behavior in kids. *Where do I sign up?*

❯ "Eight Truly Strange Christmas Customs," Mental_Floss, December 11, 2008, www.mentalfloss.com.

FACT : In Spain, a Catalonian Christmas tradition features **a statue of a little man pooping as part of the Nativity scene**. The entire town of Bethlehem, Mary, Joseph, and the baby Jesus are depicted—along with the little man, Caganer, doing his business in the corner. *We all get excited about Christmas. Some more than others.*

❯ "Eight Truly Strange Christmas Customs," Mental_Floss, December 11, 2008, www.mentalfloss.com.

FACT : In Dutch tradition, Sinterklass (Santa Claus) is accompanied by a slave named Zwarte Piet (Black Pete). Children are warned that if they don't behave, **Black Pete might take them back to Spain**. *And put them to work cleaning up all the Caganer shit in the Nativity scenes.*

❯ "Eight Truly Strange Christmas Customs," Mental_Floss, December 11, 2008, www.mentalfloss.com.

FACT: Ancient custom in Fiji dictated that when a man died, **his wives, slaves and friends should all be strangled**. *The custom was discontinued when they started running low on Fijians to kill.*

❯ "History Of Funeral Customs," Wisconsin Funeral Directors Association, *www.wyfda.org*.

FACT: India's Brahmin once practiced sati, or wife burning. When her husband died, a widow would dress in her finest clothing and **lie with his body on the funeral pyre** to be burned alive. *I hope sati isn't the same thing as satay. I've had satay, and come to think of it, it was a little charred.*

❯ Erin McHugh, *The 5 W's: Why? An Omnium-Gatherum of World Wars and World Series, Superstitions and Psychoses, the Tooth Fairy Rule and Turkey City Lexicon and Other of Life's Wherefores* (Sterling Publishing Company, 2005).

❯ Jyotsna Kamat, "The Origins of the Sati System," Kamat's Potpourri, *www.kamat.com*.

FACT: Chinese authorities are cracking down on **the practice of hiring strippers to perform at funerals**. Family and friends hire the women in order to draw more people to a funeral, since many Chinese believe that the larger the crowd, the more luck will come to relatives of the departed. *I've always heard that one should go out with a bang. You won't—you'll be dead—but maybe your friends will get laid in your honor.*

❯ "Take A Trip Around The World," My Funky Funeral, *www.myfunkyfuneral.com*.

❯ "China Acts on Funeral Strippers," BBC News, August 23, 2006, *www.news.bbc.co.uk*.

FACT: Among some North American Indian groups, a husband has the right to bite **or cut off** the nose of an adulterous wife. *Her nose isn't the problem.*

❯ George Monger, *Marriage Customs of the World: From Henna to Honeymoons* (ABC-CLIO, 2004).

FACT: According to Sharia (Islamic) law, **a girl should marry soon after puberty** to ensure that she is a virgin at her wedding; girls as young as nine or ten can be married off. *Their weddings are hideous, though; girls that age have absolutely no sense of style.*

> George Monger, *Marriage Customs of the World: From Henna to Honeymoons* (ABC-CLIO, 2004).

FACT: Hindu Laws of Manu state that a man should ideally be **three times older** than his wife; by this standard, the wife of a twenty-four-year-old man should be eight years old. *No bride should have to plan her wedding around Brownie meetings.*

> George Monger, *Marriage Customs of the World: From Henna to Honeymoons* (ABC-CLIO, 2004).

FACT: In Samoa, it was once custom for a virgin bride's hymen **to be broken publicly** by the village chief. *Sometimes the chief was her dad. Awkward.*

> George Monger, *Marriage Customs of the World: From Henna to Honeymoons* (ABC-CLIO, 2004).

FACT: Laos, Thailand, and Cambodia are working to build a golf course in the Emerald Triangle, an area where the three countries' borders meet, with nine holes in each country. The only problem: **the region is covered with minefields** left over from the Vietnam War and other regional conflicts. *"What's your handicap?" "Both legs below the knee and a hand."*

> Brent W. Ritchie and Daryl Adair, *Sport Tourism: Interrelationships, Impacts and Issues* (Channel View Publications, 2004).

CHAPTER 18

Do You Believe?

*Facts and Claims
about Aliens, Ghosts,
the Olsen Twins,
and Other Realms
of the Unexplained*

FACT: U.S. citizens are not legally permitted **to come into contact with extraterrestrials** or their vehicles, according to Title 14, section 1211 of the Code of Federal Regulations, implemented in 1969. *Does that include sex? What if you weren't aware of the law at the time?*

> Mary Bennett and David Percy, *Dark Moon: Apollo and the Whistle-Blowers* (Adventures Unlimited Press, 2001).

FACT: In July 1947, the U.S. Army Air Forces announced that **they had recovered a flying saucer** that crashed near Roswell Air Army Field in New Mexico. Within hours, however, the Army dismissed the statement, claiming the flying saucer was a misidentified weather balloon.

> Thomas J. Carey, Donald R. Schmitt, *Witness to Roswell: Unmasking the 60-Year Cover-Up* (Career Press, 2007), 27–29.

FACT: Since 1947, the U.S. government has

changed its explanation of the Roswell crash four times.

It remains one of the most a controversial, highly publicized UFO incidents in history. *At least among the sixty–seven people who actually believe that shit.*

> Thomas J. Carey, Donald R. Schmitt, *Witness to Roswell: Unmasking the 60-Year Cover-Up* (Career Press, 2007), 27–29.

FACT: Pine Bush, New York is known as the UFO capital of the East Coast, as many residents believe that **extraterrestrials have been frequenting their town for the last decade**. A support group was founded there in 1993 for locals who believe they've had encounters with these aliens. *"Hi, my name's Leo and I'm an alien shagger." (Group): "Hi, Leo."*

❯ Chris Gethard, Mark Moran, and Mark Sceurman, *Weird New York: Your Travel Guide to New York's Local Legends and Best Kept Secrets* (Sterling Publishing Company, 2005).

FACT: Ten percent of Americans claim **they have seen a ghost.** *They probably just saw one of the Olsen twins or Joan Rivers.*

❯ John E. Mack and others, *Unusual Personal Experiences: An Analysis of the Data from Three National Surveys Conducted by the Roper Organization* (Bigelow Holding Corp., 1992).

FACT: Guests at the Myrtles Plantation in St. Francisville, Louisiana should be prepared to see ghosts, a piano that plays itself, an oil portrait that becomes animated, and other unexplained phenomena. The bed and breakfast is **among America's most haunted houses**. *By its own PR staff, in a thinly veiled attempt to drum up business.*

❯ Joe Nickell, *Adventures in Paranormal Investigation* (University Press of Kentucky, 2007), 2.

FACT: The Tower of London is said to be full of ghosts, including that of the Countess of Salisbury, who, according to legend, was **hacked to death by her pursuing executioner** as she tried to escape. Some claim that spirits reenact the grisly 16th century event on Tower Green. *If any place in the world has ghosts, the Tower of London is it.*

❯ Lionel Fanthorpe and Patricia Fanthorpe, *The World's Most Mysterious Castles* (Dundurn Press Ltd., 2005), 184.

FACT: Some residents of Taos, New Mexico report hearing a constant, low-frequency hum in the desert air. Some believe the Taos Hum is caused by unusual acoustics; **others suspect a secret, sinister purpose**. The exact source of the hum is undetermined. *People who hear the hum are called Taos Hummers, which is also the name of a local gentlemen's club.*

❯ "Top Ten Unexplained Phenomena," LiveScience, *www.livescience.com*.

FACT: On February 11, 1859, **thousands of small fish rained over the village of Mountain Ash** in South Wales, one of several recorded instances of live fish falling from the sky. *Live until they hit the ground, that is.*

❯ John Michell, Bob Rickard, and Robert J. M. Rickard, *Unexplained Phenomena: A Rough Guide Special* (Rough Guides, 2000), 18.

❯ Susan Cosier, "It's Raining Fish," ScienceLine, September 17, 2006, *www.scienceline.org*.

FACT: In January 1877, **thousands of dark brown snakes** inexplicably covered Memphis, Tennessee for several days after a violent storm. Their origin was never determined. *I'm guessing their origin was all the outhouses that got turned over in the storm.*

❯ John Michell, Bob Rickard, and Robert J. M. Rickard, *Unexplained Phenomena: A Rough Guide Special* (Rough Guides, 2000), 37.

❯ John Clark, *Unnatural Phenomena: A Guide to the Bizarre Wonders of North America* (ABC-CLIO, 2005).

FACT: In 1891, a British sailor aboard the whaling ship *The Star of the East* disappeared while trying to kill a great sperm whale. After the whale was caught and its stomach cut open, **the ship's crew found the missing sailor curled up inside but still alive**. *He was rocking back and forth, whimpering, and sucking his thumb.*

❯ Stephen Wagner, "Seven of the Weirdest Human Enigmas," About.com, *www.paranormal.about.com*.

FACT: Poltergeist events usually originate with **a prepubescent "focal person."** *Even ghosts know not to tangle with a girl going through puberty.*

❯ James Houran and Rense Lange, *Hauntings and Poltergeists: Multidisciplinary Perspectives* (McFarland, 2001), 65.

 863

FACT: In 1962, a poltergeist harassed an Indianapolis grandmother, mother, and daughter by making noises, hurling objects, and biting them. The initial string of incidents stopped after two weeks, but **the poltergeist would return several times** over the following months. *Poltergeists are German, so they're very stubborn and not easily deterred.*

❯ James Houran and Rense Lange, *Hauntings and Poltergeists: Multidisciplinary Perspectives* (McFarland, 2001), 65.

 864

FACT: From 1920 to 1950, the Glastenbury Mountains area of Vermont saw **several disappearances**, including a college student who vanished while walking in the woods, a man who disappeared from a bus, and a child who went missing from his family's farm. The region has since become known as "The Bennington Triangle." *Bus Guy probably died in the bathroom and is still there. No one would notice the smell.*

❯ Joseph A. Citro, *Weird New England: Your Travel Guide to New England's Local Legends and Best Kept Secrets* (Sterling Publishing Company, 2005), 75.

865

FACT: In 1913, satirist **Ambrose Bierce disappeared in Mexico** after traveling there to witness Pancho Villa's revolution. Scholars believe that the seventy-one-year-old man was killed in the siege of Ojinaga, while others speculate that Bierce's final letters were a ruse and that he never actually went to Mexico, but instead committed suicide. *Maybe he went for a walk in the Glastenbury Mountains in Vermont.*

› Joe Nickell, *Unsolved History: Investigating Mysteries of the Past* (University Press of Kentucky, 2005).

866

FACT: During her 1937 attempt to fly around the world, pioneering female pilot Amelia Earhart disappeared over the Pacific Ocean. Military ships scoured a wide area for any sign of Earhart, her co-pilot, or the plane, but **none was ever found**. *Did she fly over Vermont?*

› "Top Ten Famous Disappearances," Time.com, *www.time.com.*

867

FACT: On June 11, 1962, inmates Frank Morris and Clarence and John Anglin escaped from Alcatraz prison during the night. Despite one of the largest manhunts since the Lindbergh kidnapping, **the trio were never found**. *Oh, they were found. By sharks. After they drowned.*

› "Top Ten Famous Disappearances," Time.com, *www .time.com.*

FACT: After James Dean was killed in a 1955 car accident, **remnant parts of his Porsche Spyder were said to be cursed.** Subsequent owners of those parts allegedly suffered numerous injuries and at least one was killed. Following a 1960 exhibition in Miami, the wreckage of the cursed car disappeared while en route to Los Angeles. *Did the route go through Vermont, by any chance?*

> Tom Ogden, *The Complete Idiot's Guide to Ghosts and Hauntings* (Alpha Books, 1999), 251.

FACT: George Herbert, one of the men who found the tomb of King Tutankhamen in 1922, died from tuberculosis and blood poisoning shortly after, and Cairo is said to have experienced **a city-wide power outage at the time of Herbert's death.** Both events are blamed on the "Curse of the Pharoah." *According to legend, the curse stems from the fact that Tut was buried in his jammies, something the ancient king would not have wanted public.*

> S. T. Joshi, *Icons of Horror and the Supernatural: An Encyclopedia of Our Worst Nightmares* (Greenwood Publishing Group, 2007).

FACT: Since the 1991 discovery of the Ice Man, several people connected to the research of the 5,000-year-old specimen have **met their death,** giving him his own version of "The Curse of Tutankhamen." *Similarly, the discovery of Vanilla Ice in the early 1990s has led to the deaths of several hundred people, all by their own hand.*

> Brian Haughton, *Hidden History: Lost Civilizations, Secret Knowledge, and Ancient Mysteries* (Career Press, 2007).

FACT: The Roman Catholic Church still believes in diabolical possession, and has at least **ten official exorcists** in America today. *Oh come on, the Catholic Church would never believe anything so crazy.*

> Robert Todd Carroll, *The Skeptic's Dictionary: A Collection of Strange Beliefs, Amusing Deceptions, and Dangerous Delusions* (John Wiley & Sons, 2003).

FACT: A San Francisco woman was pummeled to death in 1995 by Pentecostal ministers who believed she was possessed by demons. *She wasn't possessed, just Episcopalian.*

❯ Robert Todd Carroll, *The Skeptic's Dictionary: A Collection of Strange Beliefs, Amusing Deceptions, and Dangerous Delusions* (John Wiley & Sons, 2003).

FACT: In the fall of 1888, serial killer Jack the Ripper terrorized women in the slums of London, **disemboweling and decapitating victims**, most of whom were prostitutes. The murderer, thought to be a doctor because of his surgical precision, was never identified. *Or he might've been a Pentecostal minister.*

❯ Colin Wilson and Damon Wilson, *The Mammoth Encyclopedia of the Unsolved* (Carroll & Graf, 2000).

FACT: A creature called Spring-Heeled Jack terrorized London residents in the nineteenth century. **The orange-eyed beast scratched victims mercilessly** about the face and body, then leapt away with inhuman ability. *London police put Scooby-Doo and the gang on the case. They exposed the "monster" as a local prospector trying to scare away residents. And he would've gotten away with it, too, if it hadn't been for those meddling kids.*

❯ Matt Lake and Mark Moran, *Weird England: Your Travel Guide to England's Local Legends and Best Kept Secrets* (Sterling Publishing Company, 2007), 59.

FACT: From 1935 to 1938, a serial killer dubbed the Mad Butcher terrorized Cleveland residents with a series of murders. **Several victims died by decapitation**, one body was left in pieces on the shore of Lake Erie, and the rest were dismembered. The killer was never identified. *The only thing terrorizing Cleveland today— besides being Cleveland—is its NFL team, the Browns, who are left in pieces on the shore of Lake Erie every time they play at home.*

❯ Colin Wilson and Damon Wilson, *The Mammoth Encyclopedia of the Unsolved* (Carroll & Graf, 2000).

FACT: The legendary Jersey Devil, said to stalk the Pine Barrens of New Jersey, possesses a snake-like body, the head of a horse, bat-like wings, pig feet, and a forked tail. The creature has been blamed for **hundreds of deaths and mutilations of children and animals** since the mid-1700s. *You'd have to be the devil to want to hang out in New Jersey that long.*

> Beth Scott and Michael Norman, *Haunted America* (Macmillan, 2007), 176.

FACT: In 1924, a group of miners in Washington's Mount Saint Helens range were reportedly attacked by **eight-foot tall "Bigfoot" humanoids**, who pounded on the doors, walls, and roof of their cabin from dusk until dawn. *Or maybe they were just attacked by a bad batch of moonshine.*

> Colin Wilson and Damon Wilson, *The Mammoth Encyclopedia of the Unsolved* (Carroll & Graf, 2000).

FACT: The Moehau, New Zealand's version of Bigfoot, is said **to stab victims** with a long, bony finger. *At least they hope that's a finger.*

> Jonathan Maberry and David F. Kramer, *The Cryptopedia: A Dictionary of the Weird, Strange & Downright Bizarre* (Kensington Publishing, 2007), 30.

FACT: In 1996, rural villagers in Puerto Rico reported a rash of strange deaths among goats, whose **bodies were found completely drained of blood**, with puncture wounds on their necks. Locals blamed the Chupacabra, or "goat sucker," for the still unexplained incidents. *Such fanciful attributions are typical among the uneducated. More astute observers recognized these events for what they were: the work of vampires.*

> Robert Todd Carroll, *The Skeptic's Dictionary: A Collection of Strange Beliefs, Amusing Deceptions, and Dangerous Delusions* (John Wiley & Sons, 2003), 76.

FACT: Zambia is home to Pterodactyl-like flying monsters called kongamato, which are said to have bat-like wings with four- to seven-foot spans and a long, tapered jaw filled with sharp teeth. Zambian villagers believe that **to look upon the kongamato is death**. *Others know a hang-glider when they see it and are not afraid.*

❯ David Hatcher Childress, *Lost Cities & Ancient Mysteries of Africa & Arabia* (Adventures Unlimited Press, 1989).

FACT: South Americans are terrorized by minhocão, a giant worm said to be **seventy feet long with armor-plated skin**, a pig-like snout, and two tentacles on its head. Spotted in Uruguay and southern Brazil, the minhocão lives underground but occasionally surfaces, and many blame it for collapsed bridges, tunnels, and roadways. *Others know a train when they see it and are not afraid.*

❯ Jonathan Maberry and David F. Kramer, *The Cryptopedia: A Dictionary of the Weird, Strange & Downright Bizarre* (Kensington Publishing, 2007), 30.

FACT: In 1856, a pterodactyl was discovered in France by workers blasting rocks to build a railway. The beast used its **ten-foot wingspan** to stagger out into the sunlight before it let out a hoarse cry and died. Naturalists identified the creature and the rock strata as being millions of years old. *The hoarse cry was pterodactyl for, "Christ, not France."*

❯ David Hatcher Childress, *Lost Cities & Ancient Mysteries of Africa & Arabia* (Adventures Unlimited Press, 1989).

FACT: Crystal skulls found in Mexico have long fascinated archaeologists. One specimen, sold at Sotheby's in London in 1943, is known as the "Skull of Doom" and is said **to have mystical powers**, emit blue lights from its eyes, and crash computer hard drives. *Sounds more like the Skull Of Windows Vista.*

❯ Jane MacLaren Walsh, "Legend of the Crystal Skulls," *Archaeology*, May/June 2008, www.archaeology.org.

FACT: In 1938, an archeological expedition in China discovered hundreds of stone disks in caves in the Baian-Kara-Ula mountains, each measuring nine inches in diameter and etched with miniscule hieroglyphics that tell **a story of aircrafts from distant worlds crashing in the mountains**. The disks are believed to be thousands of years old. *And a possible indication of when man discovered opium.*

❯ Stephen Wagner, "The Dropa Stones," About.com, www.paranormal.about.com.

FACT: Scientists are unable to explain a number of fossils that have been found, including one of a human handprint in limestone and a human finger found in the Arctic in Canada, **both estimated to be 100–110 million years old**. *I'm unable to explain the number of fossils driving cars around my neighborhood; I thought being able to see over the steering wheel—or at all—was required for a driver's license.*

❯ Stephen Wagner, "Impossible Fossils," About.com, www.paranormal.about.com.

FACT: The Bermuda Triangle and the Oregon Vortex are believed by some to be connected to "magnetic vortexes," in which the walls between known and unknown dimensions are so thin **people can pass through them** and seemingly disappear. *Some people believe in the Tooth Fairy, too.*

❯ Nicholas R. Nelson, *Paradox: A Round Trip Through the Bermuda Triangle* (New Horizon, 1980).

887

FACT: Some experts theorize that **time travel may be possible** by passing through black holes. *Of course they do. No one will volunteer to go through a black hole and disprove them.*

> Kevin Bonsor, "How Time Travel Will Work," HowStuff Works.com, *www.science .howstuffworks.com.*

888

FACT: Other scientists believe that **wormholes have the greatest potential for time travel**; they could, in theory, permit travel light-years away from Earth in just a fraction of the time required for conventional space travel. *I wish this were true. I'd travel ahead in time and see what joke I came up with for this entry.*

> Kevin Bonsor, "How Time Travel Will Work," HowStuff Works.com, *www.science .howstuffworks.com.*

889

FACT: In December 1862, the merchant ship *Mary Celeste* was discovered adrift in the Atlantic Ocean, **unmanned and abandoned despite fair weather**. The crew was never found, nor was any clue as to how or why they vanished. *There can't possibly be any reasonable explanation; no, it could only be aliens or magic holes in the sea or the Chupacabra. Maybe even King Tut's curse.*

> Angus Konstam, *Ghost Ships: Tales of Abandoned, Doomed, and Haunted Vessels* (Globe Pequot, 2005), 78.

890

FACT: According to legend, a Dutch sea captain who wrecked near the Cape of Good Hope in the seventeenth century was punished for blasphemy and tempting fate **by having to relive his ordeal for all eternity**. The phantom of his ship, the *Flying Dutchman*, is said to haunt the waters off the Cape of Good Hope, bringing doom to any mariner who sees it. *Cape of Good Hope–I Don't-See-That-Sumbitch.*

> Angus Konstam, *Ghost Ships: Tales of Abandoned, Doomed, and Haunted Vessels* (Globe Pequot, 2005), 62.

891

FACT: From their home on the island of Crete, the Minoans once dominated the commerce and culture of the eastern Mediterranean. But in 1500 B.C., **their advanced civilization came to a catastrophic end**: temples and palaces fell into ruin, viaducts crumbled, and residents died or mysteriously disappeared. *Maybe the* Flying Dutchman *was vacationing in the Mediterranean and they saw him.*

❯ Frank Joseph, *The Destruction of Atlantis: Compelling Evidence of the Sudden Fall of the Legendary Civilization* (Inner Traditions/Bear & Company, 2004).

892

FACT: In 1918, the U.S. Navy collier **Cyclops vanished in the Bermuda Triangle** shortly after departing Barbados for the United States. Neither the ship nor her crew of 309 sailors was ever seen again. In an official statement, the U.S. government called the *Cyclops* disappearance "one of the most baffling mysteries in the annals of the Navy," as there were no reported German submarines in the area at that time. *No reported submarines. Isn't that sort of the idea of submarines?*

❯ "Seven Disappearances In the Bermuda Triangle," HowStuffWorks.com, *www.science.howstuffworks.com.*

893

FACT: In 1587, 120 English men and women settled on Roanoke Island off the coast of Virginia, but when the colony's governor traveled back to England for more financial and material resources for the foundering settlement and returned three years later, **the entire colony had vanished**. *That fast, huh? I think a glacier could disappear in three years.*

❯ "Top Ten Famous Disappearances," Time.com, *www.time.com.*

FACT: Dinosaurs evolved slowly on Earth over millions of years, surviving two distinct periods of mass extinction before dying out completely. The cause of their **final, ultimate extinction is still unknown**. *I think I've got it figured out. The Roanoke Island colonists, tired of waiting for their governor, hitched a ride on the* Mary Celeste, *then dinosaurs ate both the colonists and the crew of the* Mary Celeste *and stole their boat so they could sail to Crete and eat the Minoans, too. Then on their way back, the dinosaurs were hijacked by the Jersey Devil and the Chupacabra, who made them sail the ship around the Cape of Good Hope, where they all saw the* Flying Dutchman *and vanished forever.*

❯ "Mass Extinctions and The Evolution Of Dinosaurs," Science Daily, September 30, 2008, *www.sciencedaily.com.*

❯ Bonnie Sachatello-Sawyer and Don and Liza Charlesworth, "Why Did All Dinosaurs Become Extinct?" in *Dinosaurs: The Very Latest Information and Hands-On Activities From the Museum of the Rockies,* Liza Charlesworth and Bonnie Sachatello-Sawyer (Scholastic Professional, 1996).

FACT: Italian ten-year old Benedetto Supino made headlines in the 1980s for his apparent ability **to set objects on fire** just by looking at them. *This became a problem when a teenaged Ben started checking out girls' asses.*

❯ *Worlds Most Incredible Stories* (Barnes & Noble Publishing).

FACT: In the mid-nineteenth century, hunters in the Ochamchir region of Abkhazan captured **a feral hair-covered woman** with ape-like features who is believed to be a survivor of the Neanderthal race. *The woman, named Zana by scientists who studied her, was tamed, shaved, and taught how to speak before moving to America and becoming a celebrity. Now she goes by a different name: Kim Kardashian.*

❯ Colin Wilson and Damon Wilson, *The Mammoth Encyclopedia of the Unsolved* (Carroll & Graf, 2000).

897

FACT : In 1971, a man who called himself Dan "D.B." Cooper hijacked a plane, then parachuted out of it somewhere just north of Portland, Oregon, **clutching a bag filled with $200,000 in stolen cash.** He was never seen again. *Maybe he parachuted right into the Mount St. Helens volcano. Talk about bad luck.*

> "D.B. Cooper Redux," Federal Bureau Of Investigation, December 31, 2007, *www.fbi.gov.*

898

FACT : In December 1966, the leg and foot of a ninety-two-year-old man was discovered in his Pennsylvania home and the rest of the body burned to a pile of ashes. **Authorities could find no evidence of how the fire started,** and no other place in the home was burned. *There's only one logical explanation: God smote him. Maybe he was Amish and secretly had a TV.*

> "Spontaneous Human Combustion," HowStuffWorks.com, *www.science.howstuffworks .com.*

899

FACT : Danish anatomist Thomas Bartholin reported **the first spontaneous human combustion** in 1663, describing a Parisian woman who "went up in ashes and smoke" in her sleep. Her straw bed was not hurt by the fire. *She probably just set herself on fire. Living in 1663 would've sucked.*

> "Spontaneous Human Combustion," HowStuffWorks.com, *www.science.howstuffworks .com.*

900

FACT : In 1951, a widow in St. Petersburg, Florida was **found dead in a chair encircled by soot.** Her head was burned to the size of a teacup. Every other part of her body was charred to ash, save her backbone and a portion of her left foot. *Spontaneous combustion is one of the most burning mysteries of our time, an incendiary topic which often leads to heated debate and flying sparks on both sides of the issue. Thank you. I'm here all week.*

> "Spontaneous Human Combustion," HowStuffWorks.com, *www.science.howstuffworks .com.*

CHAPTER 19

We're Toast

Bad News about Our World and Why We're All Headed the Way of the Dodo

FACT: Every year approximately

500 meteorites strike the Earth.

The trick is knowing where.

> John S. Lewis, *Physics and Chemistry of the Solar System*, 2nd ed. (Academic Press, 2004).

FACT: **The moon is moving away from Earth** at a rate of 3.8 centimeters per year. *We have a guy up there measuring it. You should see his ruler.*

> Neil F. Comins, *Discovering the Essential Universe*, 4th ed. (Macmillan, 2008).

FACT: In 1908, an explosion 1,000 times stronger than the bombing of Hiroshima occurred near the Tunguska River in Russia, **most likely caused by a meteor or comet fragment** that burst prior to hitting Earth. The blast leveled 80 million trees in a matter of seconds. *They call it the Tunguska Event. A company picnic, prom, a pay-per-view boxing match—those are events. A comet flattening a gazillion acres sounds a little more eventful.*

> David Wallechinsky, *The New Book of Lists: The Original Compendium of Curious Information* (Canongate U.S., 2005), 397.
>
> "The Tunguska Event–100 Years Later," Nasa.com, *www.science.nasa.gov*.

FACT: Many of the gases that make up Earth's atmosphere are **slowly leaking into space**. Hot gases evaporate away, chemical reactions and particle collisions eject atoms and molecules, and asteroids and comets blast out chunks of atmosphere. *My dogs slowly leak gas, too. You don't hear anything, but you know it's there, trust me.*

> Kevin J. Zahnle, David C. Catling, and Alfred T. Kamajian, "Our Planet's Leaky Atmosphere," *Scientific American*, May 2009, www.scientificamerican.com.

FACT: In the future, **the depletion of hydrogen will dry out our oceans** and all but shut down geologic cycles that stabilize our planet's climate. Life might continue, but only in the polar regions. *The polar bears are ready. Eating seals gets old after a while.*

❯ Kevin J. Zahnle, David C. Catling, and Alfred T. Kamajian, "Our Planet's Leaky Atmosphere," *Scientific American*, May 2009, www.scientificamerican.com.

FACT: Within a million years, the star Eta Carinae could go supernova. Though it is 7,000 light years away from Earth, Eta Carinae's gamma ray burst could be powerful enough **to destroy the Earth's protective ozone layer** and kill all humans with radiation. *And then, finally, Abe Vigoda will die.*

❯ Peter Douglas Ward and Donald Brownlee, *The Life and Death of Planet Earth: How the New Science of Astrobiology Charts the Ultimate Fate of Our World* (Macmillan, 2003).

FACT: The Andromeda galaxy is **on a collision course** with our galaxy, speeding at 720,000 miles per hour. When the two likely collide in 3 billion years, the results will be catastrophic. *That gives you just enough time to get your driver's license renewed, so go ahead to the DMV now.*

❯ Peter Douglas Ward and Donald Brownlee, *The Life and Death of Planet Earth: How the New Science of Astrobiology Charts the Ultimate Fate of Our World* (Macmillan, 2003).

bad news about our world 287

908

FACT: About 7.6 billion years from now, **the sun will reach its maximum size**, extending 20 percent beyond Earth's orbit and shining 3,000 times brighter than it does today. In its final stage, the sun will collapse into a white dwarf and engulf the Earth. *Mark your calendars!*

❯ Peter Douglas Ward and Donald Brownlee, *The Life and Death of Planet Earth: How the New Science of Astrobiology Charts the Ultimate Fate of Our World* (Macmillan, 2003).

❯ David Appell, "The Sun Will Eventually Engulf Earth—Maybe," *Scientific American*, September 2008, *www.scientific american.com.*

909

FACT: Every year, **more than 28 million gallons of oil** from human activities pour into our rivers, lakes, and streams, an amount more than twice the size of the Exxon Valdez oil spill. *Human activities = oil changes and frying chicken.*

❯ "Why Are Our Oceans in Trouble?" Environmental Defense Fund, August 19, 2005, *www.edf.org.*

910

FACT: 80 percent of the waste that humans produce **ends up in our oceans**, including everything from solid garbage and sewage to fertilizers, oil, and toxic chemicals. *This is why I never feel guilty about pissing in the ocean. Like it's going to hurt anything.*

❯ "Problems: Ocean pollution," World Wildlife Federation, February 29, 2008, *www.panda.org.*

911

FACT: Raw, untreated sewage flows into the ocean in many areas of the world, including **80 percent of urban sewage** that ends up in the Mediterranean. *If you're reading this on the toilet, congrats, you just made a nice float for some kid in Crete.*

❯ "Problems: Ocean pollution," World Wildlife Federation, February 29, 2008, *www.panda.org.*

FACT : For decades, circulating ocean currents have picked up trash from shorelines and boats and corralled it into **two vast masses of decaying, soupy waste**, which have been dubbed the Great Pacific Garbage Patch. *This spawned the late '80s toy craze, Great Pacific Garbage Patch Kids, which shot decaying, soupy candy out of their noses and butts when squeezed.*

❯ "View: The Truth about Trash," *Scientific American*, January 9, 2009, *www.sciam.com.*

FACT : About **half of the carbon dioxide** emitted by humans in the last 200 years has been absorbed by the Earth's oceans, causing fish migration routes to alter, sea levels to rise, coastal erosion to intensify, and currents that move nutrients upward from the deep sea to become disturbed. *If there were oceans on other planets, we could send it there, but we haven't found any yet.*

❯ Dan Shapley, "Natural Resources Being Depleted at Record Rates," The Daily Green, September 13, 2007, *www .thedailygreen.com.*

FACT : If emission rates continue as projected, the level of mercury in the Pacific Ocean will **increase 50 percent** by the year 2050. *The level of Mercury cars in the ocean is increasing, too, as about thirty-eight people a day drive them off a pier because they're sick of having to fix that shit. Most collect the insurance money and buy a Toyota.*

❯ Dan Shapley, "Natural Resources Being Depleted at Record Rates," The Daily Green, September 13, 2007, *www .thedailygreen.com.*

❯ "How Mercury Emissions Reach Tuna And Other Seafood, And Why Mercury Contamination Is Likely To Worsen," Science Daily, May 3, 2009, *www.sciencedaily.com.*

FACT : Acid rain is caused by both natural sources like volcanoes and decaying vegetation, and artificial sources like emissions from fossil fuel combustion. It threatens both animal and plant life through **acidification of lakes and streams** and damage to forests and forest soils. *The brown acid rain is particularly bad, so avoid it. It's giving a lot of people bad trips.*

❯ "Effects of Acid Rain," U.S. Environmental Protection Agency, *www.epa.gov.*

FACT: China's Gobi desert is expanding at **the rate of over 10,000 square kilometers per year**, overtaking productive soil and threatening the livelihood of many villages. *The ants are loving it, though.*

❯ Larry West, "Scholars Predict 50 Million Environmental Refugees by 2010," About.com, *www.environment.about.com.*

FACT: Experts say more than 1,000 square kilometers of productive land is **lost annually** in Morocco, Tunisia, and Libya to desertification. *Morocco, Tunisia, and Libya have productive land?*

❯ Larry West, "Scholars Predict 50 Million Environmental Refugees by 2010," About.com, *www.environment.about.com.*

FACT: The state of Louisiana loses **about sixty-five square kilometers** of productive land every year to erosion by the sea. *Louisiana has productive land?*

❯ Larry West, "Scholars Predict 50 Million Environmental Refugees by 2010," About.com, *www.environment.about.com.*

FACT: In Alaska, **more than 200 communities** are threatened by rising sea levels that cause tides to extend about three meters further inland each year. *Alaska has 200 communities?*

❯ Larry West, "Scholars Predict 50 Million Environmental Refugees by 2010," About.com, *www.environment.about.com.*

920

FACT: New Zealand has agreed to accept **the almost 12,000 citizens** of the Pacific island state of Tuvalu if rising sea levels make the island uninhabitable. *New Zealanders don't want to die alone when rising sea levels make their islands uninhabitable, too.*

❯ Larry West, "Scholars Predict 50 Million Environmental Refugees by 2010," About.com, *www.environment.about.com.*

921

FACT: Just a slight increase in sea levels could **submerge most of the Maldives**. President Mohamed Nasheed has proposed to relocate the entire 300,000 person nation to India, Sri Lanka, or Australia. *If Sri Lanka is safer than where you live, you need to move anyway.*

❯ Larry West, "Scholars Predict 50 Million Environmental Refugees by 2010," About.com, *www.environment.about.com.*

❯ Nicholas Schmidle, "Wanted: A New Home for My Country," *New York Times*, May 8, 2009, *www.nytimes.com.*

922

FACT: Category 4 and 5 hurricanes have **doubled in number** in the last thirty years. *In case you haven't watched the news. Ever.*

❯ K. Emanuel, "Increasing destructiveness of tropical cyclones over the past 30 years," *Nature*, August 4, 2005, 686–688, "What is Global Warming?" An Inconvenient Truth, *www.climatecrisis.net.*

923

FACT: Deaths caused by global warming will **double in the next twenty-five years** to 300,000 people annually. *Dying people often complain of being cold; I wonder if that happens when you die of global warming.*

❯ World Health Organization, "What is Global Warming?" An Inconvenient Truth, *www .climatecrisis.net.*

924

FACT: Libya recorded the Earth's **highest temperature** in 1922: 136°F (58°C). *But it was a dry heat.*

> "Fun Science Facts You Didn't Know," High Tech Science, *www.hightechscience.org.*

925

FACT: Over the past decade, ice flow off Greenland's glaciers has **more than doubled** due to global warming, resulting in higher sea levels. *Hey, Greenland—what the hell? Knock it off already.*

> W. Krabill and others, "Greenland Ice Sheet: Increased coastal thinning," *Geophysical Research Letters,* December 28, 2004, "What is Global Warming?" An Inconvenient Truth, *www.climatecrisis.net.*

926

FACT: Global warming could cause shelf ice in Greenland and Antarctica to melt, resulting in a global rise in sea levels by **more than twenty feet**, with devastating effects for coastal areas worldwide. *The other night my daughter and I were looking at her globe. She pointed to Greenland and asked, "What's that?" "Greenland," I said. "Greenland? Then why is it all white?" she asked. That's a good question.*

> W. Krabill and others, "Greenland Ice Sheet: Increased coastal thinning," *Geophysical Research Letters,* December 28, 2004, "What is Global Warming?" An Inconvenient Truth, *www.climatecrisis.net.*

927

FACT: Thanks to global warming, the Arctic Ocean could be **free of ice** in summer by 2050. *What if your name was "Global Warming"? That would suck. You'd get blamed for everything.*

> W. Krabill and others, "Greenland Ice Sheet: Increased coastal thinning," *Geophysical Research Letters,* December 28, 2004, "What is Global Warming?" An Inconvenient Truth, *www.climatecrisis.net.*

> Impact of a Warming Arctic: Arctic Climate Impact Assessment (Cambridge, UK: Cambridge University Press, 2004), "What is Global Warming?" An Inconvenient Truth, *www.climatecrisis.net.*

928

FACT: At least 279 plant and animal species are **moving closer to the Earth's poles**, a response to global warming. *I'm guessing the animal species will probably get there before the plants.*

> W. Krabill and others, "Greenland Ice Sheet: Increased coastal thinning," *Geophysical Research Letters*, December 28, 2004, "What is Global Warming?" An Inconvenient Truth, *www.climatecrisis.net.*

> David Bjerklie, "Feeling the Heat," *Time Magazine*, March 26, 2006, "What is Global Warming?" An Inconvenient Truth, *www.climatecrisis.net.*

929

FACT: Arica, Chile is **the driest place on Earth** with an average of 0.03 inches (0.76 millimeters) of rain per year. *Barely edging out my wife's pot roast.*

> Robert Roy Britt, "101 Earth Facts," Space.Com, *www.space.com.*

930

FACT: The 1964 Great Alaskan Earthquake created **disastrous tsunamis** from British Columbia to San Francisco. The ground was pushed up thirty feet in the air in parts of Alaska; in others, it collapsed. *Alaska sounds like a great place to live. No, really.*

> "Eight of the Most Devastating Deadly Land Disasters," WebEcoist, *www.webecoist.com.*

931

FACT: The 2008 Great Sichuan Earthquake in China was felt **as far away as Shanghai**, over 1,000 miles from the quake's epicenter. Nearly 70,000 people died, and more than 118,000 were seriously injured. Thousands of Chinese are still missing and presumed dead. *Ya think?!*

> "Eight of the Most Devastating Deadly Land Disasters," WebEcoist, *www.webecoist.com.*

FACT: In 1980, volcanic Mount St. Helens in Washington violently exploded, killing fifty-seven people and flattening 200 square miles of surrounding forestland. It was **the most deadly, economically destructive volcanic event** in American history. *Unless you count what the stock market has done in the last year, which I do, because I'm still dumb enough to look at my monthly IRA statement.*

FACT: When Colombia's volcanic mountain Nevado del Ruiz exploded in 1984, **the resulting mudslide buried the nearby town of Armero**, killing more than 23,000 people. *No one heard it coming?*

FACT: In 1902, **a landslide of boiling mud spilled into the sea** on the island of Martinique, causing a tsunami that killed hundreds. Three days later, Mount Pelee exploded, obliterating the town of St. Pierre with an avalanche of hot lava. Of 30,000 residents, only two survived. *The boiling mud would've been enough to send me packing. Why was anyone around three days later for the volcano eruption?*

FACT: More than 2,000 people died in 1960 when a tsunami pounded the coast of Chile with **a massive thirty-foot wave**, flooding 500 coastal miles and triggering the largest earthquake in the twentieth century. *The real tragedy is that all those people missed the '60s, which were a blast.*

936

FACT: At least one group of researchers predicts that **the world's production of oil will peak** in 2011. The sharp decline in oil supplies that will follow will drastically affect the world economy. *That will be fun.*

❯ Daniel Howden, "World Oil Supplies Are Set to Run Out Faster than Expected, Warn Scientists," *The Independent*, June 14, 2007, www.independent.co.uk.

937

FACT: The 1991 eruption of Mount Pinatubo on the Philippine island of Luzon caused **a sulfuric haze around the world**, a global drop in temperatures, and a spike in ozone damage. Most residents were evacuated before billions of tons of ash, magma, and debris destroyed the region. *The worldwide drop in temperature was quickly corrected by global warming, though, so no worries there.*

❯ Matt Rosenberg, "Mount Pinatubo Eruption," About.com, August 5, 2007, www.geography.about.com.

938

FACT: The world's oceans contain enough salt to cover every continent to a depth of **almost 500 feet**. *Which is the same amount needed to make grits edible.*

❯ "Fifty Weird Science Tidbits & Oddities," Science News Review, February 11, 2009, www.sciencenewsreview.com.

FACT: There are **909 billion tons of coal reserves** worldwide, enough for 155 years worth of energy. But using coal as an energy source would only increase global warming. *Burn the coal; we need it. They can worry about what to do in 155 years. None of us will be here anyway.*

❯ Daniel Howden, "World Oil Supplies Are Set to Run Out Faster than Expected, Warn Scientists," *The Independent*, June 14, 2007, www.independent.co.uk.

FACT: Ethanol from corn offers an alternative to oil, but **ethanol production negatively impacts the environment** because corn requires so much space to grow. *We have the room. What the hell else are we gonna do with Iowa and Nebraska?*

❯ Daniel Howden, "World Oil Supplies Are Set to Run Out Faster than Expected, Warn Scientists," *The Independent*, June 14, 2007, www.independent.co.uk.

FACT: Twenty-two million hectares of tropical forest and savanna in South America are on course **to be displaced by rapidly expanding soybean plantations** in the next twenty years, resulting in the destruction of tropical ecosystems, the acceleration of climate change, and the elimination of biodiversity. *I'm not sure what a hectare is, but that doesn't sound good.*

❯ Dan Shapley, "Natural Resources Being Depleted At Record Rates," The Daily Green, September 13, 2007, www.thedailygreen.com.

❯ "Global Ecological Emergency: Brazil Must Succeed in Keeping Soybeans Out of Amazon," Action Alert, EcoEarth.info, www.ecoearth.info.

FACT: Four years of deforestation shares **the same the carbon footprint** as every air flight from the dawn of aviation thru 2025. *Deforestation doesn't give you free soft drinks, though.*

❯ Debra Ronca, "How Deforestation Works," HowStuffWorks.com, www.science.howstuffworks.com.

943

FACT: Biologists believe that the flora and fauna of rainforests holds the cures to many diseases. Rainforests cover only 7 percent of the Earth but are inhabited by 50 percent of the plant and animal species of the world—**species becoming extinct** as deforestation shrinks rainforest areas. *Deforestation is named for DeForest Kelley, famed tree–cutter and actor who played Dr. Leonard "Bones" McCoy on* Star Trek.

> Debra Ronca, "How Deforestation Works," HowStuffWorks.com, *www.science.howstuff works.com.*

944

FACT: Burning rainforests account for **roughly 30 percent** of the carbon dioxide released in the air. *We shouldn't burn the rain-forests. We need to save them to burn when we run out of oil and need the heat.*

> Tom Harris, "How Rainforests Work," HowStuffWorks.com, *www.science.howstuffworks .com.*

945

FACT: Burping cows emit up to **100 gallons of methane gas per animal each day**, joining other livestock to create nearly a third of man-made methane emissions annually. Methane is a greenhouse gas that warms Earth's atmosphere at twenty-one times the rate of carbon dioxide. *You don't even want to know about their farts.*

> Bettina Gartner, "How Better-Fed Cows Could Cool the Planet," *Christian Science Monitor,* August 16, 2007, *www.csmonitor.com.*

946

FACT: Depletion of the Earth's ozone layer aggravates health effects caused by exposure to UV radiation. Even a 10 percent loss of ozone could cause an additional **300,000 skin cancers** and up to 1.75 million more cases of cataracts worldwide every year. *It's easier to get a tan now, though.*

> "Ultraviolet Radiation and Health," World Health Organizations, *www.who.int.*

FACT: One gallon of used motor oil can ruin approximately **1 million gallons of fresh water**. *Hello? That's why we seal up the barrels before we toss them in the ocean.*

❯ "Why We Should Recycle Used Oil," L.A. County Department Of Public Works, *www.dpw.lacounty.gov.*

FACT: In 1979 Skylab, the first U.S. space station, **crashed to Earth** in pieces. *So did David Bowie, but nobody cared about that, either.*

❯ "Fun Science Facts You Didn't Know," High Tech Science, *www.hightechscience.org.*

FACT: Because of time zones, if you fly from London to New York by Concorde, you can arrive **two hours before you departed**. *I knew the Concorde was fast, but damn.*

❯ "Fun Science Facts You Didn't Know," High Tech Science, *www.hightechscience.org.*

FACT: A bolt of lightning discharges up to **100 million volts** and 30,000 amperes of electricity, and at 54,000°F (30,000°C), is roughly six times hotter than the sun. *That's why it's not a bad idea to always carry Neosporin and a Band-Aid with you.*

❯ "Fun Science Facts You Didn't Know," High Tech Science, *www.hightechscience.org.*

CHAPTER 20

What the—?!

*The Worst of
the Worst and
the Weirdest of
the Weird*

951

FACT: In 2008, **an Illinois woman had her big toe chewed off** by her pet miniature dachshund while napping. Because of diabetes-related nerve damage in her extremities, the woman felt nothing and slept through the attack. *Maybe her feet smelled like cheese. Mine sometimes do.*

> ❯ "'Beloved Dachshund' Chews Off Owner's Toe," Reuters, July 4, 2008, www.news.com.au.

> ❯ "Sausage Dogs Are the Most Aggressive," *Telegraph UK*, July 5, 2008, www.telegraph.co.uk.

952

FACT: Freshly laundered towels might smell and look nice, but if they were washed with underwear, **they could be contaminated with feces.** *That's the kind of underwear you just throw out, not wash.*

> ❯ Philip M. Tierno, *The Secret Life of Germs: What They Are, Why We Need Them, and How We Can Protect Ourselves Against Them* (Simon & Schuster, 2004), 93.

953

FACT: Some of the most prestigious libraries in the United States have **books bound in human skin.** *They don't have any skin magazines, though, so don't ask.*

> ❯ M.L. Johnson, "Some of Nation's Best Libraries Have Books Bound in Human Skin," *Boston Globe*, January 7, 2006, www.boston.com.

954

FACT: In 2005, a ten-year-old boy in Perth, Australia **lost both hands and a foot** when a brick wall supporting a basketball goal gave way when he attempted a slam-dunk. *He got gimp.*

> ❯ "Boy Who Lost Three Limbs Awake and Smiling," *Sydney Morning Herald*, March 30, 2005, www.smh.com.au.

955

FACT: There are an estimated **27 million slaves in the world today**, more than were taken from Africa during the four-century long transatlantic slave trade. *Where the hell are they? My car could use a wash.*

> Andrew Cockburn, "21st Century Slaves," *National Geographic, www.ngm.national geographic.com.*

956

FACT: In 1970, a dead sperm whale on an Oregon beach was **blown up with dynamite** in an attempt to get rid of the decomposing corpse. Flying debris from the blast destroyed the roof of a nearby car, and onlookers were covered with whale particles. *Really? Because it sounds like such a great idea. Who came up with it, Gilligan or the Skipper?*

> "A Brief History of Actual Exploding Animals," WebEcoist, September 5, 2008, *www.webecoist.com.*

957

FACT: Blood in stool or diarrhea can be a sign of necrotizing enterocolitis, a condition which causes **the lining of the intestinal wall to die** allowing tissue to fall off. The disease has a death rate of almost 25 percent. *Because diarrhea wasn't fun enough already.*

> Jenifer K. Lehrer, "Necrotizing Enterocolitis," Medical Encyclopedia, Medline Plus, U.S. National Library of Medicine and National Institutes of Health, May 3, 2007, *www.nlm .nih.gov.*

FACT: Two minutes after lethal injection drugs were administered to Raymond Landry during his 1988 execution in Texas, **the syringe ejected from his vein**, causing deadly chemicals to spray across the room toward witnesses. *Ray wasn't around to see it, unfortunately, and missed all the excitement.*

> Russ Kick, *Disinformation Book of Lists: Subversive Facts and Hidden Information in Rapid-fire Format* (The Disinformation Company, 2004).

FACT: The Amazon's Uape Indians mix their recently cremated relatives' ashes with alcohol **to be imbibed** by all members of the family as they share fond memories of the deceased. *"Who wants another shot of Grandma?"*

> eBizarre, *www.ebizarre.com*.

FACT: In one case involving the lethal use of a Taser, a doctor suffered an epileptic seizure after crashing his car, and was repeatedly shocked when he failed to comply with an officer's commands. The seizure was to blame for his lack of response, and **the Taser shocks resulted in death**. *Not the cop's fault. He kept asking the doc if he wanted another jolt, and the doc kept nodding his head yes.*

> "Tasers—Potentially Lethal and Easy to Abuse," Amnesty International report, December 16, 2008, *www.amnesty.org*.

302   the worst of the worst and the weirdest of the weird

961

FACT: There are **four sunken nuclear submarines** at the bottom of the Atlantic Ocean. One, located near Bermuda, holds sixteen live nuclear warheads. *No wonder Bermuda's a little uptight.*

❯ Legends of America, *www.legendsofamerica.com.*

 962

FACT: Records show that money lenders in 1124 had **their hands and testicles cut off** by order of Henry I. *And you thought 2008 was a bad year for banks.*

❯ Jean Kellaway, *The History of Torture and Execution: From Early Civilization through Medieval Times to the Present* (Globe Pequot, 2003).

 963

FACT: In 1581, writer John Stubs was convicted of sedition for insulting Queen Elizabeth and **sentenced to public mutilation**, where his right hand was chopped off and the wound cauterized with a hot iron. *His right arm became known as Stubs' stub.*

❯ Jean Kellaway, *The History of Torture and Execution: From Early Civilization through Medieval Times to the Present* (Globe Pequot, 2003),

 964

FACT: In 1535, French Huguenot **Antoine Poile had his tongue pierced and attached to his cheek** before being burnt alive. *People pay good money for that now. Piercing, that is. Not the burning alive part.*

❯ Jean Kellaway, *The History of Torture and Execution: From Early Civilization through Medieval Times to the Present* (Globe Pequot, 2003).

965

FACT: In Russia during the time of Ivan the Terrible, it was customary for captured highwaymen **to have their heels cut off or crushed** and be dragged along by their injured ankles. *Okay, but why did they call him Ivan the Terrible?*

> Jean Kellaway, *The History of Torture and Execution: From Early Civilization through Medieval Times to the Present* (Globe Pequot, 2003).

966

FACT: In sixteenth to nineteenth century England and Scotland, women deemed "troublesome and angry" could be subjected to the "scold's bridle," **a metal helmet with a gagging strap** that prevented them from speaking. *And . . . ?*

> Jean Kellaway, *The History of Torture and Execution: From Early Civilization through Medieval Times to the Present* (Globe Pequot, 2003).

967

FACT: In medieval England, women were punished with the ducking stool, **a dangling seat on a rope used to drop them into water**. The shock of the cold water and the length of the ducking were often enough to kill. *The good news is that the ducking baptized them as well, so they all went to heaven when they drowned.*

> Jean Kellaway, *The History of Torture and Execution: From Early Civilization through Medieval Times to the Present* (Globe Pequot, 2003).

968

FACT: The Iron Maiden was **an upright coffin with interior spikes used in medieval torture**. The victim was forced inside and, as the door was closed, had his lungs and eyes pierced by the spikes. But the prongs were too short to kill instantly, so the prisoner lingered in agony for hours before expiring. *The device is no longer used; now we have the music of Iron Maiden to torture us instead.*

> Jean Kellaway, *The History of Torture and Execution: From Early Civilization through Medieval Times to the Present* (Globe Pequot, 2003).

969

FACT: During six centuries of church-sanctioned witch hunts, an estimated **100,000 people died from torture** and being burned at the stake. *That number is probably high, though, so it's not as bad as it sounds.*

> Jean Kellaway, *The History of Torture and Execution: From Early Civilization through Medieval Times to the Present* (Globe Pequot, 2003).

970

FACT: As many as **900 people died during witch hunts** in the Lorraine region of France from 1580 to 1595. Some villages cleared of "witches" were left with just a single female resident. *And she probably liked it. Women can be very competitive.*

> Jean Kellaway, *The History of Torture and Execution: From Early Civilization through Medieval Times to the Present* (Globe Pequot, 2003).

971

FACT: Pressing to death was a form of torture used in fifteenth century England in which the offender was laid naked with a board across his torso. **Iron weights were then piled on the board** each day, until the pressure was excruciating and often fatal. *I'd take my sandwich and say, "Hey, mind if I stick this in there?" Love those pressed sandwiches.*

> Jean Kellaway, *The History of Torture and Execution: From Early Civilization through Medieval Times to the Present* (Globe Pequot, 2003).

972

FACT: Just while making the bed, the average person **traverses four miles** in a year. *That's one huge bed.*

> eBizarre, *www.ebizarre.com.*

FACT: Two thousand years ago, the condemned in the Moche civilization in Peru **suffered shockingly brutal execution methods**, including being skinned alive, decapitated, drained of blood, or bound tightly and picked to death by vultures. *That's harsh, all right, but I give them points for creativity.*

❯ Jean Kellaway, *The History of Torture and Execution: From Early Civilization through Medieval Times to the Present* (Globe Pequot, 2003).

FACT: Being unmarried can shorten a man's life **by ten years**. *Being married can shorten it by a lot more.*

❯ eBizarre, www.ebizarre.com.

FACT: The pillory was a common punishment in colonial America and eighteenth century England and France. Similar to stocks, the pillory held offenders in place **as onlookers pummeled them** with rocks, garbage, food, feces, dead animals, and more, sometimes to death. In 1756, four Englishmen died after just one hour in the pillory. *That would be fun, actually. To throw stuff, I mean. Not to be in the pillory.*

❯ Jean Kellaway, *The History of Torture and Execution: From Early Civilization through Medieval Times to the Present* (Globe Pequot, 2003).

FACT: In Los Angeles, California in 1970, authorities discovered "Genie," a feral child who had spent ten years **locked alone in a room by her abusive father**. At thirteen, Genie could barely walk and talk, was not toilet-trained, could not chew solid food, and could not focus her eyes further than twelve feet. *Genie's dad—now there's a guy who needs to be pilloried. I'd bring baseballs and bricks.*

❯ "Genie: A Modern-Day Wild Child," in *Learning About Learning,* Great Explorations in Math and Science series from the Lawrence Hall of Science, (The Regents of the University of California), FeralChildren.com, www.feralchildren.com.

977

FACT: Ingested cocaine may lead **to severe bowel gangrene** caused by reduced blood flow. *Gangrene is defined as "necrosis or death of soft tissue . . . usually followed by decomposition and putrefaction," so the bowels are the ideal place for it.*

❯ "Cocaine," *Psychology Today*, www.psychologytoday.com.

❯ "Cocaine," Dictionary.com, www.dictionary.reference.com.

978

FACT: A five-year-old English girl nearly died in early 2009 after she had swallowed so much of her own hair that **it became a rope-like structure** that wrapped around her organs—a condition known as Rapunzel Syndrome. *"Hair today, gone tomorrow."*

❯ Luke Salkeld and Alison Smith Squire, "The Real-Life Rapunzel: The Moral of Millie's Grim Tale Is, Don't Chew Your Hair," *Daily Mail*, May 23, 2009, www.daily mail.co.uk.

979

FACT: A 2009 study revealed that young male children of busy or neglectful parents can feel more closely bonded **to characters from the television shows they watch**, like Bob the Builder, than their fathers. *Just another reason not to let your kids watch Barney.*

❯ "Boys Develop Closer Bonds with Bob the Builder Than with Parents," *Daily Mail*, May 25, 2009, www.telegraph.co.uk.

980

FACT: Employees at a New York City game store wound up trapped inside for hours when **thousands of bees** swarmed around the entrance in 2009. *There was a lot of buzz about a new game that had just arrived.*

❯ Associated Press, "Buzz Off! Bee Swarm Traps Workers in NY Game Store," May 23, 2009, www.newsvine.com.

981

FACT: "Jigsaw Kid" is the nickname of a six-year-old UK girl born with two left lungs, five spleens, a diseased liver, a hole in her heart, and her stomach on the wrong side. **Most of her organs face front-to-back**, and when her heart pumps rapidly, you can see it beating through her back. *On the bright side, I'm sure she loves being called "Jigsaw Kid." Children aren't sensitive to that sort of thing at all.*

> ❯ "'Jigsaw Kid' Lives with Jumbled Up Internal Organs," *Daily Mail*, May 22, 2009, *www.telegraph.co.uk.*

982

FACT: In 2009, doctors in Izhevsk, Russia found a branch from **a fir tree germinated inside the lungs of a man** suffering from seizures and coughing up blood. *I say leave it in there, let it grow. He could save some money at the holidays and be his own Christmas tree.*

> ❯ "Fir Tree Grows Inside Man's Lungs," Pravda.Ru, April 15, 2009, *www.bizarrenews.org.*

 983

FACT: One percent of the entire population in Greenland **reside in one apartment building** called Blok P. *Luckily, Greenland's population is only like, 100 people, so Blok P is really just a one-bedroom flat.*

> ❯ eBizarre, *www.ebizarre.com.*

 984

FACT: In 2009, **a Black Angus calf was born in Colorado with seven legs**, two spines, and two hooves on one leg. The calf only survived for ten minutes. *I hope they ate it. That's a lot of veal.*

> ❯ "Calf In Colorado Born With 7 Legs, 2 Spines," *Steamboat Pilot & Today*, May 23, 2009, *www.kirotv.com.*

985

FACT: A Wyoming man saved his dog's life in 2009 when he sucked venom from a rattlesnake bite **out his dog's nose**. The man required four vials of antivenin—at $3,500 a pop. *Know what would suck? If the dog got hit by a car the next day and died. I bet that guy would be pissed, not about the money so much as the mouthful of dog snot.*

> "Man Saves Dog By Sucking Venom From Nose," *Casper Star-Tribune*, May 22, 2009, *www.trib.com.*

986

FACT: The **Vatican started a Facebook page** in 2009, gathering 45,000 contacts and 500,000 page views within days of launch. *The "How Well Do You Know Saint Eusebius of Vercelli?" quiz is a big hit.*

> Ariel David, "Vatican Launches Facebook Application," kirotv.com, May 22, 2009, *www.kirotv.com.*

987

FACT: A twenty-three-year-old New Zealand mother lost 88 pounds and suffered a heart attack **after drinking nothing but Red Bull**—from ten to fourteen cans a day—for eight months. *Her friends call her "The Great Cornholio," after the beloved* Beavis & Butt-Head *character.*

> "Traces of Cocaine Found in Red Bull Cola," NEWS.com .au, May 26, 2009, *www.news .com.au.*

988

FACT: A 2009 study by a leading fossil expert suggests that **modern humans hunted and ate Neanderthals**, a sturdy species that mysteriously disappeared 30,000 years ago as modern humans migrated to Europe. *We preferred to eat wild buffalo back then, but Neanderthals were slower.*

> Robin McKie, "How Neanderthals Met a Grisly Fate: Devoured by Humans," *The Observer*, May 17, 2009, *www .guardian.co.uk.*

FACT: Protein is rare in some parts of Kenya, so **natives drink cow's blood** for nourishment instead. *I think I'd rather eat a Neanderthal.*

> Arkady Leokum and K. R. Hobbie, *The Little Giant Book of Weird & Wacky Facts* (Sterling Publishing Company, 2005).

FACT: The world's largest mammal, the blue whale, also has the largest penis in the animal kingdom, measuring about **ten feet long and a foot in diameter**. *I bet it works like a rudder. They can steer with it.*

> Shane Mooney, *Useless Sexual Trivia: Tastefully Prurient Facts about Everyone's Favorite Subject* (Simon & Schuster, 2000).

FACT: "Dork" is the proper term for **whale penis**, hence the derogatory term. *Calling someone "whale dick" just doesn't have the same ring to it.*

> Shane Mooney, *Useless Sexual Trivia: Tastefully Prurient Facts about Everyone's Favorite Subject* (Simon & Schuster, 2000).

FACT: Medorthophobia is **the fear of an erect penis**. *Must be a female thing, because guys are only afraid of the opposite problem.*

> Shane Mooney, *Useless Sexual Trivia: Tastefully Prurient Facts about Everyone's Favorite Subject* (Simon & Schuster, 2000).

FACT: Capuchin monkeys often greet each other by **showing off their erections**. *My dog does the same thing, but you have to pet him first.*

❯ Shane Mooney, *Useless Sexual Trivia: Tastefully Prurient Facts about Everyone's Favorite Subject* (Simon & Schuster, 2000).

FACT: In the fifth century, castration was believed **to cure the plague**. *It worked, too. The disease disappeared among men virtually overnight.*

❯ Shane Mooney, *Useless Sexual Trivia: Tastefully Prurient Facts about Everyone's Favorite Subject* (Simon & Schuster, 2000).

FACT: Actor Rudolph Valentino's dog reportedly **haunts his former owner's gravesite**. *Looking for his goddamn dinner.*

❯ Varla Ventura, *The Book of the Bizarre: Freaky Facts & Strange Stories* (Weiser, 2008).

FACT: In August 2007, **more than 75,000 Elvis fans** descended on Graceland to commemorate the thirtiest anniversary of the singer's death. *Most of them even fatter and on more drugs than Elvis was when he died.*

❯ Varla Ventura, *The Book of the Bizarre: Freaky Facts & Strange Stories* (Weiser, 2008).

FACT: The longest case of hiccups on record lasted **sixty-nine years**. *That's one patient hiccuper. I think I'd leap off a bridge after 69 hours.*

❯ Katharine Kenah, *The Bizarre Body* (School Specialty Publishing, 2004).

FACT: An iceberg spotted by the U.S. Coast Guard in 1956 was **roughly the size of Belgium**. *And probably a lot more interesting.*

❯ Barbara Seuling, *Earth Is Like a Giant Magnet: And Other Freaky Facts About Planets, Oceans, and Volcanoes* (Coughlan Publishing, 2007).

FACT: Queen Isabella of Spain lived to be fifty years old, but **bathed just twice** in her lifetime. *She was so dirty, even the flies refused to land on her. Even dirt wouldn't stick to her. When she walked past a pigpen, all the pigs would hold their noses.*

❯ eBizarre, *www.ebizarre.com.*

FACT: In the past ten years the "naked recreation and travel" industry has **grown 233 percent**. *And that's just the erections.*

❯ eBizarre, *www.ebizarre.com.*

FACT: Until the late 1800s, Turkish women suspected of committing adultery were **put in bags with live cats** and tossed into the ocean. *Getting rid of the cats was just an added bonus.*

❯ Varla Ventura, *The Book of the Bizarre: Freaky Facts & Strange Stories.* Weiser, 2008.